1991

MANUSCRIPTS AND TEXTS

EDITORIAL PROBLEMS IN LATER MIDDLE ENGLISH LITERATURE

MANUSCRIPTS AND TEXTS

EDITORIAL PROBLEMS IN LATER MIDDLE ENGLISH LITERATURE

*Essays from the 1985 Conference
at the University of York*

EDITED BY DEREK PEARSALL

D. S. BREWER

© Contributors 1985, 1987

First published 1987 by D. S. Brewer
240 Hills Road, Cambridge
an imprint of Boydell & Brewer Ltd
PO Box 9, Woodbridge, Suffolk IP12 3DF and
Wolfeboro, New Hampshire, 03894-2069, USA

ISBN 0 85991 231 0

British Library Cataloguing in Publication Data

Manuscripts and texts: editorial problems
in later middle English literature:
essays from the 1985 conference at the
University of York.
1. English literature—Manuscripts
2. Manuscripts—Editing
I. Pearsall, Derek
820.9′001   PN162

ISBN 0-85991-231-0

Library of Congress Cataloging in Publication Data

Manuscripts and texts.

Contents: Some sceptical observations on the
editing of The awntyrs off Arthure / Rosamund
Allen—Metrical problems in editing The legend
of good women / Janet M. Cowen—Observations
on the history of Middle English editing / A. S. G.
Edwards—[etc.]
1. English literature—Middle English,
1100–1500—Criticism, Textual—Congresses.
2. Manuscripts, English (Middle)—Editing—
Congresses. 3. English literature—Middle
English, 1100–1500—Manuscripts—
Congresses. I. Pearsall, Derek Albert.
PR275.T45M37 1987   820′.9′001   86–23315
ISBN 0–85991–231–0

Printed in Great Britain by St Edmundsbury Press,
Bury St Edmunds, Suffolk

CONTENTS

INTRODUCTION

The present volume is in large part the proceedings, suitably adapted for publication, of the third conference on Fifteenth-Century Manuscript Studies held at the University of York in July 1985 (the proceedings of the first conference were published as *Manuscripts and Readers in Fifteenth-Century England: The Literary Implications of Manuscript Study* by the present publishers in 1983). Not all the papers given at the conference are printed here. The title of the conference was 'Fifteenth-Century Manuscripts and Editing': the title of the present volume is, it will be seen, slightly changed, in recognition of the fact that a number of contributors deal with manuscripts of the fourteenth and sixteenth centuries.

The contents of the volume are presented in alphabetical order of author's surname, since any other arrangement might be in danger of over-categorising the material, or of insisting on certain connections of subject-matter at the expense of others. The cross-connections are in fact many, and the concerns addressed, if not the views expressed, remarkably homogeneous, perhaps because nearly all the contributors are practised and practising editors. Particularly prominent are the issues raised by new editions, published or proposed, of Chaucer and Hoccleve. For the former, Charlotte Morse gives an account of the experience and value of editing for the *Variorum Chaucer*, while Ralph Hanna offers some criticisms of 'best text' editing (as practised in the *Variorum*) and some sceptical reassessment of the booming stock of the Hengwrt manuscript. Janet Cowen tackles the problem of the editor of *The Legend of Good Women* in determining the nature of Chaucer's metrical practice, and particularly the question of final *e*. Metre and final *e* figure importantly also in Judith Jefferson's approach to the editing of Hoccleve, where the status of the holographs and the possible prospect of recovering Hoccleve's own orthography, matters dealt with in detail by David Greetham, constitute a special challenge to the editor. The concept of authorial revision, which has played a large part in past theories of the relationships between manuscripts (especially of Chaucer), but which is increasingly questioned, is given another knock by Peter Nicholson, who finds many deficiencies in Macaulay's account of Gower's revisions in the *Confessio Amantis*.

Behind many of the essays lies the inspiration of the striking advances in textual criticism made by the Athlone Press editors of *Piers Plowman*, George Kane and E. Talbot Donaldson, and several contributors evidently take courage from their example, whether in attributing to scribes a role in manufacturing textual variation which had long been thought to be due to the intervention of the author, or in emending on the basis of metre, or in proposing generally radical techniques of editorial reconstruction. Rosamund Allen and Thorlac Turville-Petre take two northern poems and demonstrate what can be done if an editor is prepared to trust his or her intelligence. Some problems of manuscript variation, however, still seem to be intractable to such treatment, and Dan Embree and Elizabeth Urquhart show the impossibility or at least the futility of reducing heavily revised or 'recomposed' texts to a single archetype. Meanwhile, particular issues relating to the editing of drama texts and drama records are addressed by David Mills and Diana Wyatt, and A. S. G. Edwards provides an account of a forgotten chapter in the history of Middle English editing.

The subject, it will be seen, is in the happy state of being much argued about and disagreed over. This is as it should be, and the respectfulness with which all the present contributors address their opponents should not be allowed to obscure the strength, even the vehemence, of the conviction with which they write. In fact, the health of the subject could hardly be better attested than in the vigour of the questioning of traditional editorial attitudes and assumptions that goes on throughout all these essays.

Derek Pearsall
University of York

LIST OF CONTRIBUTORS

Rosamund Allen   Queen Mary College, University of London

Janet M. Cowen   King's College, University of London

A. S. G. Edwards   University of Victoria, British Columbia

Dan Embree   Mississippi State University, Mississippi

D. C. Greetham   The Graduate School and University Center of the City University of New York

Ralph Hanna III   University of California at Riverside

Judith A. Jefferson   University of Bristol

David Mills   University of Liverpool

Charlotte C. Morse   Virginia Commonwealth University

Peter Nicholson   University of Hawaii at Manoa

Thorlac Turville-Petre   University of Nottingham

Elizabeth Urquhart   University of Sheffield

Diana Wyatt   Polytechnic of North London

SOME SCEPTICAL OBSERVATIONS ON THE EDITING OF *THE AWNTYRS OFF ARTHURE*

Rosamund Allen

The Awntyrs off Arthure [*AA*] is a satire on the chivalric ethos cast in the form of courtly romance. Structurally it is in two parts, which differ in content and to some extent in style. In the first part, the apparition from the depths of Tarn Wadling of the ghost of Guinevere's mother to an apparently dallying Guinevere and Gawain, while the rest of the Court is enjoying the ritual slaughter of the hunt in Inglewood Forest, challenges the aristocratic assumptions of an automatic right to seize from nature and from fellow men the means to luxurious living. After requesting a trental (thirty) masses for the relief of her soul from torment, the ghost advises both Gawain and Guinevere to consider the rights of the poor and the conquered in order to avoid the same retributive suffering after death. She warns against the 'luf peramour' which is the essence of the chivalric ethos, and prophesies the downfall of an unjustly acquisitive Round Table. In the second part, Guinevere puts what she has learned into practice and is instrumental in terminating a fight between the royal champion, Gawain, and a challenger, Galleron of Galloway, who claims that Gawain has usurped his territorial rights in Ayrshire. In keeping with the ghost's directive to respect others' territory, Gawain voluntarily relinquishes Galleron's land and receives from Arthur a compensatory grant of land elsewhere. The poem is rounded off with the liturgical rites initiated by Guinevere on her mother's behalf – enormously inflated, perhaps by scribal emphasis of a most extreme kind, from thirty to a million masses. As is now recognised,[1] there is organic unity in *AA*. In spite of its title, this is not a poem about Arthur, nor about Gawain;[2] as some recent critics have

---

[1] A. C. Spearing finds causal and thematic links between the episodes, '*The Awntyrs off Arthure*', in *The Alliterative Tradition in the Fourteenth Century*, ed. B. S. Levy and P. E. Szarmach (Ohio, 1981), 183–202, esp. 196f., 200; Spearing's 1982 article (see below, p. 23 and n. 74) further supports his view that *AA* is a unity, an opinion few would now dispute.

[2] Robert Thornton is the only scribe to append a title, which he seems to have concocted out of the first line of the poem: *In Kyng Arthure tym ane Awntir by tyde* T. His title: *Here By gynnes The Awntyrs off Arthure At the Terne Wathelyn* (f. 154r) itself poses one problem: there is an otiose curl over the *n* of *Wathelyn* but a similar suspension over the *n* of *Awntyrs* has been expanded as *e* in the Introduction and Title Page of the facsimile edition, *The Thornton Manuscript* (Lincoln Cathedral MS 91), D. S. Brewer and A. E. B. Owen (London 1975); since an identical symbol (semi-circle containing a dot) is used by Thornton as an abbreviation for *n* (e.g. on f. 195, where he is transcribing section 2 of Rolle's Latin *Comment on the Canticles*) it seems that the abbreviation in *AA*, if not otiose, should be transcribed 'Awnntyrs' or 'Awu*n*tyrs' rather than 'Awentyrs'.

pointed out, it concerns the role of women in upper-class society.[3]

The theme of *AA* might be summarised as 'the vanity of human ambition'. Ironically, it impressed the truth of its message on the fate of five modern editions of the poem being prepared as graduate theses during the 1960s: only two of these were subsequently published;[4] mine was one of the three which remain unpublished. Since three of the editors[5] were attempting to use the editorial methods practised by Kane and Donaldson in editing *Piers Plowman*,[6] a comparison of the results of their textual criticism of the poem affords some relevant data in the controversy over the efficacy of applying modern editorial techniques to the medieval romances.

AA is a sophisticated work with a complex verse-form. It consists of fifty-five alliterative and rhyming stanzas of thirteen lines, in which the first nine lines have four stresses and the remaining four form a *cauda* of two-stress lines. Normally there are four rhymes per stanza ($ababababc_4$-$dddc_2$) but sometimes only three.[7] There is concatenation linking stanzas by repetition of a phrase, word or syllable from one stanza to the following, and additionally iteration, a device whereby the eighth and ninth lines of most stanzas are linked, often but not invariably by means of a phrase which is repeated with some inversion of its content. The complicated verse-form implies that *AA* must have been composed by a poet with pen in hand, and not during oral performance; it is also a useful check on the presence and degree of corruption. Both factors are important for the editor. The dialect of *AA* is northern, probably that of Cumberland.

Like other romances with a largely religious content, *AA* survives in more than one manuscript.[8] Of the four known manuscripts, the earliest is possibly the Lincoln Thornton MS, Lincoln Cathedral Library MS 91 (T), dated before 1454,[9] and in the dialect of Yorkshire. The Ireland–Blackburne

[3] For example, A. C. Spearing, 'The Awntyrs off Arthure', 199–200.

[4] Robert J. Gates, ed., *The Awntyrs off Arthure at the Terne Wathelyne* (Philadelphia, 1969); and Ralph Hanna III, ed., *The Awntyrs off Arthure at the Terne Wathelyn* (Manchester, 1974).

[5] Gates, op. cit., and Hanna, op. cit., and my own, 'A Textual Study of *The Awntyrs off Arthure*', unpublished MA Dissertation, University of London, 1968.

[6] George Kane, ed., *Piers Plowman: The A Version* (London, 1960); and George Kane and E. T. Donaldson, eds., *Piers Plowman: The B Version* (London, 1975). Only the A Version and its introduction was available when the five theses were prepared.

[7] Viz. $ababababa_4ccca_2$; $abababb_4cccb_2$; $ababababc_4aaac_2$; $ababababc_4bbbc_2$. See n. 76 for distribution of these five rhyme-patterns within *AA*.

[8] Derek Pearsall, 'The English Romance in the Fifteenth Century', *Essays and Studies* (n.s.) 29 (1976), 56–83, points out the connection between quasi-religious content and high numbers of extant romance MSS in the case of *Titus and Vespasian* (13 MSS) and *Robert of Cisyle* (10 MSS).

[9] Dated by Brewer and Owen (op. cit., xvi) to 1430–50 by handwriting and watermarks; 1454 is the date of a note on f. 49v recording the birth of Thornton's grandson; Margaret Ogden (followed by Hanna) regards this as the upper date of composition of the MS, adding that 'documentary material dated as early as 1413 and as late as 1461 has been found bearing the same watermarks as those in the paper of which the Lincoln MS is composed', *The 'Liber de Diversis Medicinis'*, EETS 207 (1938), x–xi.

MS (Ir)[10] is now thought to be late fifteenth century in date[11] and is in the West Midland dialect of Lancashire; this MS is now in the Robert H. Taylor Collection in Princeton, NJ, but was in the possession of the Ireland–Blackburne family at Hale in Lancashire from at least the sixteenth century until 1945; from then until 1971 it was owned by Martin Bodmer of Geneva and was not available for consultation.[12] A third manuscript, Bodleian MS 21898, MS Douce 324 (D), is also Midland, possibly from north-east Derbyshire,[13] and dates from the third quarter of the fifteenth century; it is part of a larger MS which was dismantled in the eighteenth century by Thomas Rawlinson, who apparently had the habit of dismembering manuscripts;[14] six other fragments of the original MS survive in the Bodleian Library.[15] The fourth manuscript, Lambeth Palace MS 491 (L), was discovered in 1890 by Bülbring;[16] it may be the earliest of the extant manuscripts of *AA*, perhaps from the second quarter of the fifteenth century,[17] but it is essentially southern in dialect, probably from London.[18]

[10] The sigil J is used by Hanna; I, used by Gates is confusible with the first person sg. pronoun and hence I prefer Ir. The MS was very capably edited by John Robson, *Three Early English Metrical Romances: From a MS in the Possession of J. T. Blackburne*, Camden Soc. 18 (1842).

[11] Earlier dating to around 1450 by Bruce Dickins, 'The Date of the Ireland Manuscript', *Leeds Studies in English* 2 (1933), 62–6 is followed by Christopher Brookhouse, *Sir Amadace and The Avowyng of Arthur: Two Romances from the Ireland MS* (Copenhagen, 1968), 10, and by Helaine Newstead, op. cit., 62. But Ir is dated 'third quarter of the fifteenth century' by Hanna (ed. cit., 7) and Roger Dahood, ed., *The Avowyng of King Arthur* (New York, 1984), 13, cites Malcolm Parkes's opinion that the first part of the MS, containing *AA*, dates from the 'third quarter of the fifteenth century or perhaps slightly later' together with Philippa Hardman's impression that the hand compares with that of MS Digby 181, last quarter of the fifteenth century.

[12] For this reason, Hanna cites Bruce Dickins's description, 'The Date of the Ireland Manuscript', *LSE* 2 (1933), 62–6, and, like other recent editors of *AA*, had to use the photographic copy in the Brotherton Library in Leeds University (or another set at Harvard University) for collation. However, a recent description of both MS and binding from direct observation is found in Roger Dahood, *The Avowyng*, 11–16.

[13] Ralph Hanna records the observation in private correspondence by Professor McIntosh that Douce was copied in north-eastern Derbyshire, ed. cit., 8.

[14] See Kathleen L. Smith, 'A Fifteenth-century Vernacular Manuscript Reconstructed', *B.L.R.* 7 (1966), 234–41; noted by Hanna, ed. cit., 8.

[15] MSS Rawlinson D.82; Rawlinson D.99; Rawlinson D.913, ff. 10–21; Rawlinson poet. 35; Rawlinson poet. 143, ff. 1–12; and Rawlinson poet. 168. The original miscellany would have comprised at least 290 folios.

[16] Karl D. Bülbring, 'Über die Handschrift Nr. 491 der Lambeth-Bibliothek', *Archiv* 86 (1891), 383–92.

[17] The date is quoted by Hanna (p. 5), and was confirmed for me by Dr A. I. Doyle. T and L therefore are the earliest extant MSS, and L may, despite its corruptions, antedate T.

[18] As Professor Samuels pointed out to me in a letter dated 9 December 1968, MS L (Hand A) is almost identical in dialect with BL MS Harley 3943 Hand A (containing Chaucer's *Troilus*) and MS Huntington HM 114; the three MSS are in fact by the same scribe. In copying Lambeth 491 he does not use his normal forms *cherchis* or *ho* (*Thre Kinges of Cologne* has *chirche*; *AA* has *who* 'who'), presumably because he used a northern exemplar; *meny*, *tul* ('till'), *she*, *eche* appear regularly in all three MSS, and, as Hanna notes (p. 5, n. 1) *mich*, *þei* and *such* are invariable, typically pointing to a southern dialect which Hanna identifies as 'south-east Midlands'; Samuels, in the same letter, indicates 'south-east Essex'. The dialects of the MSS are discussed by Paul Burtness, 'A Language Study of *AA*', unpublished Dissertation, University of Chicago, 1953.

These four manuscripts do not present *AA* with any uniformity. To begin with, none of them is complete. T lacks 108 whole and 15 half lines; it was edited three times in the nineteenth century,[19] but is unsatisfactory for a copy-text, despite its date and dialect, because of its lacunae; it also displays a marked tendency to more explicit readings.[20] The Ireland MS, although more complete in lacking only one stanza plus three additional lines, is undesirable as a base manuscript because its dialect is unrepresentative of the northern original. Ir remains, however, an underrated version of *AA* and, as I shall proceed to claim in this paper, should be given more weight in textual criticism. The Lambeth MS is also fairly complete, lacking only eight lines or parts of lines through scribal error, and parts of seven more from a torn folio, but in addition to being a southern copy, it is heavily scribally sophisticated.[21] This leaves Douce as the only practical choice as base manuscript for a critical edition.[22] It has been so selected by three of the recent editors, but mainly, one suspects, because it only lacks

[19] By David Laing in *Select Remains of the Ancient Popular Poetry of Scotland* (Edinburgh, 1822), revised and partially corrected by John Small (1885), who noted the existence of Ir, but reprinted *AA* uncorrected from the 1822 edn with the addition of variants from Ir, a glossary and an extended introduction by W. C. Hazlitt (1895); by Sir Frederic Madden, *Syr Gawayne: A Collection of Ancient Romance Poems by Scotish and English Authors* (London, Bannatyne Club 61, 1839); and by F. J. Amours, *Scottish Alliterative Poems in Riming Stanzas*, STS 27 and 38 (Edinburgh and London, 1892 and 1897). Laing had been sent both T and D for transcribing, and Madden transcribed T himself and examined D; Amours relied on transcripts made by the staff of Lincoln Cathedral for T and by the Bodleian Library for D, and seems to have used Robson's edition for his variant readings from Ir.

[20] E.g. *More explicit readings*: 462 Loke nowe] sayse lukes nowe ȝe T. (Adding *inquits* is typical of Ir, which seems to have been pointed in this way for private reading, e.g. 410 Wheþer þou be] sayd quethir þou be Ir, and also 137, 159, 222, 250, 513, 551; 415 TIr, 664 TIr). 142 I am] and nowe am I, T; 302 honest] þat h.es T. *More emphatic readings*: 93 good]beste TIr. 198 ouȝt mendes] myghte oghte menden T. 504 bright] full b. T. 698 þat haþel] those hathells T. 81 ran] rane faste T. 149 tresour] *pl.*TIr. 225 frely] full f. T. 335 prince] *pl.*TIr. 380 brene] brenyes T. 450 semly] full s. T. The tendency of both T and Ir to make copy both more explicit and more emphatic accounts for much random and coincidental agreement between these two MSS.

[21] E.g. 128 on þe goost gowes ('gapes at')] on þe grene growys L. 548 burlokest blonke] best body L (and cf. 499 blonkes]bodyes L). 693 surgenes sone saned] soiournis tul þei be salvid L. L forges a link at 547: now is gay grisell L, based on 546 fro grissell þe goode. 656 þey truly vp take] a twyn þei t. L.

[22] D was inaccurately printed in an edition pirated by John Pinkerton from Douce's not very accurate transcription with plot-summary (now itself Bodleian MS Douce 309) of the MS then owned by Joseph Baynes, later his own (Douce 324), provoking an outraged comment by its would-be editor, Baynes's legatee, Joseph Ritson. Pinkerton's edition, in *Scotish Poems Reprinted from Scarce Editions* (1792), III, 197–226, was partly transferred (stanzas 1–26), with further errors, by James Sibbald to Vol. I of his *Chronicle of Scottish Poetry from the Thirteenth Century to the Union of the Crowns*, 4 vols. (Edinburgh, 1802); transcriptions from Douce 324 were made by Laing and Madden for citation in apparatus criticus; D was printed in parallel with T in Amours's edition for STS; it forms the base for the corrected editions of Gates and Hanna.

six lines, despite editorial assertions of the value of its readings.[23] It does not meet the usual requirements for a base manuscript: in dialect and grammar it does not reflect the northern original, and it is not very consistently spelled.[24] Although its scribe was zealous, he was a somewhat careless copyist, and seems to have been smoothing his text for oral recitation: its 'neatness'[25] is deceptive.

What the potential editor of *AA* cannot do, in these circumstances, is to select his copy-text by Lachmannian recension. One can construct a simple stemma;[26] it will carry us no further back in the tradition than the exclusive

---

[23] Gates remarks that T and D make fewer of the more obvious scribal errors than Ir and L (this is debatable), and that D, with better line order and fewer omissions, results from a less corrupt scribal transmission (ed. cit., 75); Hanna, besides noting the completeness of D, observes that the scribal tradition behind it 'has been tolerably honest and faithful' and that it preserves several unique original readings (ed. cit., 53–4). Hanna identifies homoeographic forms in D which suggest that scribes were recording as closely as they could without lapsing into sophistication, but many of these are simple carelessness: 112 to hit] oute D. 119 in]h*im* *with* D. 114 cholle] clolle D. 253 aure] cure D. 385 blake] brake D, etc.

In fact D frequently sophisticates, for example in Stanza 26, where the original *-ere* rhyme of Ir has been corrupted to mixed rhymes in *-ere* and *-ene* in TL: D rationalises the genetic error of DTL in lines 327 and 329 and rewrites 333 with an *-ene* rhyme; cf. also 341 and wines to wale] inewith the walle D. 523 þe laþely lord (?lede)] þe lady loude D.

[24] Dialect difference: 56 *wyrkkis* T: *worchen* D. 299, 402 *swylke* T: *sich* D. 262 *defoules* Ir: *defoulen* D; *(defoulith* L). 575 *þer* Ir (probably for N *thir*): *þes* D. 671 *are* T: *arn* D: *(be* L).

Spelling inconsistency in D: *wil* (I pers. sg) 191: *wol* 74, 430: *woll* 465. 3 pers. pl. *wyn* 176 and *wil* (same line). *aurronen* (280) cf. *ouer* in 21, 263. 458, 488 *hour*: 34 *her* (etc.): 35 *here*. 27, 70, 118 *ho*: 26, 333 *she*.

[25] Hanna describes D as 'a very clean and neat text' (Dissertation, 119). The bracketing of the 'wheel' in D, the marking off of stanzas by means of the paraph, and some twenty instances of pointing at the caesura may all indicate preparation for reading aloud.

[26] As Paul Burtness observes, the stemmata of Lübke, Amours and Smith (unpublished University of Chicago Diss., 1921) are contradictory. Mine was independently deduced and is based on the following figures for agreement of two or more MSS in a wrong reading: agreement of T with L in 97 instances; agreement of D with L in 89 instances; agreement of D with T in 68 instances; of T with Ir in 59 instances; of D with Ir in 48 instances; of L with Ir in 41 instances. The grouping of DTL in agreement in a wrong reading in 63 instances is congruent with the groupings of two manuscripts and permits the further resolution of DTL as [D(TL)]. This is challenged by the persistent agreement of Ir with T in 59 instances, but TIr is probably random, resulting from similar habits of scribal variation (see note 20). Other groupings: LIr is random of low frequency; DL is explicable as DTL grouping with T absent by further variation or physical damage, DT as DTL grouping with L absent by further variation, DIr is random or records error in the exclusive common ancestor with TL further corrupted; TL is clearly a genetic grouping. The very low frequency TLIr (22 instances) and relatively low DTIr (38 instances) confirm the impression that TIr is a random grouping, since Ir agrees with T only rarely in the type of error that T shares with other manuscripts, and significantly shows very few cases of agreement with the true genetic group TL. Similar reasons show that LIr is random, suggested by the low frequency groups DLIr (35 instances) and TLIr; equally the low frequency group DIr is supported by relatively low frequency DLIr and DTIr. This stemma is very different from the assessment of manuscript affiliation given by Hanna (Dissertation, 96ff.). Gates does not give a stemma, and Hanna's published edition also omits discussion of relationships, apart from TL. I have not used the term 'archetype' but

common ancestor of the two families <Ir[D(TL)]>, and this ancestor was itself very corrupt:

O
|
Exclusive common ancestor
Ir   α
D   β
T   L

Moreover, this stemma does not record the conflation which I shall demonstrate later in Ir, and possibly in L. Like any stemma, this records distance from the original in terms of preservation of original readings, not date: the two earliest dated manuscripts are T and L, which are the most corrupt, both because their ancestor, TL, was responsible for releasing a large number of errors into the tradition, and because T and L each independently sophisticate.

The possibilities for the editor are: (1) to edit a single manuscript diplomatically; (2) to print a parallel-text edition; (3) to attempt an edition like that of the versions of *Piers Plowman*.[27]

1. The 'single-text' edition.

For this, this editor could select Ir, which would not serve him badly: its alliteration is fairly sound and its readings sensible. How far this results from descent through an accurately copied branch of the tradition, and how far it represents the efforts of scribal 'correction' is the crux which lies at the heart of the editorial problem with *AA*. For Ir indeed does seem to have been copied by a scribe who could 'edit'. For example:

81   Thay ran to þe raches for redeles of rayn

preferred van Groningen's term 'exclusive common ancestor' ('l'ancêtre commun d'un groupe de manuscrits', *Traité d'Histoire et de Critique des Textes Grecs* (Amsterdam, 1963), 110) because, where there are only four manuscripts, three of which form a genetic group, the 'archetype' can only be the earliest of three reconstructed exemplars, those of TL, of DTL and of DTLIr (and see below, p. 20). This need only represent a very small segment of the true stemma: an indeterminate number of lost manuscripts may have intervened between the ancestor of DTL and that of Ir, and between that of DTLIr and the original, which might clarify the many problems of their relationship. Maas implies that the loss of manuscripts would increase the possible distance of the earliest reconstructible state of the text ('archetype') from the original (*Textual Criticism*, transl. Flower (Oxford, 1958), 6(f), (g), 7(h)); accordingly, using the term archetype to denote this earliest form of *AA* testified by its extant versions would give the false impression that this inferential version was close to the authorial version and hence fairly correct. In fact the e.c.a. was very corrupt.

[27] In this type of edition 'the sole source of authority is the variants themselves, and among them, authority, that is originality, will probably be determined most often by identification of the variant likeliest to have given rise to the others.' Kane, *Piers Plowman: The A Version*, 115, and cf. E. Moore, *Contributions to the Textual Criticism of the Divina Commedia* (Cambridge, 1889), xxxv.

Presumably this means: 'they ran over to the hunting-dogs because of the riddle of the rain', to leash and calm them, perhaps. It makes sense; it's not *right*. The line should read:

> 81   Thei ran fro the roches for reddoure of rayne

'they ran down from the rocks because of the rigour of the rain': supposing that the topography of the poem corresponds to reality, the hunt must be taking place on Blaze Fell, beside the Tarn Wadling, and the wood in the Petteril Valley, where the deer are being driven, is an obvious place for shelter.[28] If DTL had not happened to preserve the right reading, we should have accepted Ir *redeles* as 'original'; we might probably have identified *raches* as an error induced by context, and common sense would then suggest motion from, rather than to, the *roches*. The point is that Ir presents a good reading, probably his own.

What is more, Ir presents many good readings not shared by the other three. Editors and critics differ, however, in both their assessment and their treatment of these readings. A case in point is:

> 134   As þou ⌜was⌝ claryfiet on crosse and clanser of synne
> (*ref.* Christ)

where DTL read *crucifi(g)ed on croys(e)/crosse*, which is theologically unexceptionable, if trite, and two recent editors and a critic have accepted it. But to me Ir *claryfiet* 'glorified' looks a harder reading contextually: Gawain is confronting the hideously shivering, half-decayed corpse, and to swear by Christ reigning in majesty is a surer bet to conjure with than Christ as a dead body himself. Or is this a modern rationalisation? Can an editor ever really be certain, despite all the information provided by the dictionaries, that his criteria for assessing a 'good' or 'original' reading are not anachronistic? In this instance, was the Ireland scribe himself rationalising the reading of his exemplar? The sense is good, and I accept Ir *claryfiet* while acknowledging that my grounds for so doing may be subjective.[29] There are many such instances in Ir: this scribe was intelligent and knew alliterative technique and diction. However, apart from some good readings, he produced many instances of more explicit grammar

---

[28] The location is marked on the Gough Map, where Tarn Wadling is disproportionately large. It was sited at High Hesket on the A6 (Roman) Carlisle road (OS Sheet NY 44) and was drained in the last century and again, by Italian prisoners of war, in World War II (see A. H. Smith, *The Place-Names of Cumberland*, I, 204).

[29] Distinction between Christ crucified and Christ in majesty is a theological commonplace, e.g. St Francis, 'this is He who is not about to die, but Who is eternally victorious and glorified' (*Letter to the Entire Order*, paralleling Pseudo-Bernard of Cluny, PL 184 col. 787A and echoing Bernard of Clairvaux, Sermo I, PL 183 col. 146A; *Francis and Clare: The Complete Works*, transl. R. J. Armstrong and I. Brady (NY, 1982), 57 n. 4). Gates and Hanna both read *crucifiged*.

which are almost certainly not original.[30] Ir therefore serves best as a supplier of good readings in a corrected edition. An edition of Ir alone will be an 'authentic' version of *AA*, not of the original composition, but of a reading of the poem by someone of intelligence living fifty years after the original was written, and one hundred miles further south; this has historical validity as a critique of the poem but no claim as a contemporary witness of the text.[31] Still less instructive as evidence of the original is L, which shows how totally a southerner can misrepresent northern idioms and prosody, despite his clear enjoyment of *AA*. Because L had only once been edited,[32] one of the recent editions, that of Florence A. Paton, was a single-text edition of L.[33] An edition of D would have the advantage of a more northern dialect than L, of greater completeness and less sophistication than T, and fewer explicit readings than Ir, but would have many points of weakness where the sense is reduced to banality or cliché; these are obvious when displayed in parallel with the other manuscripts.[34]

2. *The parallel-text edition*

Amours produced D in parallel with T and with collation of Robson's edition of Ir; he did not know of L.[35] One of the five recent editions of *AA*, C. Paul Christianson's,[36] prints all four manuscripts, but as a prelude to a never-published reconstructed version. Editing in parallel is possible with a

---

[30] E.g. 109 as]as stylle as a Ir. 460 whan] as tyde as Ir. 472 if] for and Ir. 512 in]tille him in Ir. 140 God] þus god Ir. 181 al] all þe Ir. 77 Arthur] syr A. Ir. 201 in] in þe Ir. 339 in] in his Ir. (Cf. *inquits* in n. 20 above and Gates's list, ed. cit., 74.) It also makes copy more emphatic: 517 fifte]syxti Ir. 574 a lyon] ij lions Ir; but perhaps less so than T.

[31] The disadvantages of respect for the individual MS, leading to extremes of fidelity to scribal error and even line division (as in the EETS *Ancrene Riwle* texts) are pointed out by Anne Hudson ('Middle English', *Editing Medieval Texts*, ed. A. G. Rigg (NY, 1977), 38. Peter Lucas has recently observed that the facsimile now supersedes the diplomatic edition (in a paper 'Establishment of the Text' at a conference on 'The Use of Computers in Editing Medieval Texts', London, 1985). Malcolm Godden observes judiciously that 'to allow easily correctable errors to stand, on the dubious principle that a scribe's version is as interesting as the author's, not only gives undue weight to inept scribes . . . but also obscures the history of the text', 'Old English', *Editing Medieval Texts*, 23. A single-text re-edition of Ir was announced by Brookhouse in 1968, 'currently being prepared by A. B. Friedman', *Sir Amadace*, p. 9, n. 1; it did not appear.

[32] Pearl Smith, 'A Classification of the manuscripts of the Middle English poem *Awntyrs of Arthure*', unpublished PhD Dissertation, University of Chicago, 1921, gives a transcription of L.

[33] Florence A. Paton, ed., 'A Critical Edition of *The Aunturs of Arthur*', unpublished PhD Diss., University of Colorado, 1963.

[34] E.g. 120 þat sat] TLIr; all aboute D. 124 holt(es)] IrL; hillys T; wode D (allit. is on *h*). 176 þay wil leue] Ir/TL; þen lite wyn D. 184 I downe (= dwine)] T; in dongon DL. 196 wirde] Ir; wo DT. 203 is bryttenede (conjecture)] is brouȝt to be D; bryȝte is Ir; es blakenede T; now left is L. 210 sayntes] TLIr; sere men D. 271 quele wryȝte] IrT; wight DL.

[35] Ed. cit., STS 27 and 38: see n. 19. Amours should have known of L since its discovery was announced the year before his first volume appeared.

[36] C. Paul Christianson, ed., 'The Awntyrs off Arthure: an edition', unpublished Dissertation of Washington University, 1964.

short poem where there has not been major scribal rewriting.[37] But the parallel-text edition is clumsy in use, and leaves the reader doing his own editorial work; the editor risks his elaborate textual notes being ignored as the reader struggles to keep his places in a multiple of texts of the work.

(3) *The corrected text or 'eclectic' edition: 'direct-method' editing*

Here at least the editor is not left protesting unheeded in his footnotes: he will be avidly sought, if not hounded there, to explain his decisions; but the boldness of this method in elevating to the printed text the opinions of an editor living five hundred years after the composition of a work is a scandal to many. This editorial method is indeed somewhat equivocal with a class of fiction like the romance, where there is little certain knowledge of the mode of performance: were romances sung, intoned or acted out like music-hall monologues; were they performed in hall, chamber or bower, to small or large groups, and how select or mixed were these groups; were longer romances performed in instalments over a brief span of days or with long intervals; how often, like modern television programmes, were they repeated; were extracts given as encores? All these considerations affect transmission, and therefore have a bearing on how the editor reacts to variant readings.

In scrutinising the variant readings, the editor attempts to use three procedures as objectively as he can: (i) to detect among extant variants in every instance of variation the single reading which makes most sense or best fulfils the metrical requirements, and which is most likely to have generated the others as scribal errors; (ii) to reconstruct such a reading from the extant variant forms if it is not present; (iii) to conjecture, where the post-archetypal tradition is badly mangled, or the archetype itself was corrupt, the original reading in the authorial *usus scribendi*. All substantive variants from the edited text must then be recorded in an accessible *apparatus criticus* and the preferred readings accounted for in textual notes. Naturally, the conjecture is the most difficult of these procedures to operate; this difficulty is compounded in the case of romances by the quality of the tradition and, usually, its meagreness, and above all by the relatively unremarkable and non-individualistic mode of composition of

---

[37] E.g. Bliss's edition of *Sir Orfeo* (Oxford, 1966[2]); *Floris and Blauncheflur* and *King Horn*, ed. McKnight, EETS 14 (1901), and Hall's edn of *King Horn* (Oxford, 1901). It has been used for a longer narrative extant in only two MSS in Laʒamon's *Brut*, eds. Brook and Leslie, EETS 250 and 277 (1963 and 1973). The presentation of selected MSS in parallel in *King Alisaunder*, ed. Smithers, EETS 227, 237 (1952, 1957), and *Of Arthour and Merlin* (ed. Macrae-Gibson, EETS 268, 279 (1973, 1979) is neater in format than the multiple-volume editions necessary if all extant MSS were published in parallel, especially if there has been major rewriting, as in *Guy of Warwick* or *Bevis of Hampton*, for which Jennifer Fellows has prepared a parallel-text edition (unpublished PhD Dissertation, University of Cambridge, 1981). In practice, parallel-text editions are hard to handle if one witness has large lacunae, where passages are substituted from another MS, or covered by printing one MS on both facing pages (as happens with Laud Misc. 622 of *KA*).

Rosamund Allen

the genre.[38] Nevertheless, the existence of four extant manuscripts of the poem challenged three of the 1960s' graduate students to attempt an edition of this type; two of the three give conjectural emendations; all three use D as copy-text.

It is an enlightening, and not wholly indicting critique of this type of edition to compare the results of these three editions, namely: Robert Gates's edition published in 1969 [G], the edition of Ralph Hanna III, both in the form in which it was presented as a dissertation in 1967 [H1], and in its 1974 published form [H2], and finally, my own dissertation of 1968 [R].[39] A first impression of the three shows that Gates does not emend conjecturally; Hanna prints more conjectures in the thesis than in the published edition; Allen emends extensively, at a deep level (and sometimes unnecessarily, I now think). To fulfil Sisam's stricture that every doubtful reading should be signalled as such would produce an impenetrable forest of *obeli* in every edition of romances,[40] for it is rarely possible with their corrupt traditions to provide even conjectures for the swarm of errors, and many lines must be left in a battered state, even if the textual presentation misleadingly implies by the absence of square brackets or asterisks that this is a correct reading.[41]

What does emerge from closer scrutiny of these three editions is that the more editors address themselves to the cruces of a text the easier it is to determine the better readings of the manuscripts and the kind of interpretation that may (and may not) be put on them. Even three editions of *AA* of a similar type are not superfluous; nor are the many cruces yet resolved:

```
482   The king commaunded              þe                   of kent
                        kindeli Ir  ⎫     Erle IrL   ⎫
                        krudely D   ⎬     erlis son D ⎬
              dede comaunde to L     ⎭                ⎭
      (T absent)
```

---

[38] Contrast the observations made by Kane and Donaldson on the evidence for conjecture in the B Version of *Piers Plowman* (ed. cit., 191) where the length of the poem and number of extant copies afford 'countless opportunities' for contrasting presumed original and scribal readings, and editors feel confident in identifying contrasting *usus scribendi* in poet and scribes.

[39] See notes 4 and 5 above, and '*The Awntyrs off Arthure at the Terne Wathelyne*, an edition based on Bodleian Library MS Douce 324', PhD Dissertation, Yale University, 1967. Hanna refers to his editorial procedure as 'the Kane method/system' (Diss., pp. 115, 118) and the 'eclectic editorial method' (ed. cit., 53); the term 'direct method' is Miskimin's, *Susannah* (New Haven, 1969), 31; the procedure needs a name.

[40] *Studies in the History of Old English Literature* (Oxford, 1953), 43–4.

[41] Because scribal activity frequently takes the form of making copy more explicit or emphatic by the addition of adverbs, intensives, pronouns, etc., a corrected edition inevitably involves deletion of forms; I decided that the asterisk was the handiest way to signal such a deletion by directing attention to the *apparatus criticus*, but the numerous asterisks then contend with the already omnipresent square brackets signalling substitution or transposition of base MS readings, and the resulting edited text is not at all fair, even if it is honest.

G, R: *kindely*; H1: *Cradok*; H2: *Krudely*. G, H1, H2: *erlis son*; R: *erle*. It looks as if D has editorially smoothed the line by reading *erlis son* to improve metre, while Ir has edited out the inappropriate *krudely* by reading *kindeli*; it may be, as Hanna suggests,[42] that *krudely* is the vestige of a proper name, but if so the original is irretrievable: *Cradok* H1 is a plausible guess since Cradok plays a significant role in the Alliterative *Morte Arthure*,[43] a poem which the *AA* poet knew, but does this justify the emendation here? One might conjecture an alternative [*Cador þe constable*], which at least metres the line better, although less plausably since Cador's territory was Cornwall. Clearly, such conjectures cannot stand in print, but what else should? *Krudely* is grotesque, both as proper name or as adverb; the sense 'blunt, unrefined in manner' is nineteenth century: the ME sense is 'raw, unripe'; while the possibly scribal *kindeli*, 'fittingly, spontaneously' makes the best sense, the syntax suggests that the original reading was a name with title, as does the presence elsewhere in *AA* of proper names of otherwise uncharacterised personages.[44] The best one can do here is either follow copy-text in the sense its scribe presumably understood, as Hanna's printed edition does, or take the 'best' reading, even if it is scribal, as Gates's edition does. Neither 'solution' actually resolves the problems posed by the variations.

There are, in fact, four distinct dangers in applying this method of editing to romances:

(a) First, the assumption that the original was composed by 'a man with a message', writing concisely and with originality, which forms the basis of identifying original readings in this editorial method, is not necessarily valid for romances. A romance writer, intending no more than to endorse conventional opinion on the validity of the chivalric ethos, may have drawn constantly on formulaic diction to accentuate the conventional theme.[45] I can discover no method of identifying direction of variation from an original where the variation consists of alternative formulae equally valid in context.

Alliterative formulae:

607	D	grisly on gronde he groned
	T	Galleron full greuously granes
	L	to þe ground was cast þat doghty
	Ir	all grouelong*es* in gr*o*unde gronet

---

[42] Ed. cit., 128–9.
[43] Especially at the turning-point of the plot, *AMA* 348ff. See K. H. Göller, with R. Gleissner and M. Mennicken, 'Reality versus Romance: A Re-Assessment of the *Alliterative Morte Arthure*', in *The Alliterative Morte Arthure: A Reassessment of the Poem*, ed. K. H. Göller (Woodbridge, 1981), 21, 26.
[44] At lines 96 (4×), 145 (?), 595 (2×), 654 (2×), 655 (2×).
[45] Cf. Susan Wittig, *Stylistic and Narrative Structures in the Middle English Romances* (Austin, 1978), 41–6 (esp. 45).

Religious terminology:

> 230 D to mende vs wi*th* masses[46]
> T to mene me wi*th* messes
> L to mede þe wiþ messes
> Ir to mynne me wi*th* massus

(b) Second, knowing how scribes react under supervised conditions is not necessarily a guide to the kinds of variation which occur when amateurs copy romances for their own reading. The amount of variation and the extremes of sophistication seem to me to be far greater than in other vernacular traditions, such as *Piers Plowman* or the devotional prose.[47] For example:

> 252 D siþen charite is chef and þen is chaste
> Ir sethyn charite is chef to þose þat wyn be chast
> L after þis charite is chevest *and* cherisshid moost
> T for to come to that blysse that eu*er* more sall
> laste (*supplied after line 254*).

In this scribal chaos, Gates reads with D, the copy-text, while Hanna and Allen conjecture for the second half-line: H1 *and cure of the chaste*; H2 *and þew of chaste*; R *and cherses*[48] *þe chaste*. The first of these conjectures, 'and concern (glossary: 'care, spiritual charge') of those who are chaste' regards *chaste* as pl. adj. following def. art.; the second, 'and conduct of the morally pure' also treats *chaste* as adj. used substantivally, but the emendation *þew* assumes that D misread *w/u* in his exemplar as *n*: such close attention to the shape of words and letters did not necessarily occur in amateur copying, where scribes seem to have taken up large amounts of copy and repeated it aloud while copying to their own dictation. The third

---

[46] The evidence here is complicated by two factors: (i) line 230 is the ninth line of Stanza 18, which should carry iteration from the eighth line, 229, where the readings are: *mene the* T; *myn þe* Ir; *mynge þe* D; (L sophisticates); here D and L fail to complete the iteration, but T and Ir may represent scribal emendation of e.c.a. error. (ii) lines 229–30 occur in Part Ib of *AA* (see below, pp. 23–4, and n. 76), where later matter seems to be inserted, echoing Stanza 25; the line apparently echoed here is 320, where variation is: *mene* TL; *menge* D; *myn* Ir. 230 *mende* D is irregular on this evidence, and perhaps Hanna is right to prefer a corrected sp. of Ir (ON *mynna*, 'commemorate', for which the OE equivalent *mynge* occurs in 229 D; *mene* 229/230 T, 320 TL is OE *mænan* 'remember'); *mende* has a relevant sense 'alleviate distress, improve the condition of'. These are examples of Grattan's 'substitution of similars', 'The Text of *Piers Plowman*', *Studies in Philology* 44 (1947), 593–604; also *MLR* 26 (1931), 1–51.

[47] Contrast Anne Hudson's discovery of the strictly limited and anything but muddled scribal variation in the MSS (other than B) of Robert of Gloucester's *Chronicle*, 'Tradition and Innovation in Some Middle English Manuscripts', *RES* (n.s.) 17 (1966), 359–72. Nicholas Jacobs notes that 'the categories of variants in a serious didactic work and a fugitive work of fiction do not coincide, though to some extent they overlap', 'The Processes of Scribal Substitution and Redaction', *MÆ* 53 (1984), 48, n. 17.

[48] *MED cherisshen* 2b 'take care of sb', or 6a 'encourage, exhort', assuming that *þe chaste* is pl. adj. used substantivally.

conjecture (R) assumes that a stave has been lost in DTIr and that L, with loss of the following stave, either preserves or conjecturally restores a missing original third stave in [tʃ]: *cherissh*—; if this originally took the less common contracted form *cherses* (<*cherisshes*), scribal puzzlement at the unusual form could account for its loss independently in DTIr; assuming here that DIr *chaste* was originally an adverb,[49] the third conjecture proposes: 'and Christian love takes care of you chastely'. But D apparently read *chaste* as an abstract noun, rather than the far easier adj. of Ir and adj. used substantivally of H1 and H2; was D assuming that his exemplar meant 'chastity'? The form *chǎste* n(3) 'chastity' in *MED* has only two entries, both fifteenth century, but one citation does not rhyme and the other does not scan in their respective contexts, and the word seems doubtful; *chaste* n(1), a rare derivative of OF *chasti* 'teaching, instruction', would give excellent sense if L's *cherisshid* derived from original *cher(is)se* v. 'take something to heart' (MED *cherissen*, lc); the line would then have meant originally: 'Christian love is most important, then, and takes to heart the teaching' (namely, 'love one another').[50] The major problem here is that surely this reading is too hard for *AA*?

(c) The third difficulty in producing corrected editions of romances is that, except for those which Mehl calls 'novels in verse',[51] romances are not long enough to establish what the authorial *usus scribendi* might have been, if indeed the poem ever had any stylistic individuality and was not composed in formulaic manner. In addition, a low number of extant witnesses (compare the near score of manuscripts for each version of *Piers Plowman*) means that there is little evidence to go on in attempting to determine whether a reading is right or wrong.[52] A corrected edition can be produced from only two manuscripts,[53] but usually only if the variation is not extreme. In *AA* the original reading is often neither extant nor obviously reconstructible; all we can confidently do is point to error;

---

[49] The form *chaste*, apart from the adj. (as epithet and substantive) can be adv. 'chastely', or the rare nouns, n(3) 'chastity', where the two entries are suspect, and n(1) 'teaching, instruction'. The variation indicates that scribes found the line difficult; this may have been due to a rare sense or unusual form, but it may simply have been that the line was archetypally corrupted by scribal mangling of an originally easy line; the rule of *durior lectio* is not invariable in romances.

[50] Jn 13: 34, 35; Jn 15: 12, 17; Rom. 13: 10 'Plenitudo ergo legis est dilectio' exactly corresponds to the proposed emendation.

[51] *The Middle English Romances of the Thirteenth and Fourteenth Centuries* (London, 1968), 37f.

[52] Hence Kane and Donaldson observe that 'there are thousands of lines [in *PP* B Version] where originality is either not seriously in question or else is confidently determinable' which establish the poet's alliterative principles (ed. cit., 131–2) and an additional check is afforded by the long passages where all three versions correspond and 'the text of BC is effactually a *codex descriptus* of A', making assessment of the archetypal B tradition possible (ibid., 190).

[53] E.g. Bella Millett's edn of *Hali Meiðhad* (EETS 284, 1982) but here the two extant MSS may be direct copies of the archetype (or have one intermediary MS) and that archetype may be a direct copy of the author's holograph (p. lvii); the textual situation is vastly simpler.

attempts to rectify it must be conjectural. In many cases the archetype must have been corrupt:

561 And wen[d]ys   þat wo[u]nded is sare
             D   *him to quyte*
             LIr   *to his enemy*
             (T lost through tear)

Here Hanna conjectures very plausibly that the original read *to his witerwin*, 'adversary'. The complex verse form of *AA* indicates the archetypal error in this instance, which D has attempted to correct; but it cannot help where the error is not a stave-word nor a rhyme-word nor iterative, nor if it is a proper name, which scribes notoriously garble or replace with a familiar form.

(d) And this is the fourth danger in trying to edit romances by this method: scribes did rework romances, and produced quite different versions with extensive additions or deletions. Maldwyn Mills has shown how a reviser added rationalising matter to *Libeaus Desconus* which, although laxer in style, was not inferior in content to Chestre's work; nevertheless, Mills is still able to identify what he terms the 'authenticity' of the 'original text'.[54] This is not the same situation as occurs in purely oral composition and transmission, for example the composition of ballads, which have no fixed form and are of course ineditable by the direct method.[55] *AA* shows no evidence of extensive reworking by a *disour* during oral transmission, such as has been identified in the tradition of *Libeaus* and other romances; moreover, its complex form, which has survived relatively intact, rules out both oral composition and repeated acts of oral transmission.[56]

Yet there is evidence that to some extent at least *AA* was transmitted orally, and may in the process have been contaminated by unconscious associations with other romances in the reciter's repertoire. Such contaminations from other romances can, of course, also easily occur in the unconscious response of a scribal copyist. The question is, are the variations produced by memorial associations identifiable, as scribal errors are, by their inapplicability in context or inferior quality, or do they 'improve' the text by adding terms, formulaic clusters, even whole lines, from the common stock? If multiplication of copies does not in the case of romances

---

[54] 'A Mediæval Reviser at Work', *MÆ* 32 (1963), 11–23.
[55] 'A genuinely popular ballad can have no fixed and final form, no sole authentic version. There are *texts*, but there is no *text*.' G. L. Kittredge, Introduction to *English and Scottish Ballads*, edited from the Collection of F. J. Child by H. C. Sargent and G. L. Kittredge (1904), xvii.
[56] In a *disour*-transmitted text, the form may deteriorate less rapidly than the sense, or may even be improved as sense is reduced as Kihlbom claims (*E.Sts* 19 (1937) 31f.); the scribal 'improvement' of stanza-linking and 8/9th line iteration in *AA* (especially in Ir and L) is some evidence of this. However, the detectable evidence of memorial contamination in Ir (and D) indicates that both sense and rhyme have been spoiled by oral contamination, and it seems therefore that *AA* is relatively free from reworking by *disours*.

cause sense to deteriorate, then, as Mills claims, it may not be possible to edit them to a deep level, since the principle of *durior* (or *difficilior*)[57] *lectio* is doubtfully valid where transmission is mixed, i.e. there is both oral and scribal reproduction of copies.[58]

The shortness of *AA* (715 lines) makes it likely, but unprovable, that it was passed on at some points in the tradition entirely orally. We can, however, prove that one of its scribes, Ir, knew *AA* by heart, because he makes several errors of anticipating copy which is not due to appear for another hundred lines or so, and too far ahead for eye-skip:

> 186 Ir   For in wunn*y*ng place is woe for to duelle (*corr.s.m. to* welle)
> *recte*: þer folo[wes] me a ferde of fendes [ful f]elle

Ir's line 186 belongs at 316, where it should appear as:

> 316 In my wonyng [wane i]s wo [þer] to [welle];

at 316 Ir now has *welle* correctly, but again reads *place* for *wane*.[59] Some similar kind of memorial influence in D produced a hybrid of 342 with 444 in both places in that manuscript.[60] Perhaps at several stages in the transmission scribes as much as *disours* were responsible for oral contamination; perhaps a scribe would hum as he copied: *AA* would lend itself well to being sung, and a tune always aids the memory. If the memorised version had several superior variants compared to his written exemplar, a scribe would presumably write down his memorised version at those points, thus dumbfounding an editor five hundred years later. There is no proof, but it is probable that some non-genetic good readings in *AA* are from oral tradition:

> 135   Ir   wys me þou waret wy3te
> L   now wrecche sey me sothely
> T   thou spirette saye me the sothe
> D   that þou sei me þe sothe.

D, which Gates and Hanna unaccountably prefer, has corrupted a reading

---

[57] Both terms are used by Griesbach in relation to New Testament variation: 'Difficilior et obscurior lectio anteponenda est ei, in qua omnia tam plana sunt et extricata, ut librarius quisque facile intelligere ea potuerit'; 'Durior lectio praeferatur . . .' (*Novum Testamentum Graece*, lxi, quoted by Kane, *PP: A Version*, 130).
[58] Mills, 'Mediæval Reviser', 20.
[59] Other instances where Ir apparently shows memorial contamination are: (i) 354 be tuene] Ir, for *in trete*; *be tuene* belongs in 510, where Ir reads exactly as at 354; (ii) 362 where Ir takes the whole line from 415 where it is substantially correct; in both 354 and 362 the contexts are sufficiently similar to induce memorial error; (iii) 493 *And þenne Dame gaynour grette* Ir, from 597 where Ir adds *for his sake*: 493 should read *Many galiard gret*. I cannot find any such instance in L.
[60] Although Amours (Introd. to STS 27, xlii) claims that T, D and Ir all show traces of having been committed to memory, there is no evidence of this in T.

like that of T; concurrence of non-genetic Ir and L on an alliterative stave in *w* for the term of address seems to indicate that this was the original rhyme-sound and that Ir had access to a better tradition which had preserved the original reading at this point while the archetype had introduced the mixed alliteration of L.[61]

I do not think that instances of memorial transmission in a tradition necessarily prevent an editor using direct-method editing. They do, however, altogether rule out recension, in either of two ways. Take the case of Ir in the *AA* tradition. It has many good readings; these may derive quite simply from a more carefully copied tradition than DTL, more accurately preserving the original. If, on the other hand, the good readings derive from a memorised (better) version, this version is either part of the stemma DTL:Ir, a lost version antecedent to all extant manuscripts but deriving from their common ancestor, in which case we have a form of conflation; or, it is not part of the family but a version intermediate between their exclusive common ancestor and the original, in which case we are dealing not with a contaminated but with a non-archetypal tradition,[62] a feature probably common in romance transmission. But this leakage into the tradition from an oral source of the text both improves the quality of the variation and, in the case of *AA*, extends closer to the original the reach of a very limited group of manuscripts, which may only represent a fraction of the real stemma, because with trained memories oral transmission is more accurate than written.

What interests me is what the editor is to do with the occasional non-genetic good reading. He ought to accept it, whatever its (untraceable) actual source. But in editing *AA* the attitude of editors to Ir seems to have been to ignore it and go for the 'majority reading'[63] of DTL. The corollary, to claim that the reading which departs from its genetic group must be a scribal invention and hence be rejected, is post-recensionist.

Now Gates does claim that Ir 'changes the text'[64] and he respects Ir's

---

[61] Alternatively: L may be a conjectural scribal emendation, supplying *wrecche* to alliterate with *whidir* 'whither' in 135b; however L is not usually bothered about alliteration.

[62] Other kinds of non-archetypal tradition can occur. One is the usual situation in classical texts where 'two or more unrelated ancient copies survived into the middle ages to become independent fountainheads' (Martin L. West, *Textual Criticism and Editorial Technique* (Stuttgart, 1973), 38). Another is the situation described by Anne Hudson in which texts might be multiplied by dictation to a group of scribes ('Middle English', in *Editing Medieval Texts*, 46).

[63] E.g. Gates's note to 424, and Hanna's objections to the grounds for Gates's reading in line 12 ('Interpretation', 283, n. 16). Gates's attitude to Ir has been adopted by Phillipa Hardman, 'The Unity of the Ireland Manuscript', *Reading Medieval Studies* 2 (1976), 46–8; many of the readings there identified as idiosyncrasies of Ir and the result of scribal rationalisation may in fact be original (see esp. discussion of *clarifiet* in line 134 (p. 47), and p. 11 above). There is, of course, no 'majority' where the three MSS are a family group, as DTL are.

[64] Ed. cit., 74. He also frequently rejects L's readings because L is an 'inferior' MS (note to line 676, and p. 73).

readings far less than Hanna or Allen, who use it to reconstruct a probable original where they do not accept its actual readings; Gates does not 'conjecture'.[65] But does it matter if Ir, and, less often, D, T and L did 'invent', edit, or 'sophisticate' copy, perhaps supplying terms from the common romance idiom to piece damaged matter? Have we produced a historically inaccurate, a 'dishonest' text if we accept their good readings?

My heretical response to this question is a qualified 'no'. The premise of all direct method editing is that the original was better than any scribal attempts to emulate or improve it; this is not necessarily true of a romance. Moreover, no tradition, even with the carefully supervised transmission of a venerated author, is ever perfectly recoverable, and no edition can correspond exactly to the poet's original.[66] The romances did not enjoy such systematic copying and were seriously and progressively corrupted from the earliest written copy to the extant survivors of a haphazard tradition. If there was a badly corrupt archetype at the source of the written tradition, then scribes themselves will have been acutely aware of the consequent corruptions in their exemplars and will have set out to rectify them, as (some) modern editors do. Usually, in fact, when scribes do this we can see from the weak syntax, commonplace idiom, poor rhyme or lack of alliteration what is happening; in *AA* at least, the scribes do not inevitably produce copy of equal quality with the original.[67] But they do, each of them, also produce non-genetic *good* readings, which may be either 'invention' or come from oral transmission:

80 L And fled to þe *fritthes* for þe *flawis* þat *felle*
     T And fledde faste to the foreste and to þe fawe fellis
     D And fleen fro the Forest to þe fewe felles
     Ir And fled to the Forest fro þe faufellus

---

[65] Gates abstemiously dissociates himself from conjectural emendation (ed. cit., 45); he also implies that an editor who uses 'conjectural emendation rather than choosing between variants' may fail to identify original readings (ibid., 51, n. 65); this is not how an editor who employed conjecture would operate.

[66] Supposing that an editor could exactly reproduce the author's holograph is the ultimate editorial fallacy. Cf. Kane and Donaldson, *PP: B Version*, 140, n. 48: 'An edited text is essentially a hypothesis. Its individual readings must be judged as elements of the hypothesis, in which naturally the poet's *usus scribendi* is a most important consideration', and 'The edition as a whole can be viewed as a theoretical structure' (ibid., 212).

[67] Although Derek Pearsall claims that recomposition by *disours* may reproduce the processes of original composition and thus make interpretation of variation impossible, because what are considered errors may be 'survivals of a careless original' while apparently authentic readings are 'moderately intelligent acts of rewriting', so that 'the process of change continues after the poem is written down' ('Romance in the Fifteenth Century', 59), this is not the experience of Mills, who finds the 'deviations' from Chestre's poem which result from oral transmission both repetitive in style and uncertain in rhyme and metre ('Mediæval Reviser', 23 and 20). Knight, examining Chestre's own adaptation of *Sir Laundevale*, considers that Chestre knew the poem in oral form and that his own new words 'do not seem to improve the poetry in any way' ('The Oral Transmission of *Sir Launfal*', *MÆ* 38 (1969), 164–70; oral transmission and scribal redaction have produced a different poem in the case of *Launfal*).

This shows, I think, L conjecturing a plausible reading rather than supplying a right reading from oral sources.[68]

We must therefore accept the editorial activities of scribes of romances as reflecting their dissatisfaction with the state of the text. It was a more corrupt text than those of named authors tend to be, and because these scribes had memories copiously stocked with romance formulae, motifs and episodes, and even perhaps with a complete version of the actual text they were copying, they were equipped to make conjectural emendations or actual corrections in texts which even then were damaged beyond full repair. Kane has recently restated his opinion that most scribal 'editing' is in fact 'sophistication', suggesting that many such instances are not voluntary but the result of distraction caused by the very participation in the scribe's exemplar which generates association with other texts he has copied before.[69] This is no doubt true in a purely written tradition, but those who helped preserve romances were not always only operating with pen, parchment and exemplar as tools. I think we must distinguish carefully between scribal attempts at plausible conjecture – 'editing' – and the kind of line or phrase which a scribe supplies when he gives up trying to represent what he sees or thinks he sees in his exemplar, which we may fairly call 'sophistication'.

But what should the editor do if at many points all the scribes can offer him are bad readings or variant readings which cannot be analysed? If these are formulaic synonyms or equivalent terms then he must adopt the base manuscript reading: but to claim that he does so because elsewhere the base manuscript presents good readings would be recensionism; the editor simply has no choice. Favouring any reading for any reason other than its own (relative) intrinsic merit is illogical. If the variants which are unanalysable are not substantive but consist, for example, of conjunctions (*as*: *while*: *quilles*) or intensives (*full*: *so*) or alternative syntactical connectives (*ac*: *and*: *but*: or asyndeton) the editor should again follow base text.[70] But if there is no harder reading, if all variants are acceptable but so divergent that direction of variation cannot be reconstructed from them, or if we have obvious archetypal corruption – and the editor of *AA* very

[68] L has certainly been ingenious: *fritthes* was an archaic word after 1400, and *flawis* 'flakes of snow' is a Scottish word recorded in only three other ME texts, and hence a very hard word indeed in a southern copy such as L. Even so, it seems to be wrong.

[69] 'John M. Manly and Edith Rickert', *Editing Chaucer: The Great Tradition*, ed. P. Ruggiers (Oklahoma, 1984), 220.

[70] Other instances of unresolvable variation include substitution of one dialect form for another; words which are lexically similar, e.g. 219 vnder]vndrone T. 415 lenge]lende TL.; transposed word-order in lists (Ir is very prone to this); and probably intensives (*so*: *ful* [*ful* seems to be scribal in many instances]); use of titles (*sir*: *kyng*: zero); use of def. art. vs demonstrative; use of def. art/possessive pron. for attributes or parts of body; use of alternative prepositions or prep. phrases; alternation of *in*: *on*; alternation of *ou* and ʒe with no apparent significance; alternation of modal vbs (*will*: *mon*: *wol*: *s(h)all*: *mot*: *must*: *me buse*).

frequently finds himself in these dilemmas – then the usual injunction in this type of edition is to emend conjecturally following the authorial *usus scribendi*.[71]

This is the point at which *AA* poses an additional problem. Hermann Lübke claimed in 1883 that it is in fact two poems: lines 1–338 and 703–15 comprising Part I, and 339–702 Part II.[72] The theory is tentatively supported by Hanna.[73] Recently, Spearing has found a reference to the 'sovereign mid-point' in line 358 (of 715) in Stanza 27 (of 55), i.e. the exact middle of the poem:[74]

> 358   *He was the souerͅaynest sir sittand in sete.*

There is little variation (for once): *soverayn* as noun or adjective stands in all four manuscripts. However, because a second poet could have created his own 'mid-point' within his continuation of an original, the 'compilation theory' is not refuted by Spearing's argument, and if this is indeed a combined work, it will be necessary to identify two authorial scribal habits within the text.

It has seemed to me that *AA* may well have been composed in *three* stages, not necessarily by two poets, but possibly with a gap of perhaps two decades between writings:

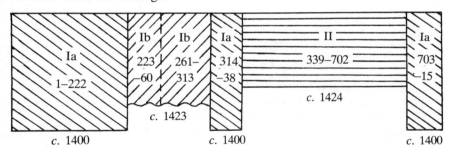

The earliest stage, which may date to about 1400, corresponds to lines 1–222, 314–38 and 703–15. This is the appearance of the ghost to Guinevere, its insistence on self-restraint and request for masses, with Guinevere's arranging of the saying of masses; it is based on a type of story current in

---

[71] 'This process consists in two operations: identifying as unoriginal unanimous or unmistakably archetypal readings of the manuscripts; and proposing in their place unattested, and therefore entirely hypothetical readings as likely or possible originals.' (Kane and Donaldson, B Version, 190). The position was earlier outlined by Kane, 'Conjectural Emendation', in D. Pearsall and R. Waldron, eds., *Medieval Literature and Civilisation: Studies in Memory of G. N. Garmonsway* (1969), 155–69.

[72] 'The Aunters of Arthur at the Tern-Wathelan, Teil I: (Handschriften, Metrik, Verfasser)', Inaugural-Dissertation zur Erlangung der Doctorwürde (Berlin, 1883), 20–27. His projected edition never appeared.

[73] '*The Awntyrs off Arthure*: An Interpretation', *MLQ* 31 (1970), 275–97, esp. 277, 293, 296.

[74] 'Central and Displaced Sovereignty in Three Medieval Poems', *RES* (n.s.) 33 (1982), esp. 248–52.

the late fourteenth century and has five close analogues.[75] The section from 223–313 is based partly on the preceding and following sections (Ia) and, in the portion from 261–313, draws allusively on the Alliterative *Morte Arthure*; this section (Ib) differs in its rhyme and alliterative patterns and use of alliteration from Ia, into which it seems to have been inserted. The remainder of the poem (II) also has differences of prosody from both Ia and Ib.[76] Ib and II may possibly date from *c.* 1423 and 1424.[77]

In other words, in this already short poem, I have designated 260 lines to Ia, 91 to Ib and 364 to II, and have found evidence that, even if a single poet were responsible for all these sections, he modified his technique over the years. In this case, while one can discriminate between variants on grounds of sense and metre and can reconstruct from extant variation a probable original form in many cases, it may be hazardous to attempt conjectural emendation in *AA* by making assumptions about authorial style and technique.

Yet I do think that it is always worth attempting to salvage the original. In practice, different editors will have different opinions about the original form for any given set of variants and will offer different inspired conjectural guesses; the literary critics may present different interpretations according

---

[75] There are at least eleven sermon exempla from the thirteenth to the fifteenth century on the theme of returning dead parents requesting masses (see D. Klausner, 'Exempla and *The Awntyrs off Arthure*', *MS* 34 (1972), 307–25) and many are related to *The Trentals of Gregory* (BL Cott. Calig. A II, 86v col. ii–88r col. i), where the ghost is a mother: *AA* apparently draws both on *Trentals* and one of its 15c derivatives in MS Harleian 219 or a similar exemplum. A third analogue is *The Ghost of Gy* (ed. Gustav Schleich, Palaestra I (Berlin, 1898)) in which a woman's husband haunts their home until a local abbot says 300 masses for his soul. A fourth, noted by Turville-Petre, is *De Tribus Regibus*, poem 54 in MS Douce 302, attributed to but not by Awdelay and based on the 13c legend of the three living and the three dead ('*Summer Sunday*, *De Tribus Regibus*, and *The Awntyrs off Arthure*: Three Poems in the Thirteen-line Stanza', *RES* (n.s.) 25 (1974), 6–9); the fifth, also noted by Turville-Petre (ibid., 4–6) is *Summer Sunday*, a wheel of fortune motif on the uselessness of pride; *De Tribus*, *SS* and *AA* all have the contrastive hunt setting, use the 13-line alliterating and rhyming stanza and present a confrontation with death or mutability; *De Tribus* and *AA* additionally use 8th/9th-line iteration and stanza-linking, while *SS* and *AA* both use the fortune *motif*, the latter from the *AMA*. The first three analogues represent appeals, the last two, warnings; *AA* combines both aspects.

[76] In Ia only 20 per cent of stanzas have three rhymes (ababababcaaac, etc.) whereas in Ib nearly 30 per cent of stanzas are of this type; whereas in Ia four-rhymed stanzas predominate, in II they are only 57 per cent. Iteration between lines 8/9 is regular in Ia and rare in II. Two- and three-stave alliteration is higher in II and Ib than in Ia and the half-lines of the wheel do not alliterate in 11 per cent of cases in II, but only 6 per cent in Ia and Ib. The frequency of *-ight* rhymes in II noted by Lübke and Hanna is, however, largely contextual: in Ia *-ight* rhyme-leashes occur 4 times, in Ib twice but in II 24 times; 16 of these involve the word *knight* in the rhyme-sequence, inevitable in context, and this generates a sequence of formulaic tags (*so right, full light, of/to sight, on hight*, etc.) which gives the superficial impression that II is less poetically dense, as Hanna claims (ed. cit., 22, 'Interpretation', 293).

[77] There is possible reference in Ib to the political situation after the 1423 Triple Alliance between Brittany, England and Burgundy, while II may possibly refer to James I of Scotland and his return north after his long exile, in 1424.

to which editor they follow,[78] but this will also happen with single- or parallel-text editions, where the critic is simply selecting which fifteenth- instead of twentieth-century editor he favours. Such minor confusions will not impair the overall impact of *AA* as a poem of considerable interest and some quality, which have not been dissipated by the corruptions of its scribal editors and will not be materially impaired by its modern ones. The more editions we have, with their editors' informed conjectures, and the more readers who are supplied with a full apparatus of variant readings so that they may both gain some idea of the individual scribes' impressions of the poem, and make their own assessments of the patterns of variation, the closer we shall approximate to what the author wrote. Meanwhile the challenge of the eclectic method of editing, which must be the hardest to operate, makes the process stimulating – and enjoyable (most of the time) – and is, for *AA* at least, a better means of uncovering and appraising the effects of the original poem than other editorial methods.

---

[78] Spearing thinks that Hanna's editorial detachment of 'the concluding stanza' from his putative second poem obscures the symmetry of *AA* as it stands ('Central Sovereignty', 250).

METRICAL PROBLEMS IN EDITING
THE LEGEND OF GOOD WOMEN

Janet M. Cowen

It is a commonplace of Chaucer scholarship that a major problem in attempts to establish Chaucer's metre is the determination of criteria for the pronunciation of unstressed syllables, in particular of final *e* where it derives from a syllabic ending. In Chaucer editing this problem can be circumvented in two ways: in a conservative edition by retaining the spelling of the base manuscript and in a modernised edition by regularising it. In both these approaches final *e* is treated as a matter of spelling, and the question of metrical emendation can be avoided. In this paper I offer a brief account of the way I have approached the metrical problem of final *e* in the editing task I am currently engaged in: an edition of Chaucer's *Legend of Good Women* in collaboration with George Kane. We take the view that final *e* is not to be treated merely as a feature of the spelling of the copy text, but must be considered in its metrical implications as a feature of the form of the poetry, and therefore demands the exercise of editorial judgement.

The Legend of Good Women differs from *The Canterbury Tales* and *Troilus* in that there is no manuscript which by virtue of dialect and spelling readily recommends itself as copy-text, either in general terms, or specifically in the matter of final *e*. This does not, however, make the problem of assessing the scansion in principle more difficult than in the case of the other texts; it simply complicates the presentation of the edited text once the question of scansion has been considered.

The critical apparatus of our edition is designed to give an indication of the situation in the manuscripts with regard to final *e* and to terminal suspensions which might stand for final *e*. In all the manuscripts there are to be found instances of final *e* in places where there is no justification for it in terms of historical grammar, and with the exception of Cambridge University Library MS Gg.4.27, which is written in a formal book hand not using otiose strokes, all manuscripts contain instances of terminal strokes indistinguishable from suspensions in places where there would be no justification for a final *e* in terms of historical grammar. Conversely, in all manuscripts are found instances where a final *e* justifiable in terms of historical grammar is neither present nor represented by a suspension. Such variation of practice is the expected result of the ongoing change in the language from the mid-fourteenth century onwards with respect to unstressed syllables. In this situation any attempt at assessing the metrical significance of final *e* in Chaucer's verse cannot depend on the evidence of the manuscript spellings alone. What is needed is an analysis of the grammatical situations in which final *e* is to be found,[1] as a preliminary to a correlation of its grammatical and metrical functions, and a distinction of these from functions which are merely orthographic.

When at an early stage of my work I was mentally reviewing attempts that have been made to read Chaucer's line as one based not on a decasyllabic norm but on a four-beat measure,[2] it seemed to me that one of the basic methodological weaknesses of such attempts to disallow any systematic syllabic value to final *e* in the scansion of the line was the failure to base the demonstration on a corpus of lines where the value of final *e* is not in question. To meet this objection I set out to find those lines in the text which wouldn't beg the question at the outset. I based my enquiry on the text of the legends and the F version of the Prologue, together with those lines peculiar in their entirety to the unique G version of the Prologue.[3] I excluded all lines where the metrical value of final *e* might theoretically be in question, that is, where there are word endings derived, in terms of historical grammar, from an original vocalic ending or a syllabic ending reducible to *e* in Middle English, including loan words ending in *e*, and situations where analogous forms with *e* are postulated. In order not to beg the question, I did this very strictly, excluding even those grammatical

---

[1] Until relatively recently the problem has been considered as one of phonology and metrical theory. Factors not adequately taken into account have been grammar and metrical variation. Work of Michael Samuels, and more recently of David Burnley, has now provided a model for investigation of the grammar of final *e* in the scribal language of particular manuscripts. See M. L. Samuels, 'Chaucerian Final -E', *Notes and Queries*, 217 (1972), 445–8, and J. D. Burnley, 'Inflexion in Chaucer's Adjectives', *Neuphilologische Mitteilungen*, 83 (1982), 169–77. Barry Windeatt's discussion of metre in his edition of *Troilus and Criseyde* takes account not only of problems presented by manuscript variation, but also of the way lines whose syllabic content is agreed by all manuscripts may be taken as indications of Chaucer's metrical practice. See Geoffrey Chaucer, *Troilus and Criseyde*, ed. B. A. Windeatt (London, 1984), 55–64.

[2] J. G. Southworth, *Verses of Cadence* (Oxford, 1954); Ian Robinson, *Chaucer's Prosody* (Cambridge, 1971); Jack Conner, *English Prosody from Chaucer to Wyatt* (Mouton, 1974).

[3] Examples below are from our edited text, for which Bodleian MS Tanner 346 is the copy-text, in the case of the legends and the F version of the Prologue, and from my transcription from the manuscript in the case of the G version of the Prologue. Line references given are as in *The Complete Works of Geoffrey Chaucer*, ed. F. N. Robinson (London, 1957), to which reference may be made for the examples not quoted here in full. A terminal stroke is shown as an expanded abbreviation only in those cases where, after consideration of the factors under consideration here, we have concluded that a sounded final *e* is necessary to the metre. The scribe of T does not consistently use or consistently avoid terminal strokes in any of the lexical or grammatical situations exemplified here. Because of this lack of consistency it is very doubtful whether the use of a terminal stroke in place of a metrically necessary final *e* is a conscious one on the scribe's part, but it nevertheless seems preferable to register such instances as expanded abbreviations rather than as emendations. For a list of textual authorities see Robinson, p. 912.

situations where received historical phonological opinion is that final *e* had
become silent by or before the late-fourteenth century. Needless to say,
since these excluded situations comprise a large part of the language, I did
not expect the resulting sample to be large, or to provide more than limited
guidance to other lines. I then made the further exclusions of lines with
manuscript variants other than morphological and spelling variants not
affecting the number of syllables, and of lines whose syllabic value is
indeterminate from considerations such as the coexistence of full and
abbreviated forms, e.g. 'neuer/ner', or the possibility of syncope in an
inflectional ending. The result was a list of nine lines: 110, 171, 995, 1290,
1532, 1904, 2002, 2315 and G Prol. 529, assuming that the two imperatives
in this last example are to be construed as singular, as the surrounding
pronouns indicate, and that 'Let' belongs among the majority strong forms
of this verb. (G Prol. 138 would also fit the conditions but must be treated
as anomalous since its defective sense indicates corruption.) Such a corpus
is of limited value as a normative model, not only because it is axiomatic
that a line on which all textual witnesses agree may yet not be original, but
because a sample so small still leaves open the question of how far variants
on any pattern it may demonstrate may be admissible. It was, nevertheless,
reassuring to see that the metrical pattern of this small sample was, as
uncontroversially as anything in Middle English studies can be, that of a
ten syllable line of five stresses with a predominantly rising rhythm, e.g.:

> 2002   Yif that he be a man he shal do soo

The addition of lines where the value of final *e* is in question at the line end
only, but which are otherwise subject to the exclusions noted above, would
add another short list of eight examples demonstrating the same metrical
pattern with the possibility of an extra unstressed syllable at the end of the
line: 9, 347, 428, 1513, 2114, 2540, 2716, G Prol. 261. (The likelihood of a
feminine ending must, of course, be assessed in each of these and similar
cases in relation to subsequent conclusions about the metrical value of final
e and with reference to the rhyme.)

This preliminary exercise had at least shown no contra-indications to
taking a decasyllabic line as a hypothetical norm when looking at the rest of
the text. On this basis I went on to consider the metrical value of final *e*
according to grammatical categories. My procedure was to exclude from
consideration in the first instance the following: lines containing more than
one word where a final *e* is justifiable in terms of historical grammar but
where the sounding of only one is necessary to produce a metrical line
according to the presumed norm; lines where a final *e* justifiable in terms of
historical grammar is followed by a word beginning with a vowel, *h* or *y*,
and where, therefore, elision might be presumed; lines with textual variants
of substance or with other variants affecting the number of syllables; and
lines containing words of indeterminate syllabic value as referred to above,

or where the question of sounding a final *e* is affected by the possibility of syncope elsewhere in the line. I did not consider rhyme words, and hence the question of variant metrical patterns at the line end, at this stage, on the presumption that this might be a peculiar situation which should be considered separately.

The resulting correlation of grammatical and metrical functions indicated that final *e* should always be sounded in two grammatical situations:

– in monosyllabic adjectives in weak position:
118 smale soft*e* swote; 136 foule; 256 fair*e*; 511 grete; 876 dede; 1329 large; 1620 right[e]; 1972 bright[e]; 1978 leue; 2330 false; 2426 brighte; 2431 wise; 2463 same (twice; the sounding of both is metrically necessary in all texts except that of Thynne, where a variant renders the sounding of one superfluous);

– in monosyllabic strong adjectives in the plural:
331 wise; 370 olde; 484 go[de]; 1117 rich*e*; 1531 Alle; 2013 queynt[e]; G Prol. 278 alle.

(There are, however, some instances of the plural of 'all' which seem to be exceptional. For instance, the sounding of final *e* is not metrically necessary in line 272. In similar instances the question is complicated by the possibility of syncope or another final *e* elsewhere in the line, but here too a sounded final *e* seems unnecessary: 546; 673; 679; 918. It is notable that in all these cases 'all' precedes a definite article, a demonstrative, or a possessive adjective. The question arises whether there is a distinction in respect of sounded final *e* between 'all' when it is used in such positions and when it is the sole modifier. Comparison of lines 272 and 1531, however, shows that if such a distinction exists, it is not a rigid one.)

By the same analysis, final *e* is sometimes metrically necessary, sometimes not, in the following grammatical situations:

– in the singular of those adjectives and nouns which historically ended, in the nominative, in *e* or in a syllable reducible to *e* in Middle English:
necessary in 464 trewe; 33 game; 670 tonge; 915 herte; 2237 name; not necessary in 1576 trewe; 112 son; 491, 498, 921, 1040, 2455, 2492, 2521, loue; 812 moone; 1893 shame; 1921 tale;[4]

– in the singular of French adjectives other than in weak position ending in *e*, and of French nouns ending in *e*:

---

[4] One further example should be noted under noun inflections, although it is affected by textual variation. The phrase 'at the gate' in line 1717 requires a sounded final *e* on 'gate' to give a regular line according to the presumed norm. The omission of 'the' in two manuscripts is an easily explicable scribal error which hardly affects the case. It is notable that this example is a fixed phrase in which the preposition has come to be closely associated with the noun in a way which has been considered to contribute to the preservation of the original inflection. See Ruth Buchanan McJimsey, *Chaucer's Irregular -E* (New York, 1942).

necessary in 1116 large; 425 prose; 839 place; 1466 ile (cf. 2167 ile, where a sounded final *e* before following *h* might be considered preferable to elision, particularly since the initial *h* is not on a lightly stressed word[5]); 2196 barge; 2251 fest[e]; 2510 terme; not necessary in 1992 quyte; 321 relik; G Prol. 202 balade; G Prol. 313 seynt (used as a title for Venus; the equivalent though not identical line in the F Prologue, 338, however, although complicated by variation, raises the opposite possibility; either it must be assumed that alternative pronunciations of the word are being used in these two lines, or 338 must be scanned as a headless line; the question of the admissibility of such headless lines in Chaucer often presents a further problem for editorial judgement, cf. the example of 562 'Make' and further discussion below);

– in the comparative adjective 'more':
necessary in 99 moore; 967 moore; (in 906 the situation is complicated by variation in two manuscripts and by the presence of a word of indeterminate syllabic value, 'trewlie', but whether this word has a medial *e* or not, the line would still be hypermetric if final *e* were sounded in the comparative);

– in the first person singular present indicative:
there are no lines unaffected by manuscript variation in which final *e* is metrically necessary, but there are cases where it will appear as necessary after the likelihood of scribal error in the variants has been assessed;
it is not necessary in 83 haue; 552 woll; 566 wole; 694 wol; 894 wol (twice); 1161 haue; 1340 haue; 2660 wil;

– in the third person singular present subjunctive:
although account must be taken of variation at another point in the line, final *e* appears metrically necessary in 1956 helpe; 2340 send[e] (the case of 'wreke' in this line is obscured by variation);
it is not necessary in 1446 wer; 1731 saue; 1921 wer; 2084 send; 2514 were;

– in the first person singular preterite of weak verbs:
necessary in 1539 myght[e]; not necessary in 279 hadde; 2106 had;

– in the third person singular preterite of weak verbs:
necessary in 605 roght[e]; 1082 seid*e*; 1397 hight[e]; 1854 kaught[e]; 1913 wende; 1978 seid*e*; not necessary in 417 made; hight; 603 thoght;

– in adverbs, prepositions and conjunctions which historically ended in *e* or in a syllable reducible to *e* in Middle English:
necessary in 1913 sore; 2553 Withoute; not necessary in 87 sore; 190

---

[5] On the distinction between degrees of stress in relation to elision before *h* see Burnley, 'Inflexion in Chaucer's Adjectives', p. 172, fn. 8. As he does, I have omitted all cases of final *e* before following *h* from my survey in order to avoid any uncertainty about the pronunciation of initial *h*.

Namor; 579 righte; 2515 ryghte; 2636 halfe; 282 Behinde; G Prol. 52 Thanne; G Prol. 200 aboute; G Prol. 263 Thanne.

In the case of the infinitive, the plural inflexions and the preterite participle of strong verbs the evidence is complicated by the alternation of forms ending in *e* and in *en*. Nevertheless there are sufficient indications that in all these parts of speech a syllabic ending is sometimes metrically necessary, sometimes not. In many cases where our copy text has a form ending in *e* which may elide with the following word, emendation to *en* is preferable, but such emended forms are not included in the following examples. Thus final *e* is metrically necessary in the infinitive in 183 call*e*; 326 serue; 1800 fight*e*; 2170 tell*e*; not necessary in 663 haue; 729 haue; 1595 gete; G Prol. 312 forgete; necessary in the indicative plural in 17 mote; 754 wold*e*; 761 myght*e*; not necessary in 756 wolde; 1557 wole; 1710 shul; G Prol. 263 blame, wete; necessary in the preterite participle in 1901 come; not necessary in 1103 come.

In the case of the imperative singular of weak verbs and the imperative plural there is only one instance which I could use according to the conditions of my investigative survey: 562 Make, sg. If the final *e* justifiable in terms of historical grammar is sounded here, the result is a line with a modulated initial stress pattern consisting of ten syllables plus a feminine ending; if it is not sounded the result is a headless line of nine syllables plus a feminine ending.

The text provided no examples of a superlative adjective which I could use, but one instance is worth comment. If in line 229 the omission of 'first' in one manuscript is discounted as scribal error, a final *e* on 'fresshest' is metrically unnecessary. It should be noted that the superlative here, although preceded by the definite article, is positioned after the noun it qualifies, and cannot therefore be taken as typical of the behaviour of superlatives in the weak adjective position.

For grammatical categories not noted above, the indications were that sounded final *e* is never metrically necessary. (I exclude proper names from this discussion.)

The exercise had provided support for decisions in some of the situations where the reader or editor has to take account of the variables which I excluded from my exploratory survey: the operation of elision, syncope and manuscript variation. There was encouragement to regard as original a reading with a sounded ending on a weak monosyllabic adjective where there is a question of syllabic value elsewhere in the line, e.g. in line 108,

And th[i]s was now the first*e* morwe of May,

to value the final *e* on the adjective, where our copy-text has a terminal stroke on *t*, rather than reading, with some manuscripts, 'the first morow'

with full disyllabic value on the noun and no elision. There was encouragement to regard as original a reading which values a weak adjective ending
where textual variants provide an extra syllable instead, e.g. in line 2628,

> 'My ryghte doghter tresour of myn herte,'

where one manuscript reads 'My right dere doghter'. There was encouragement to emend, e.g. in line 1620,

> 'My right[e] lady,' quod this Iasoun tho,

where no manuscript has an *e* spelling. There proved to be no situations in
the text where to value a weak adjective in this way would produce a
hypermetrical line or a line with a stress pattern which seems at all
awkward, and the same was so for strong adjective plurals (with the
exception of 'all', discussed above).

Such situations seemed unproblematical. But what were the problems in
lines where my delimited survey had left me with apparent confirmation of
indeterminacy in certain grammatical situations? In such cases the possibility of a sounded final *e* must be weighed in each case against other
variables in the line, attention must be paid to the rhythmical pattern of the
whole line, not just to the number of syllables, and an explanation must be
sought for scribal variants which alter the scansion of the line. It is here
that considerations other than metrical ones will enter in.

A further general problem remains: if sounded final *e* in certain grammatical situations can be an option, then the question which remains open
is whether certain variant line forms which can result should be regarded as
available and acceptable options for the poet, specifically, lines with extra
unstressed syllables in mid-line positions, lines with a pause instead of an
unstressed syllable at a syntactic break in mid-line, and so-called 'headless'
lines, that is, lines of nine syllables lacking an initial weak stress. In the
nature of the case the evidence on these points is often going to be obscure,
because the metrical positions which are in doubt are most likely to be
occupied by words whose syllabic value is itself in doubt.

I will confine myself here to the question of headless lines. My check list
had not provided me with any examples of possibly headless lines uncom-
plicated by the doubtful status of final *e* or by manuscript variation (cf. the
discussion of lines 338 and 562 above). But evaluating the evidence of the
manuscript variants is just what an editor has to do. Metrical questions
cannot in the end be considered without reference to other considerations
of textual criticism. One consideration in the matter of headless lines is that
the manuscript variants reveal marked signs of divergent scribal attitudes
to such lines. Some textual variants otherwise explicable as scribal errors
on other grounds create the need to scan as headless a line which does not
otherwise read so, whereas in other cases variants read as systematic
attempts to smooth lines either originally headless or appearing so to the

scribe because a final *e* in the line was not given metrical value. Among the latter there may also in some instances be an additional inducement to mechanical error. Line 725 illustrates the interrelated issues:

Tisbe highte [the] maide, Naso seith thus,

Tisbe highte] And Tysbe he\i/t (i *above line by correction*) G; the] FBSTrThA[1]FfG; *om* T.

Here 'the' is present in all manuscripts except T, where its omission can be explained as a visual error caused by the similar endings of adjacent words. This is not the immediate point I wish to comment on, although we may infer from it that the scribe of T thought of the scansion of the line as admitting one and no more than one unstressed syllable at this point. The variation of substance which is to my immediate point is that of G, whose reading smooths what is otherwise scannable as a headless line. (The above-line correction does not alter this situation.) There is here, as in similar examples elsewhere in the text, an additional, non-metrical inducement to error, in that the following line has initial 'And'. The reading of G thus appears from more than one point of view to be questionable. A further question is whether the scribe of G is smoothing a line originally headless or one which appeared headless because of failure to value a syllabic final *e*. In other words, could the line as it reads in the manuscripts other than G be acceptably scanned not as a headless line but as a modulated ten syllable line in which the final *e* on 'highte' is sounded but where the word stress in the second two syllables runs counter to an iambic stress? Many readers to whom a headless line would be acceptable will probably decide that this second alternative sounds forced and awkward,[6] but the evidence from other lines for the variable metrical value of final *e* on this verb obliges us to consider both scansions before discarding either of them. I hope that an introductory discussion such as I have outlined above will encourage readers of the text to weigh such possibilities. In Robinson's text, which is based on G, this line stands in the text with the metrically smoothest reading, retaining G's initial 'And' (though with G's spelling of the verb normalised to 'hight'), and the selective nature of the textual apparatus (this line does not appear in it) precludes consideration of other scansions in this instance. In our text, as quoted here, the line will require of the reader a scansion varying from the norm, and the G reading will stand in the apparatus.

I take it for granted that an edition of a verse text should encourage, or provoke, the reader into thinking about the scansion of the lines. I hope that our text will be provocative and that our textual apparatus will provide material for thought.

---

[6] For comment on the infrequency of such a metrical pattern in this line position in English five-beat metres see Derek Attridge, *The Rhythms of English Poetry* (London, 1982), p. 174.

OBSERVATIONS ON THE HISTORY
OF MIDDLE ENGLISH EDITING

A. S. G. Edwards

No history of Middle English scholarship exists – a situation made all the more striking by the extended study of Old English scholars and their achievements. This deficiency is particularly felt by the student of Middle English editing and its history, who finds himself working in territory marked only by isolated signposts and the occasional local map of his terrain.[1] This is of particular importance because, until the publication of Warton's *History of English Poetry* in 1776 (and, indeed, for some time after its publication), the history of Middle English scholarship *is* substantially the history of Middle English editing. We are, admittedly, albeit only quite recently, quite well served with respect to Chaucer's editors;[2] but elsewhere we rely on occasional studies of the history of specific works, such as Robert of Gloucester's *Chronicle*[3] and Layamon's *Brut*,[4] or of particular genres and periods.[5] The notes that follow can be most charitably seen as a preliminary sketch of some significant aspects of the history of Middle English editing, chiefly between the late sixteenth and early nineteenth centuries.

My narrative begins towards the end of the first phase of such editing, the period from (roughly) Caxton to Stow, when we see the problems of rendering Middle English manuscripts into printed forms first confronted, and resolved in a variety of ways. We now have a clearer sense of the factors involved in Caxton's editing of Chaucer and Malory, for example: the editorial judgement that led him to accept a superior manuscript for his

---

[1] The extremely provisional nature of the following account must be stressed. It is quite probable that future research (which I hope to undertake) will lead to the modification of a number of the assertions made here.

[2] See P. Ruggiers, ed., *Editing Chaucer: The Great Tradition* (Norman, Okla.: Pilgrim Books, 1984).

[3] See Anne Hudson, 'Robert of Gloucester and the Antiquaries', *Notes & Queries*, 214 (1969), 323–36.

[4] R. Willard, 'Layamon in the seventeenth and eighteenth centuries', [University of Texas] *Studies in English*, 27 (1948), 239–78.

[5] See most notably the brilliant account of romance in the eighteenth century in Arthur Johnston's *Enchanted Ground* (London: Athlone Press, 1964) and Anne Hudson's discussion mainly of nineteenth- and twentieth-century editing in 'Middle English' in *Editing Medieval Texts . . .*, ed. A. G. Rigg (New York: Garland Publishing Inc., 1977), pp. 34–57. I am indebted to both these works.

second edition of the *Canterbury Tales*[6] and the extremely methodical ways in which he edited Malory's Winchester manuscript for publication.[7] We also have some information about de Worde's treatment of his copy-texts and other aspects of his editorial role.[8] And we are beginning to appreciate more the quite sophisticated editorial activities of Thynne,[9] who, in his 1532 Chaucer seems, at times, to have collated and conflated readings from more than one witness, and also to have introduced conjectural readings of some intelligence.[10] Stow may also have adopted a critical approach to problems of multiple authority to create an eclectic text.[11]

But much of this activity is, of course, ad hoc and pragmatic, uninformed by any methodological sense. There are few explicit indications of the problems of textual transmission. Caxton enumerates the textual differences between his first and second editions of the *Canterbury Tales*;[12] and we find Berthelette in his 1532 Gower criticising Caxton's edition of Gower for omitting 'lynes and columnes, ye and sometymes holle padges'.[13] But these are rare passages. If one is to seek a convenient signpost, marking a consciousness of some need to formulate a distinctive approach to the editing of Middle English works, Speght's 1598 Chaucer is a suitable one. This remained the standard text of Chaucer until Urry's edition in 1721. It was also the first to be accompanied by a glossary, the first significant indication of a response to the growing sense of linguistic distance separating Chaucer from a contemporary audience.[14]

Speght's glossary was followed by other responses to this problem of linguistic distance between text and audience. Thus, in 1613, there appeared

---

[6] See Lotte Hellinga, 'Manuscripts in the Hands of Printers', in *Manuscripts in the Fifty Years after the Invention of Printing*, ed. J. B. Trapp (London: Warburg Institute, 1983), esp. pp. 6–8.
[7] See N. F. Blake, 'Caxton Prepares his Edition of the *Morte Darthur*', *Journal of Librarianship*, 8 (1976), 272–85.
[8] See e.g. G. Bone, 'Extant Manuscripts printed from by Wynkyn de Worde with Notes on the Owner, Roger Thorney', *Library*, 4th ser. 12 (1931–32), 284–306; R. W. Mitchner, 'Wynkyn de Worde's Use of the Plimpton Manuscript of *De Proprietatibus Rerum*', *Library*, 5th ser., 6 (1951–52), 7–18; T. J. Garbaty, 'Wynkyn de Worde's *Sir Thopas* and Other Tales', *Studies in Bibliography*, 31 (1978), 57–67; and Carol Meale, 'Wynkyn de Worde's Setting-Copy for *Ipomydon*', *Studies in Bibliography*, 35 (1982), 156–71.
[9] See J. E. Blodgett, 'Some Printer's Copy for William Thynne's 1532 Edition of Chaucer', *Library*, 6th ser. 1 (1979), 96–113 and his chapter on Thynne in Ruggiers, *Editing Chaucer* . . . , pp. 35–52.
[10] See, e.g. line 1721 of the *Legend of Good Women*: where all other authorities read either 'oure bok' or omit this phrase, Thynne reads 'Liui'.
[11] See Anne Hudson, 'John Stow' in Ruggiers, *Editing Chaucer* . . . , pp. 53–69.
[12] The relevant document is printed in *Caxton's Own Prose*, ed. N. F. Blake (London: Deutsch, 1973), pp. 61–3.
[13] Quoted in *The Complete Works of John Gower*, ed. G. C. Macaulay (Oxford: Clarendon Press, 1901), II, clxix.
[14] See H. G. Wright, 'Thomas Speght as a Lexicographer and Annotator of Chaucer's Works', *English Studies*, 40 (1959), 194–208 and Derek Pearsall, 'Thomas Speght', in Ruggiers, *Editing Chaucer* . . . , pp. 71–92, esp. pp. 81–2.

the first volume of William Browne's *Britannia's Pastorals*, the first eclogue of which bears abundant testimony to Browne's wide reading of medieval literature, which achieves its fullest and most curious expression in his modernisation of Thomas Hoccleve's *Tale of Jonathas*. This undertaking merits more examination than is possible here. Most directly relevant to my present enquiry is the note Browne appends to his translation:

> THOMAS OCCLEVE, one of the Priuy Seale, composed first this tale, and was neuer til now imprinted. As this shall please, I may be drawne to publish the rest of his workes, being all perfect in my hands.[15]

That this was a serious promise is established by Ashmole 40, a manuscript of Hoccleve's *Regement of Princes*, which Browne seems to have worked over quite systematically, transcribing and inserting missing leaves, and supplying missing lines and even words, as well as glosses and notes.[16]

Browne's interest in Hoccleve can be seen to embody two distinct, indeed contradictory tendencies. In the first place, we see his sense of the linguistic distance that separates Hoccleve from his own time, a distance which he seeks to reduce by modernisation in the *Tale of Jonathas*. In contrast, we see in Ashmole 40 his desire for textual accuracy – or, at least, completeness – that expresses itself in the collation of this manuscript against at least one other copy. The history of Middle English editing for the rest of the seventeenth century seems to be, very largely, the history of these contending claims: on the one hand, the perceived need to make Middle English texts accessible to audiences with little or no knowledge of their grammar, orthography or syntax and, on the other, the need to retrieve and preserve the text.

The more conservative response to these claims may be conveniently represented by William Bedwell's edition of *The Tournament of Tottenham* in 1631. It is possible to assess his work as editor with relative precision since his copy-text has survived in CUL Ff.5.48, ff. 62–6, a manuscript brought to his notice, he claims, by the poet George Wither.[17] A collation of Bedwell's text against the manuscript suggests that he was relatively accurate, apart from a little trouble with Middle English forms like thorn and yogh, and an intermittent tendency to tinker with orthography. He is,

---

[15] *The Whole Works of William Browne*, ed. W. C. Hazlitt (1869), II, 198.

[16] For a description of this manuscript see M. C. Seymour, 'The Manuscripts of Hoccleve's *Regement of Princes*', *Transactions of the Edinburgh Bibliographical Society*, IV, pt 7 (1974), 278–9.

[17] *The Tvrnament of Tottenham . . . Taken out of an ancient Manuscript, and published for the delight of others, by Willelm Bedwell . . .* (1631). The preface 'To the Courteous Reader' announces that 'It is now seauen or eight yeares since I came first to the sight of the copy, and that by meanes of the worthy, and my much honoured good friend, M. *Ge. Withers*: Of whom also, now at length I, haue obtained the vse of the same . . . I thought it worth the while . . . to transcribe it, and for the honour of the place [i.e. Tottenham], to make it publicke'. (A 4)

in the main, content to 'transcribe' (his term) to produce a tolerably faithful representation of his exemplar. But he is conscious of problems; he notes that 'many, not onely words, but phrases, are so obsolete and outworne, that few, except such as are well versed in the writynges of the Auncients, may easily vnderstand them'.[18] These are not problems he is disposed to resolve. He makes no attempt at eludication, either through modernisation or through notes or a glossary.

One might contrast this conservative attitude with the one revealed in William Stansby's edition of Malory's *Morte Darthur*, which appeared in 1634. The 'Preface . . . to the *Reader*' announces that

> in many places this Volume is corrected (not in language but in phrase) for here and there, King *Arthur* or some of his knights were declared in their communications to sweare prophane, and vse super-stitious speeches, all (or the most part) of which is either amended or quite left out, by the paines and industry of the Compositor and Corrector at the Presse; so that as it is now it may passe for a famous piece of Antiquity revived almost from the gulph of oblivion, and renued for the pleasure and profit of present and future times.[19]

Stansby may be adjudged guilty of excessive optimism and also lack of candour. His was to be the last edition of Malory until the early nineteenth century.[20] And his text, far from being improved, is often notably corrupt.[21] But he does indicate the growing sense of a need to do something about Middle English texts if they were to be printed for contemporary audiences.

Others who confronted this problem during the seventeenth century were often content to implement what might be termed the Stansby solution of frequent, extensive emendation, amounting to virtual modern-isation. Serenus Cressy's edition of Hilton's *Scale of Perfection* (1659) describes this solution neatly; according to the title page, the text is ' . . . by the changing of some antiquated words, rendred more intelligible'.[22] But not everyone was content with a process of simple, linguistically distorting modernisation. Towards the end of the century, there were one

---

[18] Ibid., A 3.

[19] *The Most Ancient and Famovs History of The Renowned Prince Arthur King of Britaine* (1634), A 4v.

[20] See further on the role of Stansby's edition in the later history of Malory's text, Barry Gaines, 'The Editions of Malory in the Early Nineteenth Century', *Papers of the Bibliographical Society of America*, 68 (1974), 1–17.

[21] Gaines, 1.

[22] A similar process of modernisation can be seen in other contemporary treatments of Middle English texts; cf. e.g. the various renderings of Rolle, Hilton and the *Cloud of Unknowing* by Fr Augustine Baker (on which see Fr Peter Salvin and Fr Serenus Cressy, *The Life of Augustine Baker*, ed. Dom Justin McCann (London: Burns, Oates & Washbourne, 1933), esp. Appendix II) and the seventeenth-century versions of the Middle English translation of Deguileville's *Pelerinage de la Vie humaine* extant in Cambridge University Library Ff.VI.30 and Magdalene College, Cambridge, Pepys 2258.

or two more sophisticated reflections on the problem. For example, Henry Wharton in 1688 produced an edition of Pecock's *Treatise Proving Scripture to be the Rule of Faith*. His text is based on Trinity College, Cambridge MS B.14.45, which he tells us

> was by me transcribed . . . which seemed to have been written with Bishop *Peacock*'s own hand, as may be conjectured from the frequent Emendations and Additions inserted in the Margin, and bottom of the Page by the same hand. (xxxix)

Such reasoning (and the assurance that Wharton did his own transcription) suggest a degree of editorial care that is further evidenced in his response to the problem of linguistic distance:

> I will not so far presume upon the Judgement of the Reader, as to make an Apology for the old and obsolete stile of our Author. If it wanteth the Elegance and Beauties of our modern Language, that must be imputed to the fault of the Age, not any deficience [*sic*] of the Author. I had once intended to represent his Arguments in our modern Language, and publish both together in distinct Columns, but the fear of inlarging these Papers too much, deterred me from pursuing that design. However, I have drawn up an Alphabetical Catalogue of the more obsolete and unusual words, and affixed their significations to them. (xl)

The notion of facing page translations was not a new one. It was actually employed in the editing of Old English texts in the sixteenth century in Archbishop Parker's *A Testimonie of Antiquitie* (1566), where a homily of Aelfric's appears side by side with a modern rendering. But even if the method is derivative – and here aborted – there is some interest in Wharton's sense of the problems of attempting to reconcile fidelity to his author (particularly in what he felt to be an autograph manuscript) with the problem of the editor's responsibility in presenting an antique text to a modern audience.

The pressing nature of these related concerns of linguistic accessibility and textual integrity can be brought a little more clearly into focus by a consideration of the textual history of the poem *Christ's Kirk on the Green*, attributed variously (and on wholly insubstantial grounds) to either James I or James VI of Scotland. A convenient starting point is the edition by the precocious Edmund Gibson included in the second edition of Drummond's *Polemo Middinia* in 1691. It is sometimes incorrectly asserted that this is the first edition of this poem. In fact it seems to have had a history as a broadside during the second half of the seventeenth century;[23] some seventeenth-century manuscript copies also survive.[24]

[23] See e.g. Wing J 412–13, M 1851.
[24] E.g. Edinburgh University La. III. 501, Bodleian Ashmole 36, 37 and BL Lansdowne 740.

Gibson's edition is set out in a form that is both authoritative-seeming and also innovative. The use of black letter (not yet abandoned for editions of Chaucer) is coupled with explanatory notes at the foot of the page, with illustrations from, for example, Chaucer and Gavin Douglas. This is the first Middle English edition of which I am aware to adopt this modern-looking shape to the page.

But if the design of Gibson's edition has a modern look, his text is less to be commended in its modernity. We see that the scholarly apparatus of his text supports an edifice that is rather shoddy, and seeming to derive from a heavily-anglicised source, probably the broadside tradition mentioned above. The text is extensively distanced from any putative Scottish original. Thus, Gibson expends his annotational efforts on a text that has already been made distortingly accessible linguistically. Black Letter becomes in itself a sufficient warranty of linguistic antiquity, and Gibson is not disposed to enquire into the antecedents of his text.

One can contrast Gibson's edition, with its scholarly form but textually unsound substance, with the various editions of *Christ's Kirk* produced by Allan Ramsay. He first produced two editions in 1718. The first was in two cantos (the first the original poem, the second his own addition). The text of this edition seems to derive from that published by James Watson in his *Choice Collection of Comic and Serious Scots Poems* which derives in its turn from Gibson's edition.[25] Later in 1718, Ramsay brought out another edition of *Christ's Kirk*, this time in three cantos; once again, only the first, containing the original poem, is relevant to the present purposes. In the interval Ramsay had made some forays into textual criticism. In the Advertisement to this edition he writes

> This Edition of the first CANTO, is copied from an old Manuscript Collection of SCOTS POEMS wrot an hundred and fifty Years ago; where it is found to be done by KING *JAMES* I. Besides its being more correct, the VIIIth STANZA was not in print before; the last but one, of the late Edition, being none of the King's, gives place to this. (A 2r)

There seems no reason to doubt Ramsay's claim that he had access to a manuscript of the poem, although I have been unable to identify it. It is sufficient to note the editorial enterprise that led him to reject a text he had recently printed in preference to one he could feel, on reasoned grounds, to be superior. Nor did he stop there. The second 1718 edition of *Christ's Kirk* reappeared in subsequent collections of Ramsay's poems, with relatively few alterations. In the 1721 edition of his *Poems* Ramsay adds explanatory notes, continuing the process of producing what was, for its

[25] See further Burns Martin, *A Bibliography of the Writings of Allan Ramsay*, Records of the Glasgow Bibliographical Society, Vol. XI (1931), pp. 21–3 to which the following account is indebted.

day, a creditable edition of a Middle English poem. The process was carried still further in Ramsay's final editorial effort on *Christ's Kirk* in *The Evergreen* (1724), where he elects to print a different text, this time that of the Bannantyne Manuscript, in what he claims to be a strict representation of 'the old Orthography', with explanatory and glossarial notes.

I recount the history of Ramsay's continuing engagement with this poem because it suggests a serious concern with editorial responsibility, both in the authority of his choice of text and in matters of orthography and elucidation. It also suggests a notion of the text that imposed considerable limitations on the editor. For Ramsay, the text was not an entity capable of at least partial construction out of the variety of surviving witnesses, but a series of independent artefacts, from among which the editor must choose one in its entirety.

While the notion of eclectic, conflated texts is one that seems to have been foreign to Ramsay, the first intimations of the concept were beginning to emerge at roughly the same time – once again, in Scotland. The 1710 edition of Gavin Douglas's *Eneydos* is a notable example of scholarly collaboration, involving at least five men of letters whose energies were channelled by the Edinburgh printer, Thomas Ruddiman.[26] Nowadays the edition is generally viewed as having some cultural importance (it contains a glossary that marks the beginnings of Scottish dialectal studies), but no editorial interest. Certainly, it has little intrinsic value as a text. Ruddiman used the 1553 edition by the London printer William Copland as his base-text. He supplemented it, however, with some readings from the Ruthven manuscript, as well as by some of his own conjectures. The process is a somewhat random one; Ruddiman did not become aware of the Ruthven manuscript until he had printed off the first forty-four pages of his edition.[27] It seems to have been the first effort since the middle of the sixteenth century (in the editions of Thynne and Stow of Chaucer) to use more than one authority to establish the text of a Middle English work.[28]

The implications of the 1710 *Eneydos* can be seen more intelligibly in the context of other near-contemporary efforts to deal with the problems of multiple authority. Two works are of some relevance. The first is John Fortescue Aland's edition of *The Difference between an Absolute and a Limited Monarchy*, by his ancestor Sir John Fortescue, which first appeared in 1714. Fortescue Aland seems to have been prompted by a conspicuous

---

[26] See the helpful discussion of Ruddiman's edition in L. M. Watt, *Douglas's Aeneid* (Cambridge: Cambridge University Press, 1920), pp. 18–20. Ruddiman's collaborators were Bishops Thomas Nicholson and John Sage (the latter wrote Douglas's biography), Sir Robert Sibbald, the antiquarian, the bookseller, Robert Freebairn and John Urry.

[27] Urry also seems to have collated the Longleat manuscript with the 1553 edition, but the relationship of his work to the printed text is unclear; see Watt, p. 140.

[28] Mrs Felicity Riddy has, however, drawn my attention to Andrew Hart's 1616 edition of the *Bruce*, which is described on the title page as 'Newly corrected and conferred with the best and most ancient Manuscripts'. The validity of this claim would merit more enquiry.

devotion to his ancestor's reputation. He had a transcript made of Bodleian Digby 145, which he 'collated'[29] with other copies in the Laud and Digby collections and with one in the Cotton Library, Cotton Claudius A. VIII. After this effort, he decided to base his text on the Digby manuscript, for reasons it is not easy to endorse in their entirety:

> This copy [Digby 145] is the fairest, most perfect and complete of them all, and was transcrib'd by Sir Adrian Fortescue's own hand, who was a Descendant from our Author, and lived in the Reign of King Henry the Eighth.[30]

Even though, as he notes, 'Archbishop Laud's copy [Laud Misc. 593] seems to be the most ancient' he chooses to adopt a substantially later text. But he does claim to include 'all the various Readings' from the manuscripts he has collated, 'which are material to the curious Antiquary'.[31] While this amounts to much less than a full collation, we do see for the first time a consciousness of the need to present variant textual evidence in a clear form. Variants appear in the margins at the appropriate points. Explanatory notes and some glosses appear at the foot of the page.

Thomas Hearne's edition of Robert of Gloucester's *Chronicle* in 1724 has been acclaimed as the 'first workmanlike edition of a Middle-English text'[32] and the accuracy of his work has earned the admiration of modern scholars. Once again, though, the actual choice of base text is rather peculiar: Hearne used an incomplete manuscript, Harley 201, which he then had to supplement by another, Cotton Caligula A. XI, when it might have seemed more reasonable to have used Cotton throughout. He also includes extensive variant readings from College of Arms MS LVIII.

Both Fortescue Aland's and Hearne's editions share a randomness of editorial method, combined with considerable care and restraint in the execution of that method. In both, the reasons for the selection of a base-text are – at best – unconvincing. Yet the text, once selected, is presented in an extremely scrupulous manner, with great attention to accuracy. The editors' sense of the purposes of recording variant readings is unclear, apart from Fortescue Aland's desire to serve the 'curious Antiquary'. They do not provide, for instance, any basis for the activity so central to our modern sense of the editorial role, emendation. The notion of recording variants is not part of any larger strategy for establishing the relative authority of particular readings. In this respect, Middle English editing stands in striking contrast to the editing of classical texts, where

---

[29] The only earlier use of the word in this textual sense recorded by *OED* is in Thynne's 1532 Chaucer.
[30] *The Difference between an Absolute and Limited Monarchy . . . Faithfully Transcribed from the MS. Copy in the Bodleian Library, and Collated with three other MSS.* Published with some Remarks by John Fortescue-Aland (London, 1714), xxxvi–vii.
[31] Ibid., xxxvii.
[32] D. C. Douglas, *English Scholars, 1660–1730*, 2nd edn (London: Eyre and Spottiswoode, 1951), p. 188; see also Hudson, 'Robert of Gloucester', 331.

emendation had enjoyed a central role since the Renaissance. But the implications of the activity for vernacular texts were not swiftly perceived, and when applied at all in the early eighteenth century, were applied with some perversity.[33]

One reason for this slightly eccentric conservatism seems to lie in the lack of any methodology for establishing departures from a base-text, for indicating the actual use of variant readings or editorial conjectures. The convention of square brackets to indicate such departures is now sanctioned by scholarly convention. But we lack a history of the conceptions of the function of square brackets at least in so far as it was applied to and manifested in vernacular texts. The first edition of a Middle English work of which I am aware that employs them is Ruddiman's of Douglas's *Eneydos*. They are employed at a scattering of points,[34] and their function is never clearly stated. But it seems that their purpose is not so much to alert the reader to altered readings in the text as to indicate additions to it, from the Ruthven manuscript. (Most of Ruddiman's emendations are silent ones.)[35]

The first person (to the best of my knowledge) who sought to use square brackets systematically to indicate all departures from his base-text, apart from omissions, was John Pinkerton in his *Ancient Scotish Poems* (1786), based largely on the Maitland Folio Manuscript. He announces

> Where in one or two places, a word, a line was palpably lost, the editor has supplied them; but every the most minute supplement, or alteration of an evidently wrong word, tho' it be but a *That* for an *And*, is always put in brackets [thus]. And the reader may depend upon finding thro-out a *literal* transcript of the MS. save in these very rare instances, as far as human fallibility would permit.[36]

Human fallibility would permit quite a lot. Pinkerton silently regularises thorn and yogh, adds punctuation, and changes capitalisation, as well as making a number of transcriptional errors. And while he uses square brackets with great frequency, he does not always explain the reasons for his emendations or their (at times) conjectural basis. But he seems to have been the first editor to be conscious of the appropriateness of alerting readers in a regular way to forms of editorial intervention.

[33] The most obvious example is Bentley's editing of *Paradise Lost* applying classical techniques of conjectural emendation; for recent discussion see R. G. Moyles, *The Text of Paradise Lost* (Toronto: University of Toronto Press, 1984), pp. 59–71. One may contrast his activity with Edward Capell's work on the text of Shakespeare a generation later which has earned him the accolade of 'the first systematic editor of Shakespeare' and, one might suggest, the first systematic editor of any English writer; see further Alice Walker, 'Edward Capell and his Edition of *Shakespeare*', *Proceedings of the British Academy*, 46 (1960), 131–45 (the quotation is from p. 132).

[34] E.g. pp. 105–6, 138, 190, 200, 213, 429.

[35] See further, Watt, p. 138.

[36] *Ancient Scotish Poems Never Before in Print but now Published from the MS. Collections of Sir Richard Maitland*, 2 vols. (1786), I, xvi.

He was also among the first to intone a formal claim of fidelity to his manuscript witness. That such a claim was necessary probably derives from a growing recognition of the activities of Bishop Percy in the several editions of his *Reliques*, first published in 1765. There is no need to rehearse Percy's editorial excesses in detail; Bate summarises the matter admirably. For example, from his own Folio manuscript he printed forty-six ballads.

> Approximately half of these he printed substantially as he found them. The remaining ballads were altered in varying degrees; some received an addition of only a few stanzas and the insertion of one or two new incidents in the narrative; others were altered beyond all recognition, containing scarcely an incident or even one line that might be found in the manuscript version.[37]

In one case he expanded the 'Ballads of the Childe of Elle' from thirty-nine lines to two hundred.[38]

Percy was, of course, simply drawing on a lengthy tradition of 'improving' the works of medieval writers going back at least to Thomas Alsop's modernisation of the *Man of Law's Tale* in the *c.* 1520s[39] and continued in William Browne's work on Hoccleve and John Lane's mid-seventeenth-century efforts to continue Chaucer's *Squire's Tale* and Lydgate's *Guy of Warwick*, a trend continued in various later seventeenth- and eighteenth-century rewritings of works by (among others) Chaucer, Lydgate and Hoccleve. But the temper of the times was against Percy, and indeed, he himself in his later editorial career showed that he was capable of much more responsible editing than that shown in the *Reliques*.[40] But he was forced into public acknowledgement of his editorial excesses in the fourth edition of the *Reliques* in 1794:

> The Second Poem in this Volume, intitled THE MARRIAGE OF SIR GAWAINE, having been offered to the Reader with large conjectural Supplements and Corrections, the old Fragment itself is here literally and exactly printed from the Editor's Folio MS. with all its defects, inaccuracies and errata; that such austere Antiquaries, as complain that the ancient copies have not been always rigidly adhered to, may see how unfit for publication many of the pieces would have

---

[37] W. J. Bate, 'Percy's Use of the Folio-Manuscript', *Journal of English & Germanic Philology*, 43 (1944), 336–7.

[38] Bate, 345–8.

[39] Printed and discussed by F. B. Williams, *English Literary Renaissance*, 6 (1976), 351–68.

[40] See Cleanth Brooks, 'The History of Percy's Edition of Surrey's Poems', *Englische Studien*, 68 (1933–34), 424–30. Brooks concludes that 'had his Surrey appeared in 1775, Percy's reputation as an editor would stand much higher today' (428). Percy certainly seems to have become conscious of the need for careful collation; BL Add. 39547 includes (ff. 88–107v) his text of Lydgate's *Churl and Bird* with variants recorded from a manuscript and two early printed editions.

been, if all the blunders, corruptions and nonsense of illiterate Reciters and Transcribers have been superficially retained, without some attempt to correct and emend them.[41]

A comparison of this literal and exact transcript with the version previously printed, indicates that Percy had added some forty-six stanzas and made numerous other changes.[42]

This belated concern with editorial candour was not to save Percy from becoming a whipping boy for subsequent Middle English editors, and also helping to stimulate a growing refinement in the enunciation of concepts of editorial responsibility. Joseph Ritson, in his *Ancient Engleish Metrical Romances* (1802), generally lays about him with sneers about Percy's 'elegant and refin'd work', but he does go on to give a sense of the role of the editor that is detailed and valid:

To correct the obvious errors of an illiterate transcriber, to supply irremediable defects and to make sense of nonsense, are certainly essential dutys of an editour of ancient poetry; provided he act with integrity and publicity; but secretly to suppress the original text, and insert his own fabrications for the sake of provideing more refin'd entertainment for readers of taste and genius, is no proof of either jugdment, candour, or integrity.[43]

Ritson's edition is itself not altogether free from the imputation that it sought 'secretly to suppress the original text'. His sense of the relationship between the activity of emendation and its indication is not always very clear. He does provide at the end of his collection a list of 'Original Readings Corrected in this edition', and does place a number of readings within square brackets. But there seems no connection between the two activities; readings that appear in square brackets in his text are not noted in the 'Original Readings Corrected . . .', and it is not possible to discover the forms of the rejected readings elsewhere. It appears that, as in Ruddiman's 1710 edition of Douglas, square brackets indicate only interpolations, not other forms of emendation.

The problem of accuracy and the role of the editor seems to have achieved its first wholly systematic formulation in Middle English editing in Frederic Madden's remarkable edition, *Syr Gawayne, A Collection of Ancient Romance Poems*, published by the Bannantyne Club in 1839.[44] The introduction contains a statement that enunciates clear and consistent procedures for the presentation of texts:

---

[41] *Reliques of Ancient English Poetry*, 4th edn (1974), III, 350.
[42] See further, Johnston, *Enchanted Ground*, p. 81.
[43] *Ancient Engleish Metrical Romances Selected and Publish'd by Joseph Ritson* (1802), I, cix.
[44] For discussion of this edition see R. W. Ackerman, 'Madden's Gawain Anthology', in *Medieval Studies in Honor of Lillian Herlands Hornstein*, eds. J. B. Bessinger and R. R. Raymo (New York: New York University Press, 1976), pp. 5–18.

The poems here taken from original manuscripts are printed with a scrupulous regard to accuracy, and the abbreviations left as written, but, for the convenience of the reader, a list of them is annexed, and the words written at length [i.e. expanded in full] in the Glossary and Notes. The truth is, that editors of our old poetry have, with few exceptions, paid too little attention to the system of writing used by the early scribes, and the consequence is, that but a small portion of all that have been published will bear collation with the originals . . . It is time this were remedied. (xlv)

The magisterial tone is justified by Madden's palaeographical genius which is reflected in his scrupulous methodology. In his edition, the problem of presenting the 'original text' is tackled by the ultimate solution before the age of photography, the type facsimile, retaining the manuscript contractions and letter forms. Madden was not the first to apply this method to Middle English texts,[45] but he seems to have been the first to employ it as part of an overall strategy that could lead one to claim his collection as the first completely scrupulous edition of Middle English works. His concern for the accurate presentation of his texts does not preclude emendation; but emendations are regularly indicated within square brackets; rejected readings are systematically recorded in a textual apparatus at the foot of the page; and there are substantial notes, glossary and introduction. In Madden's work we see merged the components of a genuine critical edition: accuracy, collation, emendation, a systematic procedure for indicating emendations of whatever size, as well as the necessary supporting explanatory materials. Such an edition placed Madden at the forefront of the medievalists of his age. It was the first in a series of major editions – followed by those of Layamon's *Brut* and the Wycliffe Bible – in which Madden sustained his new editorial standards to produce works that retain their importance to our own day.[46]

In Madden's work we see the demonstration of a sustained application of editorial method that is valid and ably executed. In an important sense he established a tradition of Middle English editing that continues to our own day in ways that are not very advanced. It is a tradition marked first by a conservationist cast, a consciousness of a need to represent the surviving forms of a text as scrupulously as possible, both in transcription and collation, as well as by a clear sense of the relationship between these activities and emendation.

This tradition of editing is one within which much of the competent editing of Middle English texts has gone on. When one considers the

---

[45] The earliest type facsimile of which I am aware of a Middle English text is Samuel Pegge's of the *Forme of Cury*, which appeared in 1786.

[46] On Madden's achievements as editor see further R. W. Ackerman 'Sir Frederic Madden and Medieval Scholarship', *Neuphilologische Mitteilungen*, 73 (1972), 1–14.

evolutions in method that have taken place in the editing of texts of other periods it is noteworthy that Middle English editing should be marked by tendencies that are often cautiously pragmatic. Inevitably one compares the formulations of W. W. Greg, in his 'Rationale of Copy Text',[47] itself a development of positions first adumbrated by R. B. McKerrow in the early years of this century in his edition of Nashe[48] and later in his *Prolegomena to Shakespeare* (1939), formulations which have recently been elaborated and applied more extensively to post-Renaissance literature by Fredson Bowers and Thomas Tanselle.[49] These attempts to formulate general editorial principles which combine methodological coherence with flexibility have not evoked much interest from editors of Middle English works.

This is most apparent in the editorial treatment of Chaucer's works, particularly the *Canterbury Tales*. My account so far has bypassed the central figures of the Middle English tradition. This is because, apart from Chaucer, none of the major, textually complex authors, such as Langland, Gower, Lydgate and Hoccleve was edited in any real sense before the latter part of the nineteenth century. (In the case of Gower and Hoccleve we still rely on these same editions.) But the example of Chaucer is interesting because it reveals tendencies that run directly counter to the conservationist ones I have been chronicling. What we can perceive is the way in which, in the editing of Chaucer, the pursuit of method has become steadily more confused with a lust for order. It is possible to trace an evolving sense of the function of the editor, not as restorer, but inventor of the forms of the text he seeks to edit.

A pivotal figure in such tendencies is Thomas Tyrwhitt, whose great edition of the *Canterbury Tales* appeared in 1775. Recent scholarship has articulated his achievement with admirable clarity.[50] But Tyrwhitt was not an editor committed to method in the sense of the enunciation of formulable principles that sought to address such questions as the actual form of his text or the evidential basis for resolving a disputed reading. In spite of his claim that he had 'formed the text throughout from the Mss', the actual form of his edition is the 1687 reprint of Speght.[51] Variants are not recorded regularly; nor are emendations signified in the text; nor does it seem to have been Tyrwhitt's practice to do so when actually examining

[47] First published in *Studies in Bibliography*, 3 (1950–51), and reprinted in his *Collected Papers*, ed. J. C. Maxwell (Oxford: Clarendon Press, 1966), pp. 374–91.
[48] *The Works of Thomas Nashe*, ed. R. B. McKerrow (London: A. H. Bullen and Sidgwick & Jackson, 1904–10).
[49] Much of the relevant material is conveniently reprinted in Bowers, *Essays in bibliography, text, and editing* (Charlottesville: University of Virginia Press, 1975), and Tanselle, *Selected Studies in Bibliography* (Charlottesville: University of Virginia Press, 1980).
[50] See the excellent essay by Barry Windeatt in *Editing Chaucer . . .*, pp. 117–43.
[51] See A. L. Hench, 'Printer's Copy for Tyrwhitt's Chaucer', *Studies in Bibliography*, 3 (1950), 265–6.

manuscripts; and he follows the example of Urry in imposing a large number of conjectural metrical emendations on his text.[52]

I offer such criticisms not out of any inclination to disparage Tyrwhitt's achievement. His editorial activity was sufficiently imposing as to inhibit the critical editing of Chaucer's works again for nearly a hundred years. He set new standards in editorial judgement and the use of manuscript evidence for the editing of Middle English texts. But these standards reveal a degree of ambiguity in Tyrwhitt's attitudes towards the treatment of Chaucer's texts that may have had its roots in his training as a classical scholar. While he is far from being a slashing Bentley he is much more interested in the *interpretation* of manuscript evidence than its presentation and hence more preoccupied with emendation than with fidelity to a particular manuscript form of his text.

Tyrwhitt's intellectual heir was Skeat, who frequently expresses his admiration for the earlier editor. Skeat develops in his own editing many of the tendencies inherent in Tyrwhitt's work, so that editorial method becomes further subordinated to the manifestation of editorial genius, genius manifested through the application of thought to textual problems. As I have tried to show elsewhere,[53] Skeat came to regard his own secure confidence that he knew what Chaucer meant to say even when the manuscripts did not as a sufficient basis for editing Chaucer. Thus he silently changed Chaucer's orthography, regularised his verse, made silent emendations and offered unsystematic collations. Such confidence in his own powers that he did not need to present evidence or offer cautionary indications of his activities stems from this confidence in the capacity of the right editor to arrive at the right solution by the exercise of reason. Much more so than did Tyrwhitt, Skeat seems to have believed in the final accessibility of the variant forms of a text to rational editorial conjecture to produce a form that enacts authorial intention.

In some ways, the recent edition of the B Text of *Piers Plowman*[54] lies in a line of descent from Tyrwhitt and Skeat. It is edited out of a clearly articulated belief in the necessity and the efficacy of conjectural emendation to recover Langland's original intention. Editorial method – the use of recension – is abandoned in preference to editorial judgement. This involves extensive emendation, and the establishing of a number of readings unsupported by any authority.

The role of the editor becomes in this context potentially at least a vatic one, in which he casts himself as confidante of the author's shade, glossing the mysteries of intentionality. It must be said that the editors are conscious of such implications in their position and, indeed, discuss them. They also

---

[52] See Windeatt, esp. pp. 132–3.
[53] In my essay on Skeat in *Editing Chaucer . . .*, pp. 171–89.
[54] *Piers Plowman: The B Version*, edited by George Kane and E. Talbot Donaldson (London: Athlone Press, 1975).

seek to set themselves apart from traditions of editorial invention both by the fullness of their editorial apparatus, their scrupulous attempts to indicate all forms of editorial intervention and their lengthy introduction which discussed many of the changes they have made. Such candour and intellectual honesty require the fullest response of which any reader is capable.

It may be that this edition marks a methodological advance that will set a new standard and provide a new model for editions of Middle English texts. Less optimistically, it may be seen as a *tour de force* that lends itself to misapplication through imitation. If so, it may constitute a methodological impasse, or, in the worst hands, a return to the inventive techniques of Bishop Percy. The lesson of history seems to suggest a different lesson: the more durable value of the editorial achievement when the virtues of Kane/Donaldson's edition – accuracy, candour and full presentation of evidence – are joined to restraint.

THE SIMONIE: THE CASE FOR A PARALLEL-TEXT EDITION

Dan Embree and Elizabeth Urquhart

In working on our parallel-text edition of *The Simonie*,[1] we have occasionally found ourselves at odds with some of the received assumptions of our craft. Not that we have found those assumptions themselves to be fundamentally or generally in error – just that they seem not to fit very comfortably our observations of the texts with which we are working. Indeed, it is the refusal of our facts to fit some of the conventional assumptions about medieval composition and transmission that led us to decide on a parallel-text edition in the first place.

That such a decision needs to be defended is suggested partly by the relative absence of similar editions, partly by the occasional sceptical looks of our colleagues, and partly by Kane and Donaldson's characterisation of any edition which stops short of a fully reconstructed original as a 'poor-spirited and slothful undertaking'.[2]

But before we proceed any further with this apologia for sloth, we had better say what the main facts of the manuscript tradition are.

The Simonie is a Middle English evil-times complaint – that is, a poem which attacks the ecclesiastical, political, and social abuses of the poet's society and which despairs of that society's moral condition. Because of its concern with the contemporary and the secular, it can be somewhat more loosely classified as one of R. H. Robbins's 'poems on contemporary conditions';[3] and because it analyses society according to traditional medi-

---

[1] We are preparing this edition for the *Middle English Texts* series, eds. Manfred Görlach and Oliver Pickering. Each of the three known manuscripts has been previously edited: *A* by Thomas Wright, *Political Songs of England*, Camden Society, 6 (London, 1839); *B* by Thomas W. Ross, ' "On the Evil Times of Edward II": A New Version from MS Bodley 48', *Anglia* 75 (1957), 173–93; and *C* by Charles Hardwick, *A Poem on the Times of Edward II*, Percy Society, 28 (London, 1849). There is also a 'composite edition', made by conflating all three texts, by Ross, *A Satire of Edward II's England*, Colorado College Studies 8 (Colorado Springs, 1966).

[2] George Kane and E. Talbot Donaldson, eds., *Piers Plowman: The B Version* (London, 1975), p. 129.

[3] R. H. Robbins, 'Poems Dealing with Contemporary Conditions', in *A Manual of the Writings in Middle English, 1050–1500*, ed. Albert E. Hartung, 5 (New Haven, 1975), p. 1437. Several 'evil times' complaints are to be found in Robbins, *Historical Poems of the XIVth and XVth Centuries* (New York, 1959), and T. Wright, *Political Poems and Songs*, Rolls Series, 14 (London, 1859–61).

eval hierarchies and divisions (in this case, bishop, archdeacon, clerk, parson, monk, friar, physician, baron, knight, squire, bailiff, beadle, justice, lawyer, merchant, tradesman, labourer), it can also be classified as an 'estates satire'.[4] The thesis of the poem is that greed is the common motivation behind the peculiar abuses of each estate. Greed, personified from time to time as 'Simonie' or 'Coveytise', is shown to be victorious over personified Truth and, in an unpersonified form, to seduce men of all estates from their true obligations and allegiances.

The Simonie survives in three manuscripts, which present three distinct texts in three different contexts. The earliest or *A*-version occupies the remains of what is now the last quire of the famous Auchinleck Manuscript, National Library of Scotland, Edinburgh, Advocates MS 19.2.1.[5] It is in the hand of Scribe 2, who was responsible for two other, widely separated items in the manuscript. Although Scribe 2 was probably not a Londoner by origin, the manuscript seems to have been put together in London, probably for one of those educated and aspirant middle-class citizens of whom London had a plentiful supply by the 1330s.[6] At first sight, *The Simonie* seems rather an odd bedfellow for the romping romances and sturdy saints' lives which dominate Auchinleck, but it shares the moral concerns, more or less clearly stated, of many items in the manuscript – particularly the other two pieces copied by Scribe 2 (the homiletic *Speculum Gy de Warwike* and a short macaronic political poem). And, in its concern for the state of the nation, 'al Engelond, boþe souþ and norþ' (l. A 417), it emphasises some aspects of the whole manuscript's 'Englishness'.[7]

The *B*-version of the poem occupies the last quire, plus preceding verso, of Bodleian Library MS Bodley 48. That manuscript seems to have been put together during the second quarter of the fifteenth century as materials and exemplars came to hand, written by a capable, conscientious, but probably non-professional scribe.[8] (Scribe, compiler, and owner may well

[4] See Ruth Mohl, *The Three Estates in Medieval and Renaissance Literature* (New York, 1933), and Jill Mann, *Chaucer and Medieval Estates Satire* (Cambridge, 1973) for discussions of this genre.

[5] Available in a Scolar Press facsimile, with an introduction by Derek Pearsall and I. C. Cunningham (London, 1977). For the work of Scribe 2 and the composition of the manuscript, see A. J. Bliss, 'Notes on the Auchinleck Manuscript', *Speculum* 26 (1951), 652–8; Cunningham, 'Notes on the Auchinleck Manuscript', *Speculum* 47 (1972), 96–8, and the introduction to the facsimile edition; Cunningham and J. E. C. Mordkoff, 'New Light on the Signatures in the Auchinleck Manuscript', *Scriptorium* 36 (1982), 280–92. We are also grateful to the staff of the Gayre Institute, Edinburgh, for the information they have provided on dialectal features of the manuscript, and to I. C. Cunningham for advice on its palaeography.

[6] See Pearsall, introduction to the facsimile edition, and L. H. Loomis, 'The Auchinleck Manuscript and a Possible London Bookshop of 1330–40', *PMLA* 57 (1942), 595–627, and reprinted, with several other essays concerning this manuscript, in *Adventures in The Middle Ages* (New York, 1962).

[7] Pearsall, *Old English and Middle English Poetry* (London, 1977), pp. 115–16.

[8] We are grateful to Dr A. I. Doyle, University of Durham, and Dr Bruce Barker-Benfield, Department of Western Manuscripts, Bodleian Library, Oxford, for palaeographical information on this manuscript.

have been one and the same person.) The first section consists of four of Rolle's less 'difficult' and more expository Latin works; the second contains William of Nassyngton's *Speculum Vitae* (a long catechetical poem in English),[9] and *The Simonie*. All the items preceding *The Simonie* offer clear and easily assimilated definitions of theological concepts, the kind of works a secular priest might find useful for his duty of instructing the laity.[10] But while the *Speculum* offers a static analysis of sin, *The Simonie* presents a picture of sin in action, sin in its social context. Its vigour and vividness proved too much for a later reader, who excised three leaves of the attack on the clerical hierarchy. But this manuscript may represent the intellectual and social context in which the poem best flourished.

The *C*-version also occupies the tail-end of a manuscript, in this case the last two leaves of Peterhouse College Cambridge MS 104, dating from the last quarter of the fourteenth or first quarter of the fifteenth century.[11] The bulk of the manuscript is taken up with a series of dominical sermons, in Latin, ascribed to Ralph Acton, a (putative) early fourteenth-century theologian.[12] After the sermons were completed, a scribe (most probably the same one), seeing that there was space available, continued with *The Simonie*, which received the same style of decorative initial as the sermons (but upside-down). Although the manuscript is plain and workaday in its appearance, it resided in a distinguished home. It was assigned to Peterhouse by the executors of Thomas Beaufort, Duke of Exeter, who died without heirs in 1427. His will had provided that his chapel books should be sold to provide pensions for the chapel servants.[13] It seems probable that the great service-books fetched the sum required, leaving a residue of plainer, more technical books – like this one – to be disposed of at the executors' discretion. Evidently they agreed that a college library would make a suitable and grateful recipient of such a book. Although the Old Register of Peterhouse, which records the manuscript's entry into the college library, does not note the presence of *The Simonie* in the manuscript, it seems on balance most likely that manuscript and poem reached the college together, and it was only the registrar who thought the poem

---

[9] V. Nelson, 'The Middle English *Speculum Vitae*: A Critical Edition of Part of the Text, from 35 MSS', unpublished Ph.D. thesis (University of Sydney, 1974).

[10] Private communication from Dr M. Moyes.

[11] We are grateful to Dr A. I. Doyle and to Dr D. Smith of the Borthwick Institute, University of York, for palaeographical information on this manuscript.

[12] The earliest references to Acton that we know of are mid-fifteenth century: one is a colophon to a fifteenth-century set of Acton's sermons in Manchester, John Rylands Library, MS 367, the other is a reference to 'Acton *super Evangelias*' in a booklist in Cambridge, Peterhouse Library MS 203.

[13] J. Nichols, *A Collection of all the Wills now known to be Extant of the Kings and Queens of England, Princes and Princesses of Wales, and Every Branch of the Blood Royal, from the Reign of William the Conqueror to that of Henry VII* (London, 1780), 246–64. The *Old Register* of Peterhouse entered the book as '*Liber sermonum collatus Collegii per manus Executorum nobilis Domini Thomae dudum Ducis Exonie Henrici Regis Quarti Fratris*'.

insignificant. Later readers thought it was 'well worth decyphering'.[14]

All versions are composed in six-line stanzas, rhyming aabbcc, in which the first four lines have four to seven stresses, and the fifth and sixth are a one-stress bob and a four- to seven-stress wheel. Alliteration is haphazardly and half-heartedly employed in fewer than a third of the lines. *A* breaks off in mid-stanza after 476 lines – probably very near its end; *B* once had 630 lines, but is missing 216 (3 leaves) which have been cut from the manuscript; *C* is complete at 468 lines.

The versions vary radically from one another, both in the order and in the content of their stanzas. Each has unique inclusions and unique omissions, so that, though the longest version has just 476 extant lines, only 178 lines (or 37 per cent) are common to all three – as compared, for example, with the first two passus of the *C*-text of *Piers Plowman*, in which 233 of the 436 lines (or 53 per cent) are shared by the other two versions.

In the ordering of stanzas too, the versions show substantial differences. Five stanzas on the corruptions of the lawcourts appear in three widely separated sections in *A*, in two sections in *C*, and in a single section in *B*; a stanza on the starvation of the poor which appears in the last third of *A* and *B* is a part of the prologue of *C*; a stanza on the corruptions of bakers and brewers occurs together with an attack on merchants in *B* and *C*, but is widely separated from it in *A*.

The conventional vocabulary for describing the relationship of variant texts is a vocabulary of degeneration. It posits a single act of composition by an *author* whose text is said to embody *authorial intent* and thus to have *authority*. Subsequently, this *original* text is *copied* by *scribes* who, however well intentioned, inevitably make *errors* which lead to the *corruption* and *debasement* of the text. The editor's job is to detect *inferior readings*, to *recover the original*, to *reconstruct the archetype*, and thus to *restore the historical truth of the text*. Variants make up the editor's forest; the single reading is his holy grail. Or to put it less romantically, truth is original and sin is scribal.

Now, in fact, such a vocabulary serves us well enough for *Troilus and Criseyde* or for the *Confessio Amantis* or, with due provision for John But, for *Piers Plowman* – in short, for any work in which our interest centres on the original act and product of composition – that is, for any work which (because of the excellence of thought or expression we attribute to the original author or because of altered historical or literary contexts or because of our suspicion that the revisers did not fully understand or sympathise with the sentiments of the original author) we consider to be so much better or bolder or truer or more authentic than any of its later revisions that we do not think it worthwhile to place any other version before our readers. And that is probably most of the time.

---

[14] An opinion expressed in a note tucked into the pages of the MS.

But what of a work in which the scribe seems to have participated on a footing nearly equal to that of the author? – a work which the scribe has assumed licence to retitle, to abridge, to expand, to reorder, to reframe, to alter not just the words and phrases of, but the lines and stanzas of, to change the characters of, to redirect the satire of – in short, to rewrite according to his own tastes and biases? Is the term *scribe* adequate to the role he has assumed?

And what of a work whose conventional subject, popular sentiments, and proverbial expression seem to have invited adaptation, illustration, extrapolation, accommodation by whatever conventional, popular, pro-verbial materials lay to hand? What of a work whose own internal claims of authority are based finally on assertions like 'Euerich man nou bi dawe may sen þat þus hit is' (1. *A* 66)? Is *corruption* an accurate characterisation of the resultant text?

A careful study of the variations in the three versions of *The Simonie* has led us to believe, though it has not allowed us to prove, that each version is independently derived from a lost original. We posit, then, four separate acts of composition – one of creation and three of revision. Only the revisions survive, but comparison of corresponding stanzas often allows us to infer both the text of the original and the nature of the revisions – as in the following more or less typical instance:

> And if þe king in his lond makeþ a taxacioun,
> And eueri man is iset to a certein of raunczoun,
> Hit shal be so forpinched, totoilled, and totwiht
> Þat haluendel shal gon in þe fendes fliht
>   Of Helle.
> Þer beþ so manye parteners may no tunge telle.
>
> (A 301–6)

> And ȝif þe kyng in his lond make a taxion,
> And euery man schal þe set to his porcion,
> Hit schal be so pyncheþ, foretold, and foretwiȝt,
> Þat hit goþ more þan halfendel in þe fendis fliȝt
>   Of Helle.
> Þer beþ so many gaþereris þer may no tong telle.
>
> (B 403–8)

> Whan þe kyng into his werre wol haue a taxacion
> To help hym at his nede, of eche toun a porcioun,
> Hit shal be totolled, hit shal be totwyȝt,
> Hit shal halfdel be go into þe deueles fliȝt
>   Of Helle.
> Þer beþ so many parteners ne dar no pore man telle.
>
> (C 349–54)

It is obvious at a glance that no one text is the source for the other two, since each possible pair agrees against the remaining text in at least one key word: *A* and *B* agree against *C*'s 'develes'; *A* and *C* agree against *B*'s 'gaþereris'; *B* and *C* agree against *A*'s 'rauncʒoun'. But *A* has far fewer unique elements than either *B* or *C* – besides 'rauncʒoun' only 'certein' – so it is reasonable to assume that the original was substantially like *A*.

The changes wrought upon the putative original in the revisions reveal an assumption of not only the usual scribal licence to alter forms, word order, and the use of function words, but a broader editorial licence to make more substantive changes. *A*'s 'rauncʒoun' emphasises at the expense of the rhyme the coercive nature of the king's taxes, whereas the apparently original 'porcioun' and the accompanying stanzas suggest that the original author had no quarrel with the king himself – just with his corrupt officials. *B*'s 'gaþereris' seems to miss (or, at any rate, to alter) the point about these officials: the problem in the original was not that the number of the collectors has impoverished the people (a complaint made in 'Song of the Husbandman'),[15] but that the number of 'parteners', officials who expect a part of the proceeds, has impoverished the king. *C*'s last line shifts the point from the impossibility of estimating so great a number to the danger of attempting to do so.

This last idea has been picked up from two stanzas further on in the original. And indeed, the stanza is characteristic of *C* in making use of ideas or phrases caught from surrounding stanzas. The first half of each of the first two lines of *C* are taken almost intact from the previous stanza in the original.

The effect of the *B* and *C* revisions upon the poetry is also suggested by these stanzas. *A*'s trim and forceful lines 'Pat haluendel shal gon in þe fendes fliht/ Of Helle' probably preserves the original. But the lengthening and reordering of the earlier line (with consequent impairment of its rhythm), the too-easy heightening of the claim by the gratuitous 'more þan', the changing of 'halfendel' from a potent pronoun to a flaccid adverb, and the pointless loss of the alliteration in 'fendes fliht' all tend to show that the revisers lacked the original poet's modest technical skill.

Occasionally, such comparisons permit us to glimpse the revisers at work – as in the following stanzas about the blasphemies of swaggering squires:

> Godes soule is al day sworn; þe knif stant astrout.
> And þouh þe botes be torn, ʒit wole he maken hit stout.
> Þe hod hangeþ on his brest as he wolde spewe þerinne.
> Ac shortliche al þis contrefaiture is colour of sinne
> And bost.
> To wraþþe God and paien þe fend hit serueþ allermost.

> (A 277–82)

---

[15] Robbins, *Historical Poems*, 7–9.

Now Godis soule is al day suore; þe knyf schal stonde astrout.
And þow his botes be totore, ȝit he wil maket stout.
Þe lokkis schul hang adoun of boþe half þe hoþ.
At ylk a word can he noȝt suere but Godis soule and blod
      Fore pride.
But Y rede hem beleue þe woue þat walket now so wide.

                              (B 349–54)

Goddes sowle shal be swore; þe knyf shal stond astrout.
Þow his botes be al totore, ȝet he wol make it stout.
His hod shal hang on his brest, riȝt as a draueled lowt.
Alas! þe sowle worþe forlore, for þe body þat is so prowd
      In felle.
For soþe, he is deseyued: he wenyth he doþe ful welle.

                              (C 325–30)

It is impossible to be very confident about the shape of the original beyond
the first two and a half lines. But if we suppose on the evidence of other
stanzas, that A is closest to the original, then we can make a guess about
what happened here. The probably original image of the squire vomiting
into his hood may have proved too gross for the revisers of B and C, and
when they altered the line, they lost their rhyme and thus their way. Forced
to finish out the stanza on their own, they fell back separately but with
equivalent awkwardness on the cliches of popular medieval theology.

Often, however, we simply lack the basis for such an assessment – as, for
example, in the case of B and C stanzas on the persecution of Truth for
which there is no corresponding A stanza:

God pleynet hym on al men; forȝetet he noȝt on
Þat falsliche han slawe Trewþe, and skile haue þei non.
Wel awey! What haþ he do? Ne may he nowhere duelle.
No man loueþ his companye þat schal bye or selle,
      Alas!
Fore while he myȝt in londe lyue, a frensom fere he was.

                              (B 301–6)

Þe pope gret wel al lewed men – William, Richard, and Ion –
And doþ hem to vnderstonde þat trewþ is þer non,
And seyþ þat he wer worþi to be hanged and drawe
Þat haþe dryue Trewth out of lond without proces of lawe,
      Alas!
Certes whil Trewth was in londe, a gode frend he was.

                              (C 271–6)

There is just enough resemblance here to demonstrate that both are derived from an original. But it would be a reckless editor indeed who would attempt to restore that text.

On the solider ground of medieval politics, however, a comparison reveals not mere technical differences, but philosophical or at least tactical biases. That *B* is the most safely moral of the three and *C* the most boldly political is suggested by the following stanzas on the corruption of local and royal officials:

> And iustises, shirreues, meires, baillifs, if I shal rede ariht,
> Hii kunnen of þe faire day make þe derke niht.
> Hii gon out of þe heie-wey. Ne leuen hii for no sklaundre,
> And maken þe mothalle at hom in here chaumbre
> Wid wouh.
> For be þe hond iwhited, it shal go god inouh.
>
> (A 289–94)

> And ȝif we speke forþermore of men of more myȝt,
> Of iustises, scherefes, stywardes þat schold mayntene þe riȝt,
> Ȝif ȝe loke þer after Trewþe, he nys bote litel founde.
> Fore Couetise is mayster þere, and Riȝt goþ al to grounde
> With wo.
> Fore be þe hond wel [ywiteþ], hit shal wel ynow.
>
> (B 391–6)

> Mynystres vnder þe kynge, þat shuld meynten ryȝt,
> Of þe fair clere day þei maken derke nyȝt.
> Þei goþ out of þe hy-way. Þei letten for no sclandre.
> Þei makeþ þe motehalle at home in here chawmbre
> With wronge.
> Þat shal pore men abygge euer more amonge.
>
> (C 337–42)

B's omission of mayors from the list of offenders would seem to shift the target of the attack prudently downward, while *C*'s substitution of the inclusive phrase 'Mynystres vnder þe kynge' would seem to shift it recklessly upward. The *B*-reviser discards the imagery of subtlety and error in favour of straightforward moral allegory, and he discards the perhaps too specific charge of conducting public business as if it were a personal matter. The *C*-reviser, probably not understanding the metaphor in the last line, substitutes for it a characteristically sympathetic reference to the poor.

The same tendencies are evident in many of the passages apparently added separately by the *B*- and *C*-revisers – as, for example, in the following:

> Fore al is long on lordis þat suffre þus hit go.
> Þey scholde mayntene þe porayle, and þey do noȝt þerto.

But take meþe and sle þe folc in as moche as þey may.
Þe pore han here her purgatorie; þe riche kepe her day
     In Hell.
Þat so scorneþ God and hise can Y non oþer telle.

(B 457–62)

Þei byggeþ with þe kynges seluer boþe londes and ledes,
Hors as fair as þe kynges saue grete stedes.
Þei take þus with a pore man þat haþ but half a plowland
Oþer of a wreched laborer þat lyueþ by hys hond,
     I trowe.
Þis my3t help þe kyng and haue hemself inow.

(C 385–90)

The *B*-reviser is not hesitant to state his sympathy for the poor or his criticism of the powerful (these poles are, after all, implicit in the poem), but he is careful to keep his criticisms unspecific. He makes rather extreme, if general, charges, but assigns their resolution to the next world. The *C*-reviser on the other hand, makes at least a tentative motion toward resolution of virtually the same charges by suggesting a worldly remedy which even today retains some of its appeal – that all taxes should be paid by the rich.

There is little doubt, then, that the *B*- and *C*-revisers had tastes and biases of their own which they did not hesitate to act upon. But how premeditated were their alterations? Were they the impulsive interventions of scribes suddenly discovering that they had something of their own to say on the matter of the current stanza? Or were such alterations part of a planned revision of the poem?

Many of the alterations of *B* and *C* do have an impulsive, *ad hoc* look about them. There are several single-stanza expansions of ideas suggested in *A*; in *C*, these are frequently built up out of phrases (or even whole lines) borrowed from near-by stanzas of *A*. But there is evidence, as well, that both the *B*- and *C*-revisers planned their revisions. The *B*-reviser moved four stanzas on officials of the law courts forward more than a manuscript page in order to have them precede an attack on justices – a more logical position than they have in *A*. And the *C*-reviser, knowing in advance that he would omit the long section on wars and famines (probably because it no longer made sense to his audience), borrowed one of these stanzas, adapted it to a wholly new purpose, and moved it forward some sixty-five stanzas to become part of the prologue.

Finally, the vocabulary of corruption and degeneration seems particularly inappropriate to a poem which is in fact improved by some of the additions of its revisers.

A includes, in a poem whose ordinary tone is carefully contrived despair, a stanza of dry, ironic wit:

> Summe bereþ croune of acolite for þe crumponde crok
> And ben ashamed of þe merke þe bishop hem bitok,
> At euen he set vpon a koife and kembeþ þe croket;
> Adihteþ him a gay wenche of þe newe iet
>   Sanȝ doute.
> And þere hii clateren cumpelin whan þe candel is oute.
>
> (A 115–20)

The 'croune' is, of course, the simple tonsure worn by the minor orders – an unbecoming 'merke' which these dandies are at some pains to cover by kerchief or carefully combed croket. The *MED* suggests that the phrase 'claterin cumpelin' is 'used humorously with regard to chatting and snoring', but we suspect that there is more to this candleless service than that.

B includes among its many unique passages the following lines on the swindling of poor labourers by rapacious merchants:

> A sely werkman in a toun þat wolþe lyue in trewte
> And haþ a wif or children, peraunter to or þre,
> He sueteþ many a suetes drope, and swynk he neuer so sore
> Al day fore a peny or fore a peny more,
>   Be cas.
> At eue whan he setteþ hit, half is stole, alas!
>
> (B 439–44)

Alongside this stanza might be placed the stanza from *C* given above on the oppression of the poor by the king's officials. These vignettes are, like the best of those in *A*, built up out of the solid nouns of daily medieval existence – out of 'werkman', 'children', 'suetes drope', and 'peny', out of 'seluer', 'londes', 'hors', 'stedes', 'plowlond', 'laborer', and 'hond'. They add vividness and force and concreteness to the proposition – all too often in Middle English complaint an empty and formulaic claim – that virtue is driven down.

The case for a parallel-text edition of *The Simonie* rests, then, on the recognition of the three versions as quite distinct though closely related texts which need to be understood in relation to one another before they can be very seriously studied.

And it rests, as well, on a consideration of the alternatives: to publish three separate editions would simply make the task of comparison physically awkward; to 'restore' the archetype would be to discard dozens of stanzas and scores of lines of Middle English verse; to combine all the stanzas of all three versions into a single 'composite' edition would be to edit a text that never was.

While it is implicit in our interpretation of these texts that at least the latter two of our three poets could not have objected to our thus recasting their poem to suit ourselves, we consider ourselves scribes – not revisers – and prefer to remain as simultaneously faithful as possible to all three versions of the poem.[16]

---

[16] Our edition prints corresponding stanzas on the same page, occasionally repeating (in boxes) stanzas out of their MS order to permit comparison with the differently ordered versions. Thus each version can be read in its own order. Except where no reading seems possible, we have not 'corrected' the text.

CHALLENGES OF THEORY AND PRACTICE IN THE EDITING OF HOCCLEVE'S *REGEMENT OF PRINCES*[1]

D. C. Greetham

There is one rhetorical device which is no longer necessary in Hoccleve studies – the *apologia*. Hoccleveans no longer need to explain why they are interested in the poetry of a self-confessed 'dull' and derivative writer, for, as the work of John Burrow[2] and others has shown, Hoccleve's *oeuvre*, while mercifully brief compared to Lydgate's, and frequently uneven in quality, often contains a fluidity and sensitivity to language reminiscent of his master Chaucer. As is now well known, access to the specific charac- teristics of this language is, for much of the Hoccleve corpus, fairly direct, for there are three manuscripts of his own works generally accepted as holographs.[3] In fact, except for the notoriously idiosyncratic Orm and his *Ormulum* Hoccleve is the only author writing in Middle English verse for whom there is a substantial body of material extant in the author's own hand. The prose *Equatorie of the Planetis* attributed to Chaucer is obviously a special case. While he frequently complained about his duties as scribe – the unreliable and scanty remuneration, the backache caused by stooping over a desk – Hoccleve's dual role as both author and copyist doubtless assisted in the preservation of this documentary evidence for auctorial intention. With Hoccleve, therefore, modern editors are presented with a situation rare in Middle English studies but more common in literature of later periods – the possibility of the consistent editorial recreation not only

[1] This article is indebted to the work of several medievalists and textual scholars. The Hoccleve editors (Charles R. Blyth, Peter P. Farley, Burt Kimmelman, Marcia Smith Marzec, Jerome Mitchell, Gale Sigal, and David Yerkes) have provided much of the textual material on which its conclusions are based, and John Burrow, Fredson Bowers, W. Speed Hill, and G. Thomas Tanselle have given valuable criticism of the textual principles followed by the Hoccleve edition. I would particularly like to thank Judith Jefferson, whose work has proved to be of enormous value to the Hoccleve editors in their attempt to establish the accidentals of the *Regement*; we are very grateful to her for having allowed us to consult her findings before publication.
[2] See, for example, 'Hoccleve's *Series*: Experience and Books', in *Fifteenth-Century Studies*, ed. Robert F. Yeager (Hamden, Connecticut, 1984), pp. 259–73 and 'Autobiographical Poetry in the Middle Ages: The Case of Thomas Hoccleve', Sir Israel Gollancz Memorial Lecture, *Proceedings of the British Academy* 63 (1982), 389–412. For other recent appraisals of Hoccleve, see Jerome Mitchell's 'Hoccleve Studies 1965–1981', in Yeager, pp. 49–63.
[3] Huntington Lib. MS HM 111, MS HM 744, and Durham MS Cosin V.III.9. In addition, BL MS Add. 24062 contains materials in Hoccleve's hand, though not in verse (or in English).

of the 'meaning' of a text (i.e., its lexical, substantive status), but also of the so-called 'accidentals', the surface features (primarily spelling, but also including punctuation and capitalisation) about which so much textual blood has been shed in the criticism of the texts of the Renaissance and later periods.

It is only fair to admit that an editorial desire to attend to accidentals might seem to testify more to a modern (i.e. post-eighteenth century) concern for consistency in morphology and orthography than to a valid invocation of auctorial will. For some authors such a concern might plausibly fulfil auctorial intention (think of Spenser with his highly personal orthography, Ben Jonson carefully overseeing the printing of his *Works* in folio, Pope designing and controlling the very typography of simultaneous editions of his Homer in different formats). But for other authors, attention to the original surface features of the text has sometimes been regarded as an anachronism (defenders of 'modern' or 'normalised' spelling editions often citing Wordsworth's sending of the second edition of *Lyrical Ballads* to Humphry Davy to punctuate, or Shakespeare being unable to decide how his own name should be spelt).

A recent article of mine in *Studies in Bibliography*[4] details the editorial methods of dealing with the problems of the Hoccleve text – and specifically the accidentals. Rather than repeat the substance of that article, I propose in this account to concentrate on the theoretical implications of the editorial method, and thus to draw Hoccleve textual studies into the main current of textual discussion, just as Hoccleve critical studies can now be regarded as a firm part of the criticism of late medieval literature. My plan is to sketch briefly the actual textual conditions of the Hoccleve canon, then to cover the theoretical options available to an editor, moving on to the actual practice adopted by the Hoccleve edition and the relevance of this practice to the theoretical options. To avoid repetition of previously-published material, the practical account of the actual editing will be kept as brief as possible, while still (I trust) being comprehensible, my purpose being to place the editorial theory and methodology within the broader context of both medieval and modern textual criticism.

What are the textual conditions in the case of the *Regement*? By the testimony of the manuscripts, the poem was easily Hoccleve's most popular work, indeed was among the most popular of all late Middle English metrical works. Its more than forty manuscripts, however, do not display the range of scribal ingenuity, invention, and conscious 'editing' which, for example, Chaucer and Langland were subjected to by the copyists of the fifteenth century. Quite the contrary in fact, for the textual transmission is, with a couple of idiosyncratic exceptions, remarkable for its conservatism

---

[4] 'Normalisation of Accidentals in Middle English Texts: The Paradox of Thomas Hoccleve', *Studies in Bibliography* 38 (1985), 121–50.

and its determined preservation of the text rather than for its recreation, rationalisation, and determined 'improvement'. We doubt that this conservative attitude is the result of any scribal acceptance of the sanctity of the *Regement* text, for as is well known in Biblical textual criticism, sacred texts such as the New Testament seem to encourage rather than forbid scribal licence. It might simply be that the *Regement*, half personal confession (like the so-called *Series* poems) and half pedagogical and political polemic, did not offer the same opportunities for invention and reconstruction as did the texts of Chaucer and Langland. The issues covered in the *Regement* (the rights and responsibilities of kingship) were clearly in much debate during the internecine struggles of the fifteenth century – hence the popularity of the work – but the form of Hoccleve's verse remained almost frozen.

Given these textual conditions (and before having attempted any charting of the filiation of the extant witnesses) what theoretical options are therefore available to the editor? In declining degrees of 'fidelity' to the documentary state and history of the work the possibilities could be arranged as follows:

1. First, of course, there is the photographic facsimile, which, as Derek Pearsall points out in his study of the desiderata of fifteenth-century editing,[5] can be particularly useful not only in making available the bibliographical nature of the work (its make-up, foliation, etc.) but can also serve as a register of taste, especially in anthology manuscripts. Some of the *Regement* manuscripts are indeed anthologies (several manuscripts, for example, contain works by other authors in addition to Hoccleve, and some manuscripts are apparently attempts at a Hoccleve 'complete works')[6] but none of these manuscripts has a codicological value or a transmissional status to justify its being the *only* representative of Hoccleve's text. We do not argue that a facsimile of, say, Society of Antiquaries MS 134 (which contains, in addition to the *Regement*, Lydgate's *Life of Our Lady*, Gower's *Confessio Amantis*, and Walton's

---

[5] 'Texts, Textual Criticism, and Fifteenth Century Manuscript Production', in Yeager, pp. 121–36 (esp. pp. 128–30).

[6] The 'anthology' manuscripts include BL MSS Arundel 59, Harley 116, Harley 372, Harley 4826, Add. 18632 (with Harley 7333 as a 'general' miscellany); Bodley MS Digby 185; Trinity College Cambridge MS 602; Fitzwilliam Museum MS McClean 185; Society of Antiquaries MS 134; Coventry Record Office MS; Huntington Lib. MS 135; Rosenbach MS 1083/30; and Yale University MS 493. The 'complete works' manuscripts include BL MS Royal 17.D.vi; Bodley Laud Misc. 735; Selden Supra 53; Bodley 221 (and the Coventry MS again). See M. C. Seymour, 'The Manuscripts of Hoccleve's *Regiment of Princes*', *Transactions of the Edinburgh Bibliographical Society* iv, Part 7 (1974), 255–97; A. S. G. Edwards, 'Hoccleve's *Regiment of Princes*: A Further Manuscript', *Trans. Edinburgh Bibl. Soc.* v, Part 1 (1978), 72; R. F. Green, 'Notes on Some Manuscripts of Hoccleve's *Regiment of Princes*', *The British Library Journal* 4, number 1 (Spring, 1978), 37–41; and Kate Harris, 'The Patron of BL MS Arundel 38', *Notes and Queries* 229 (1984), 462–3.

Boethius) would not be a codicological, palaeographic, and historical aid to fifteenth-century studies, but rather that such a facsimile would not serve in place of a critical edition; the facsimile would preserve *scribal* rather than auctorial intention, and no matter which *Regement* manuscript were selected, would not represent either a *textus receptus* or a state of textual transmission interesting in its own right.

2. Next in line of fidelity would be the diplomatic transcript, whereby the substantive and usually the accidental features of the document would be retained, but in a modern typography. Such editions, best exemplified by the Malone Society reprints, do serve an honorable textual purpose, but are perhaps most valuable in the recording of historical material where such questions as the actual visual features of palaeography and auctorial orthography are less significant than the modern researcher's access to original *content*. In multi-witness works such as the *Regement* (where no single document can display this historical content with complete reliability), the value of the diplomatic transcript becomes much less – compared, say, to the eclectic edition with a complete record of substantive variants.

3. The next level of fidelity is probably a 'best-text' edition, and (excepting occasional editorial emendation), the Furnivall, Seymour, Burrow, Pryor, and O'Donoghue editions of part or all of the Hoccleve *holograph* material[7] could be viewed as best-texts or editions 'in the form of' a specific witness. I cannot deal here with the characteristics of all these earlier Hoccleve editions, but the least scholarly of them all (or, I suppose, the most 'popular') will serve as a *caveat*. I speak of Bernard O'Donoghue's 1982 *Selected Poems*,[8] where the editor adopts an apparent 'best-text' stance in the editing of the works contained in the holographs, but then paradoxically selects as copy-text a non-holograph (MS Selden Supra 53) simply because 'The Complaint' and part of the 'The Dialogue' are not extant in the holograph used by Furnivall, Durham Cosin V.iii.9. This is a denial of authority with a vengeance. When it comes to his selections from the *Regement* (where best-text theory loses the specific claims it might have had for the works represented in holograph), O'Donoghue normalises quite arbitrarily several of the orthographic features of his copy-text (HM 135): for example, substituting 'y' for initial *yogh*, employing modern 'w'/'wh' usage, and substituting 'is' for 'ys' throughout. This would seem like the shades of

---

[7] *The Minor Poems*, ed. F. J. Furnivall, EETS, ES No. 61 (1892), rev. A. I. Doyle and Jerome Mitchell (1970); *Selections From Hoccleve*, ed. M. C. Seymour (Oxford, 1981); *Selected Poems*, ed. Bernard O'Donoghue (Manchester, 1982); *English Verse 1300–1500*, ed. J. A. Burrow (London, 1977), pp. 265–80; M. R. Pryor, *Thomas Hoccleve's 'Series': An Edition of MS Durham Cosin v. III. 9* (Diss. UCLA, 1968).
[8] O'Donoghue, esp. p. 102.

Donaldson's 'Chaucer' for the 'modern reader'[9] except that quite ironically (and doubtless by accident), O'Donoghue produces by whim some of those normalised forms which we have discovered to be most characteristic of Hoccleve's idiolect. His rationale, however, is suspect at best: for example, initial 'y' is preferred to *yogh* because the latter 'looks odd in a way that the MS does not' and modern 'w'/'wh' is used because the manuscript form could be 'confusible with another modern word'. Whatever opportunities for genuine best-text there might be are lost in a spurious normalisation on modernising principles. I should note that there is initially a suspicion of similar whimsicality in Furnivall's *Regement*, for he chooses his copy-text (Harley 4866) on no better grounds than its containing 'the best portrait of Chaucer'[10] (which he reproduces in the edition with great pride), but his editing in general obeys the usual EETS mandate of documentary fidelity. The criticisms of the O'Donoghue edition are not introduced here in order to denigrate best-text editions as a whole, but rather to point to a perhaps extreme example of the truism that there is no such moral security as a perfect loyalty to a document, for even the act of transcription (especially into a modern type-face) involves editorial intervention, and O'Donoghue simply intervenes inconsistently and under false pretences. The point for the current Hoccleve edition is that none of the extant witnesses provides (for both substantives and accidentals) a totally trustworthy mechanism for the reconstruction of auctorial intention; furthermore, none of the witnesses can be justified as the *sole* repository of even an acknowledgedly corrupt transmission of that intention. Arundel 38 (copy-text for Seymour's edition) and Harley 4866 (copy-text for Furnivall) come closest to that condition, but they both fail the accidentals test, as Furnivall admits when he apologises for the 'northern forms' present in Harley.[11]

4. I suppose that our descending hierarchy brings us next to another orthodoxy, the genealogical text created by recension. Until recently, this was, of course, the prevailing norm in most Anglo-American textual criticism of multi-witness Middle English works, just as Bédier's 'best-text' was the norm in Old French and in other, unrelated disciplines (e.g. music). The neat stemma (see fig. 1a) we have constructed for the *Regement*, with both inferred and extant manuscripts plotted according to their putative filiation, might suggest that recension is the dominating practice in the Hoccleve edition, and I must confess that the pull of this modern version of the old Alexandrian faith in 'analogy' is a powerful

---

[9] E. Talbot Donaldson, *Chaucer's Poetry. An Anthology for the Modern Reader* (New York, 1958), esp. 'A Note on the Spelling of the Edition', pp. 848–9. Like O'Donoghue, Donaldson normalises according to *modern*, not *medieval* accidence: 'the forms of individual ME words have been assimilated to the forms of their ModE descendants' (p. 848).

[10] Furnivall, *Regement*, p. xvii.

[11] Ibid.

one, particularly in a textual transmission as conservative as the *Regement*'s. I have argued elsewhere[12] that the Hoccleve edition is in fact a marriage of two orthodoxies – the Lachmann stemmatic (for substantives) and the Greg–Bowers copy-text (for accidentals) – of which more anon. But here I must offer some cautions. Any stemma is (*pace* Harold Bloom) a map of *misreadings*, for it depends upon misinterpretation and error for its surety. This particular 'map', artfully constructed through the diligent work of one of our editors, Marcia Smith Marzec,[13] is, however, surer in some places than in others (for example, the filiations drawn in the branches to the *left* of the stemma are more consistently demonstrated than those on the *right*, and there are some witnesses – Hh, Ha3, Ra1, and Sj [see fig. 1b for sigla] – which cannot be located in one position only, since they display various degrees of contamination). But the major drawback of this stemma (and of all such stemmata using the Lachmann system) is its uselessness as a vehicle for the reconstruction of accidentals, the functional ideal around which copy-text theory (as opposed to base-text theory) has been built.[14] Therefore, while a genealogical system of recension might still offer some assistance in the restoration of *substantive* readings in the text, it cannot yet provide the mechanism for the recreation of auctorial idiolect.[15] While Greg copy-text theory might employ Lachmann stemmatics in order to arrange witnesses genealogically, this procedure is (with regard to accidentals) usually only a means of identifying the states of text from which copy-text will be selected.[16]

5. The remaining editorial options in the hierarchy, although rarely (if ever) used in medieval and classical editing, ought properly to be

[12] Greetham, 'Normalisation', p. 127.

[13] Marcia Smith Marzec, 'The Genealogy of the Manuscripts of Hoccleve's *De Regimine Principum*' (forthcoming). For ancillary information on filiation, see Marzec's 'The Latin Marginalia of the *Regiment of Princes* as an Aid to Stemmatic Analysis', *TEXT* 3 (1986).

[14] See W. W. Greg, 'The Rationale of Copy-Text', *Studies in Bibliography*, 3 (1950–51), 19–36. The literature on copy-text theory is enormous, but see esp. G. Thomas Tanselle, 'Greg's Theory of Copy-Text and the Editing of American Literature', *SB*, 28 (1975) 167–229, Tanselle's 'Recent Editorial Discussion and the Central Questions of Editing', *SB* 34 (1981), 23–65, and his 'Historicism and Critical Editing', *SB*, 39 (1986), 1–46, and Fredson Bowers, 'Greg's "Rationale of Copy-Text" Revisited', *SB*, 31 (1978), 90–162.

[15] However, some progress has recently been made in this area. Francis I. Andersen has, for example, demonstrated that *plene* and *defective* spellings in the Old Testament can be used to establish the chronology of biblical books (and, by extension, the putative filiation of the documents containing their texts) – 'Orthography and Text Transmission: Computer-Assisted Investigation of Textual Transmission through the Study of Orthography in the Hebrew Bible', *TEXT* 2 (1985), 25–53 – and, in a conference paper from York 1985 not included in this collection ('Dialectal Analysis and the Editing of Middle English Texts: Some Thoughts'), Michael Benskin provided some examples where the evidence of accidentals might indeed be employed in the genealogical mapping of Middle English texts.

[16] Exceptions to this rule might occur where it could be demonstrated that there was auctorial interest in, and control over, the accidentals of stages of the text later than the 'fair copy'. For a discussion of this and other problems relating to the status of 'multiple' texts, see Fredson Bowers, 'Mixed Texts and Multiple Authority', *TEXT* 3 (1986).

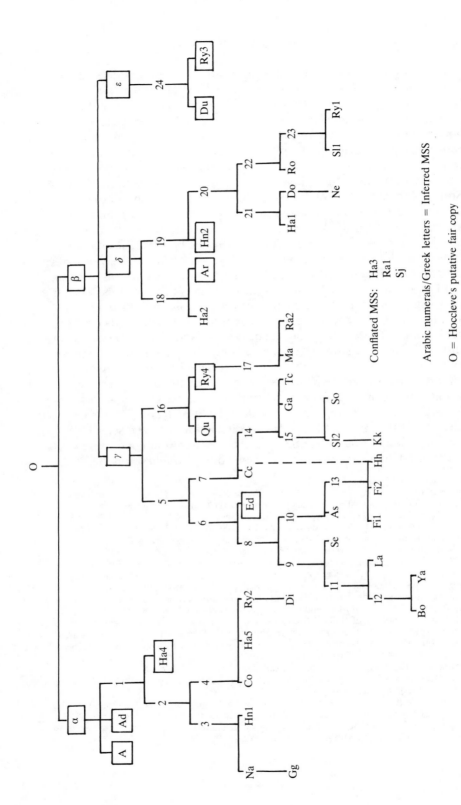

Fig. 1a   The Genealogy of *Regement of Princes* Manuscripts

Conflated MSS: Ha3
Ra1
Sj

Arabic numerals/Greek letters = Inferred MSS

O = Hoccleve's putative fair copy

MSS cited in substantives apparatus are in boxes

Fig. 1b   Manuscript Sigla

A	British Library MS Arundel 38
Ar	British Library MS Arundel 59
Ad	British Library MS Additional 18632
As	Bodleian Library MS Ashmole 40
Bo	Bodleian Library MS Bodley 221
Cc	Corpus Christi College, Cambridge, MS 496
Co	Coventry Record Office MS
Di	Bodleian Library MS Digby 185
Do	Bodleian Library MS Douce 158
Du	Bodleian Library Dugdale 45
Ed	University of Edinburgh MS 202
Fi1	Fitzwilliam Museum, Cambridge, MS McClean 182
Fi2	Fitzwilliam Museum, Cambridge, MS McClean 185
Ga	Princeton University MS Garrett 137
Gg	Cambridge University Library MS Gg.vi.17
Ha1	British Library MS Harley 116
Ha2	British Library MS Harley 372
Ha3	British Library MS Harley 4826
Ha4	British Library MS Harley 4866
Ha5	British Library MS Harley 7333
Hh	Cambridge University Library MS Hh.iv.II
Hn1	Huntington Library MS El. 26.A.13
Hn2	Huntington Library MS HM 135
Kk	Cambridge University Library MS Kk.i.3, pt 10–12
La	Bodleian Library MS Laud Misc. 735
Ma	Magdalene College, Cambridge, MS Pepys 2101
Na	National Library of Scotland Adv. MS 19.I.II, pt 3
Ne	Newberry Library MS 6
Qu	The Queens' College, Cambridge, MS 12
Ra1	Bodleian Library MS Rawlinson Poet. 10
Ra2	Bodleian Library MS Rawlinson Poet. 168
Ro	Rosenbach Foundation MS
Ry1	British Library MS Royal 17 C. xiv
Ry2	British Library MS Royal 17 D. vi
Ry3	British Library MS Royal 17 D. xviii
Ry4	British Library MS Royal 17 D. xix
Se	Bodleian Library MS Arch. Selden supra 53
Sj	St John's College, Cambridge, MS 223
Sl1	British Library MS Sloane 1212
Sl2	British Library MS Sloane 1825
So	Society of Antiquaries of London MS 134
Tc	Trinity College, Cambridge, MS R.3.22 (602)
Ya	Yale University MS 493

considered by an editor, and should be briefly touched on here, since they could be of greater value to other Middle English editorial projects than they proved to be for the Hoccleve. For example, Hans Walter Gabler's arguments in favour of a *diachronic* (as opposed to the conventional *synchronic*) apparatus – with presumably a clear-text facing page as in his edition of Joyce's *Ulysses* – could be a plausible way of approaching medieval works with variant *auctorial* drafts, or with post-publication revisions by the author or a 'licensed' scribe.[17] Such a 'synoptic' apparatus, which represents in documentary form the dominant Franco-German genetic text ideology, could be employed in, say, *Troilus and Criseyde*, in the F and G versions of the 'Prologue' to *The Legend of Good Women*, possibly in the Caxton and Winchester versions of Malory, Layamon's *Brut*, *The Owl and the Nightingale* or even (with horrendously complex diacritical formulae) in *Piers Plowman*.

6. Next might come the Slavic textological model, with its emphasis on the potentially equal status of all remaniements as textual witnesses, and this model is, I would claim, implicitly (and perhaps unconsciously) invoked in the EETS *Ancrene Riwle* series and, in a very different sense, in the Athlone *Piers Plowman*,[18] where copy-text has no *prima facie* 'presumptive authority'[19] but is just a vehicle for editorial emendation. The difference, of course, is that, like the geneticists, the textologists are content to record the degree of variance but not to wager a critical judgement on the basis of this documentary evidence. Such reticence would be unthinkable in the likes of George Kane and Talbot Donaldson, whose ironic castigation of the 'editorial death-wish'[20] is a well-known defence of the editor as co-creator of the work.

7. Finally, one might consider a 'social' textual theory such as that envisaged by Jerome McGann in his *Critique of Modern Textual*

---

[17] Hans Walter Gabler, 'The Synchrony and Diachrony of Texts: Practice and Theory of the Critical Edition of Joyce's *Ulysses*', *TEXT* 1 (1984), 305–26.

[18] A brief note of explanation is called for on what may seem a paradox. As Anne Hudson observes ('Middle English' in *Editing Medieval Texts*, ed. A. G. Rigg (New York, 1977), p. 38), the EETS *Ancrene Riwle* series 'exalts palaeography as sole editor . . . [in] a dutiful recording of [every manuscript's] idiosyncrasies . . . even down to the splitting of a word between one line and the next'. This type of editing – if it can be so called – is a far cry from the eclectic licence adopted by the Kane/Donaldson *Piers Plowman*, but both responses to the array of documents deny a specific privilege to any *one* state of the text, regarding all as *potentially* useful (or useless) in the representation of intention. Lachmann genealogy endorses privilege and hierarchy, whereas the textology of the *Ancrene Riwle* and the Athlone *Piers Plowman* (with very different results) holds such authority in abeyance, in the manner of the 'remaniement' school of Slavic textology.

[19] See, for example, G. Thomas Tanselle, 'Classical, Biblical, and Medieval Textual Critics and Modern Editing', *Studies in Bibliography* 36 (1983), 21–68 (esp. 65 on the concept of the 'presumptive' or 'residual' authority of copy-text, i.e. 'the status of the copy-text as the text one falls back on when no . . . reason exists to dictate the choice among variants').

[20] E. Talbot Donaldson, 'The Psychology of Editors of Middle English Texts', in *Speaking of Chaucer* (New York, 1970), p. 105.

Criticism[21] (although paradoxically *not* exemplified in his edition of Byron). In works where post-publication transmission is long, varied, and demonstrably non-auctorial, such a method has its attractions, for it transfers to subsequent history the prerogative of composition and recomposition, in a textual implementation of Fish's 'interpretive communities'.[22] Within the conservative (and historically very limited)[23] career of the *Regement*, such an approach would offer no great insights (unless, of course, one raises scribal invention to the prerogative of auctorial, as Nicholson suggests has happened with the *Confessio Amantis*);[24] but one could argue that the success of Anne Hudson's edition of the 'socially-produced' *factory*-disseminated Wycliffite tracts depends in fact if not in theory upon a McGann-like methodology.[25] Within the general area of 'social' texts or 'reader/editor response', perhaps the greatest degree of radical editorial restructuring of text that has so far been offered is in the computer editing of Yugoslav and Old English oral epics by John Foley,[26] where the textual/narrative elements or formulae may be infinitely combined and recombined at an editorially-controlled terminal. It could be argued that the substantive eclecticism of Kane–Donaldson does no more than this, but the difference is that Foley's electronic apparatus is continually reader-defined, whereas the Athlone *Piers Plowman*, in common with almost all other editions of Middle English works, is always striving towards a perhaps unreachable textual security rather than to textual dissolution as valid in its own right. The preservation of the Hoccleve edition's historical collation in a pouch containing a separate microform or floppy disk format (what John Burrow has dubbed the 'kangaroo Hoccleve') could appear to be a concession to infinite variety, but we doubt that the comparatively colourless invention recorded in this apparatus is likely to lead to much playing of the collational odds by our readers.

[21] Jerome J. McGann, *A Critique of Modern Textual Criticism* (Chicago, 1983). McGann's six-volume *Complete Poetical Works of Byron* (Oxford English Texts Series) was begun *before* his conversion to a reader-response textual ethic. See also McGann's *Textual Criticism and Literary Interpretation* (Chicago, 1985) for a collection of essays by various hands, each offering a re-evaluation of the various 'orthodoxies' of current textual criticism.

[22] Stanley E. Fish, *Is There A Text in This Class?* (Cambridge, Mass., 1980), esp. 'Interpreting the *Variorum*', pp. 147–73. Some of the implications of Fish's reader-response theories for *textual* scholarship are explored in Steven Mailloux's *Interpretive Conventions* (Ithaca, NY, 1982), esp. chapter four, 'Textual Scholarship and "Author's Final Intention"'.

[23] Hoccleve was, of course, a 'popular' medieval writer who was promptly ignored by Caxton and the other fifteenth–sixteenth-century printers who fixed the early canon of vernacular literature. The *first* edition of any Hoccleve material had to wait over three centuries (George Mason's *Poems by Thomas Hoccleve, Never Before Printed* (London, 1796)) and the first edition of the *Regement* was Thomas Wright's for the Roxburghe Club in 1860. The 'transmission' of the *Regement* text in its 'primary' documents thus occupied a very short period.

[24] For Nicholson, see below, pp. 130–42.

[25] See Hudson, op. cit. (pp. 45–7) for an account of the dissemination of Lollard texts.

[26] John Miles Foley, 'Editing Oral Epic Texts: Theory and Practice', *TEXT* 1 (1984), 75–94.

The conservative turned radical always seems to feel that his earlier conservative credentials need a greater demonstration of their frailty than do his new radical precepts, which can be regarded as articles of the revealed truth. So George Kane proved in excruciating detail why a conventional recension editing of the *Piers Plowman* A-text would *not* work before embarking on a method that would allow a critically-motivated documentary eclecticism.[27] In a similar manner, several of the original Hoccleve editors had cut their editorial teeth on the Clarendon edition of Trevisa's translation of Bartholomaeus Anglicus' *De Proprietatibus Rerum*, under the general editorship of M. C. Seymour.[28] This edition, representing an orthodox genealogical rationale, relied very heavily upon the demonstration of palaeographic transmission of error, which, despite the strictures of A. E. Housman,[29] has remained as one of the primary defences of editorial emendation in Middle English studies – it is defended at length, for example, in Vinaver's edition of Malory. This system is, of course, inferentially based on the notion of the historicity (and therefore the *vertical* variation) of documents, and does not allow for horizontal variation or contamination. It gives some opportunity for the demonstration of an editorial aesthetic (i.e., the creation of forms without documentary confirmation, based primarily upon a sense of the auctorial 'rightness' of a reading), but its defence is inevitably historical, palaeographic, and transmissional, not creative, aesthetic, and conjectural. It embodies, indeed, Donaldson's 'editorial death-wish' already mentioned in its reliance upon a *techne* of orthographic, bibliographic, or linguistic *probability*.[30] Coming from such a background, it was perhaps inevitable that the Hoccleve editors should originally have embarked upon a similarly orthodox methodology, where the reconstruction of the substantives of the archetype was to delimit the responsibilities of the editor, and where these substantives were to be resurrected from a close mapping of the putative genealogical relationships of the extant witnesses. Higher witnesses in the tree were to

---

[27] *Piers Plowman: The A Version. Will's Visions of Piers Plowman and of Do-Well*, ed. George Kane (London, 1960), esp. chapter 3 of the introduction ('Classification of the Manuscripts', pp. 53–114). It is here that, after exploring the possibilities of orthodox Lachmann recension (chiefly through a detailed criticism of the Knott/Fowler edition), Kane comes to the conclusion that 'the comfort and the appearance of authority afforded by recension are denied to the editor of the manuscripts of the A version of *Piers Plowman*' (p. 114).

[28] *On the Properties of Things. John Trevisa's Translation of Bartholomaeus Anglicus 'De Proprietatibus Rerum'*, ed. M. C. Seymour *et al.*, (Oxford, 1975), 2v. (text); two additional volumes of notes and Latin sources are forthcoming.

[29] A. E. Housman, 'Preface to Manilius I 1903', in *Selected Prose*, ed. John Carter (Cambridge, 1961), p. 50, 'a conjecture which alters only a single letter may be more improbable palaeographically than one which leaves no letter unaltered'.

[30] For a recent account of the scope of the Lachmann system, see Paul Oskar Kristeller, 'The Lachmann Method: Merits and Limitations', *TEXT* 1 (1984), 11–20. The standard history of Lachmann genealogical thinking is S. Timpanaro, *Die Entstehung der Lachmannschen Methode* (1971), trans. & rev. version of *La genesi del metodo del Lachmann* (1963).

be seen as more trustworthy, less corrupt, than lower, employing the moral terminology which Pearsall notes as the conventional defence of ortho-doxy[31] (itself a morally loaded term, of course). Our stemma recording the putative genealogical relationships is perhaps the last vestige of this earlier orthodoxy, but as I shall demonstrate, its value to the Hoccleve edition is very different from that previously envisaged for stemmatic evidence.

Despite the orthodoxy of the Trevisa edition, with its faith in the validity of the archetype and its acknowledgement (or assumption) that the auctorial accidentals were irrecoverable,[32] there was a (sometimes-disputed) employ-ment of an extra-textual 'control' over the process of emendation: this was the citing of two witnesses of the *Latin* text which Trevisa translated (one early manuscript, one early printed edition) as parallel (even paramount) evidence for the reconstruction of the *Middle English* archetype.[33] I think it only fair to say, in retrospect, that some of us now regret the use of these non-vernacular controls, for the value of their evidence rested upon two dubious assumptions – one, that Trevisa had worked from a Latin source textually very close to either or both of the cited Latin witnesses, and two, that he had both the competence and the desire to transmit the exact content of this Latin text into English. The merits of the position are being argued elsewhere (I have, for example, attempted to construct theoretical models for the transmission of translation and the editorial prerogatives arising out of the implementation of these models)[34] but their implications for the Hoccleve are fairly clear. Like Trevisa, Hoccleve claims to be a translator, although he does not argue quite as strongly as Trevisa does for the *verbal* accuracy of his translation. Thus, while the *Regement* (from its very title) might appear to be a translation,[35] Hoccleve is no more a simple 'translator' of Aegidius or his other sources than is Chaucer a translator of *his* sources, appeals to 'myn auctour' notwithstanding. Even leaving aside the 2,000-line 'Prologue' to the *Regement* – which comes primarily from his own experience and from an observation of the times – Hoccleve is, in the body of the *Regement* itself, more of an adapter like his master Chaucer.

---

[31] 'Having been tested for error by the editors of critical texts, those [MSS] that have failed have been dismissed to a kind of codicological limbo, labelled "worthless", "corrupt", or "degenerate" to mark their inferior status.' Pearsall, in Yeager, p. 22.

[32] Only occasionally was the putative (dialectal) orthography of the author used as a critical tool (e.g., in the support of emendation or the rationalisation of the direction of textual corruption based on the assumption that, say, the author's original initial voiced consonantal 'v' would have been 'normalised' by SE Midlands scribes to initial 'f'). For a discussion of a crux involving such alternation, see D. C. Greetham, 'Models for the Textual Transmission of Translation: The Case of John Trevisa', *Studies in Bibliography* 37 (1984), 146–7.

[33] These are MS Bodley 749 (late fourteenth century) and the Vatican copy of the 1485 edition by Georg Hausner of Strassburg.

[34] See Greetham, 'Models for Textual Transmission', 131–55.

[35] H. S. Bennett, for example, simply assumes 'he translates the *De Regimine Principum* of Aegidius Romanus' (*Chaucer and the Fifteenth Century* (Oxford, 1947), p. 148) without further comment – or, it would seem, understanding of what actually happens in this 'translation'.

As Jerome Mitchell[36] and others have shown, he freely omits and amplifies, comments on and ignores his supposed sources. So, the editorial implications of this condition were totally different from those in the Trevisa: there was no reliable extra-textual 'control' to be invoked as a means of confirming (or even creating) the 'meaning' of Hoccleve's text. Latin sources, therefore, do not appear in the apparatus of the Hoccleve edition, except, of course, where they are actually cited in Hoccleve's own marginalia.

However, while the unorthodox employment of extra-textual sources was not to be countenanced in the Hoccleve edition for the reconstruction of the substantives, there was ironically another extra-textual control lurking in the wings – this time for the reconstruction of accidentals. This control is, of course, the holographs of the *other* works which Hoccleve 'wrote' (in both senses, as author and as scribe).

The existence of this potential control inevitably calls into question the ambiguous status of the archetype (and the issue of editorial fidelity to its resuscitation), with a very clear connection to the equally problematic status of the accidentals in medieval texts, and to the validity of copy-text theory as it relates to those accidentals. The Hoccleve editors have been forced to confront an unusual question: is it possible, considering the peculiar conditions of Hoccleve's texts, to combine orthodox 'classical' base-text theory (stemmatics) with orthodox 'modern' copy-text theory to produce for the first time an edition of a Middle English work (surviving only in scribal copies) with *all* its auctorial features – accidentals and substantives alike – still intact in the edited, eclectic version?

The *SB* article on Hoccleve responds to this challenge as follows:

> Clearly, the immediate and sensible answer to this question would be 'No', for the forty-three scribal copies of the *Regement*, even though displaying a remarkable degree of conservatism in copying, should not logically provide access to auctorial accidentals in a work which, like virtually all other mediaeval texts, does not exist in holographs, in rough drafts, in annotated first edition, or in any other 'authorised' form [commonly encountered by the theorists from later periods who have produced the doctrine of copy-text theory]. The major qualification to the question, however, is that nearly all of Hoccleve's other works do survive in holograph, and that it might therefore be worth looking at the accidentals of these manuscripts to determine whether there were patterns of auctorial usage that could be employed in the editing of the *Regement*. The process, if successful, would certainly take us beyond the archetype of the *Regement*, but in accidentals, not in substantives. (pp. 123–4)

---

[36] Jerome Mitchell, *Thomas Hoccleve: A Study in Early Fifteenth-Century Poetic* (Urbana, Illinois, 1968), esp. chapter 4, 'Handling of Sources'.

In other words 'classical' base-text Lachmann theory would be used for the editorial reconstruction of substantives and 'modern' copy-text theory would be used for the reconstruction of accidentals. The likelihood of *consistency* in auctorial accidentals depended in part upon current research into the much wider question of the movement towards standardisation of orthography in the fifteenth century and, of course, Hoccleve's place in any such movement.[37]

In theory, then, with a careful analysis of the holograph manuscript practices, the accidentals of the bulk of Hoccleve's corpus are just as recoverable a part of auctorial intentionality as are the substantives. The problem, of course, is the translation of the system of accidentals discernible in the holographs on to the scribal base-text of the *Regement*. The editing of the *Regement*, if it is to respond to both aspects of intention, must therefore operate under Greg's doctrine of divided authority: the actual documentary evidence may be very dissimilar from that normally associated with the implementation of Greg's theory, but none the less it will be based on the concept of separate authorities for substantives and accidentals.

Here, in brief, is the editorial methodology involved: first, a theoretical normalisation model (see Appendix A, pp. 81–3 below) is constructed in order to test the potential range of editorial intervention in the forms of any given copy-text. As can be seen from the hierarchy of values, the model could very well apply to any normalisation of a copy-text from external authority, although it is obviously dependent immediately on the documentary circumstances of the Hoccleve canon. There is no space here to rehearse the various levels of editorial prerogative, but I trust that the notes will provide sufficient guidance for those interested in pursuing the matter. The primary principle is that, despite the apparent radical motivation and results of this model, its employment should be based on a very conservative evaluation of the evidence of copy-text, holographs, and the lexicons derived from both.

Since I am to draw further theoretical inferences from it later, the only part of the model I would emphasise here is that referring to the residual authority of copy-text, which, as can readily be seen, operates only under level 14, and is therefore heavily constrained.

The next figure (fig. 2) consists of the editorial flow-chart, demonstrating the actual process whereby a normalised form is created with reference to the documentary evidence, the various steps being analysed through a specific example in Appendix B (pp. 84–6 below). I would emphasise that the system has sufficient safeguards (represented by the several backtrackings to other evidence) to prevent a too-licentious editorial enthusiasm. I have to admit, however, that once editors have got a whiff of normalisation, they are often tempted to take off with abandon, casting off all constraints,

---

[37] Greetham, 'Normalisation', 125.

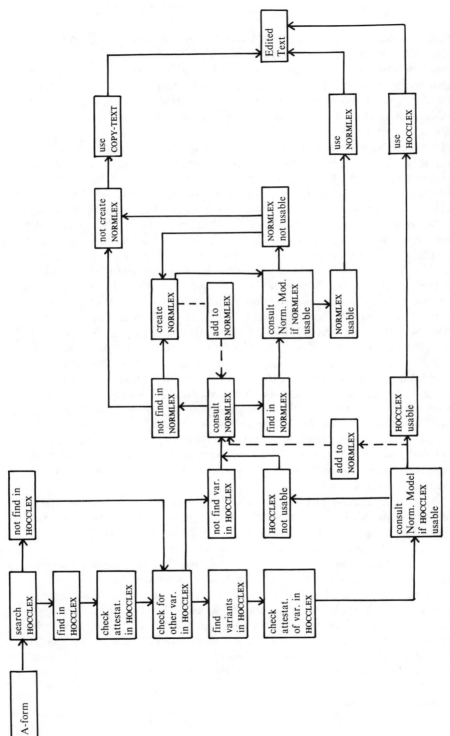

Fig. 2   Editorial Flow-Chart for Normalisation

so heady is the power given! It is then that the structured format of the flow-chart becomes most chastening. I would also suggest that this process model might be of value wherever normalisation via a previously created lexicon is contemplated.

One final part of our editorial equipage must be mentioned briefly, and that is the reverse lexicon (an extract from which is included in Appendix B). Quite simply, this is a computer listing of all forms in HOCCLEX in reverse alphabetical order. The implications are, I hope, fairly obvious. The reverse lexicon would theoretically enable us, given enough inflectional inspiration, to recreate an entire system of auctorial accidence. Our aims are not so presumptuous, however, for it is only rarely that we attempt such a wholesale invocation of analogy. Rather, we regard the unit of lexical comparison and reconstruction as the morpheme itself, not the putative inflectional system in which it is embedded.

For the other part of the 'divided authority' of our edition – the substantive emendation – we began, as I have already suggested, with an orthodox Lachmann model of recension. However, while it might appear that the genealogical rationale is therefore a perfect vehicle for the resuscitation of Hoccleve's text (using, say, Anne Hudson's criteria from her Toronto article on Middle English editing)[38] in fact the prominence of the extant patronic copies, and the comparatively conservative copying already mentioned, place copy-text in a much more visible position substantively than would be expected in such a well-witnessed transmission. To put it rather crudely, an editor needs the evidence of other extant witnesses in order to emend Arundel fairly infrequently, whether such emendation is carried out under the relatively austere code of McKerrow's 'contextual' errors or under the more liberal auspices of Greg's collational system, algebraic or otherwise.[39] Furthermore, where such emendations might occur, the surety of the genealogical model begins to dissolve. With the possible exceptions of two or three extremely idiosyncratic witnesses, it

---

[38] Hudson, 'Middle English', p. 45. The two 'genealogical' assumptions are: 'First, that extant (and, implicitly, lost) manuscripts all descend from a single author's copy . . . and . . . second . . . that nothing other than the author's original text . . . will be of any interest.' Both assumptions *might* be appropriate for the *substantives* of the *Regement*, but for the *accidentals*, the principles are very problematical (i.e., according to Greg, subsequent copying will obscure auctorial orthography irrecoverably, so that the first criterion is irrelevant; but, in the absence of an independent value in the accidentals of the scribal copies – and, given the putative characteristics of the lost accidentals of the auctorial fair copy – it is inevitably the 'author's original text' which is the major focus of our editorial practices).

[39] R. B. McKerrow, *Prolegomena for the Oxford Shakespeare. A Study in Editorial Method* (Oxford, 1979). McKerrow's principle of emendation is that an editor should depart from the 'originals . . . only when they appear to be certainly corrupt' (p. 20). This corruption is defined as 'any form which, in the light of our knowledge of the language at the time when the text in question was written, was "impossible", that is, would not have been, in its context, an intelligible word or phrase' (p. 21). Greg questions this 'contextual' rule in *The Editorial Problem in Shakespeare*, 2 ed. (1951), p. xxvii, and posits an algebraic charting of collation as a means of mapping the transmission of error in *The Calculus of Variants* (Oxford, 1927).

is virtually impossible to exclude any of the extant texts from active consideration on such conventional grounds as their lowly hierarchical status or their inherently corrupt nature. I suppose this means that we endorse by implication the motto, 'Recentiores non deteriores', in a reaction against a strict rendering of the Lachmann–Maas model. However, it should be noted that Marzec's mapping of the genealogy using Maas does itself lend support for the Pasquali view. That is, the number of demonstrably *derived* manuscripts is very few, and elimination on these grounds is therefore very tenuous. Similarly, as the stemma displays, the number of inferred witnesses (almost as many as the extant, in this most conservative of transmissions) is so great that an editorial reliance on the reconstructed readings of these inferred witnesses is just as common as is a reliance upon a variant actually preserved in documentary form. Tanselle has made the valid point[40] that the editorial use of an inferred reading is no more or less conservative or conjectural than the use of documented scribal readings: both require an editorial leap of faith as well as careful transmissional analysis. The fact that one manuscript happens to exist and the other does not is not in itself an argument for the validity of one reading over another. This argument should be of particular value to editors of medieval texts, who almost always have to deal with scribal copies (all labouring under the same 'corrupt' stigma) as opposed to auctorial drafts.

After substantive and accidentals emendation, the next area of editorial responsibility is to produce the evidence – i.e., historical collation. As can be readily seen, any historical collation can provide the basis for either a synoptic apparatus (for recording putative auctorial revision) or a social text of post-publication non-auctorial transmission. Indeed, as the recent exchanges in the popular press between John Kidd and Hans Walter Gabler over the *Ulysses* edition would suggest,[41] the placing of such variants in either a

---

[40] Tanselle, 'Classical . . . Editing', 62–3 (in defending 'modern' textual theories and methods of eclectic editing against those typically used in 'ancient' editing): 'the [modern] idea that all alterations made in the selected copy-text are emendations – whether they come from other documentary texts or from the editor's (or some other editor's) inspiration – gives rise to a fundamentally different outlook from that which has often prevailed in the textual criticism of earlier material. It leads to a franker acceptance of the centrality of critical judgement because it calls attention to the similarity, rather than the difference, between adopting a reading from another text and adopting a reading that is one's own conjecture. Both result in a form of the text unlike that in any known document and therefore represent editorial judgment in departing from documentary evidence.'

[41] See the newspaper article by Isabel Wilkerson, 'Textual Scholars Make Points about Points in Books' (*New York Times*, 29 April 1985) and the report by Jeremy Treglown, 'Editors Vary' (*TLS*, 10 May 1985). The contention lying behind this public coverage of the third Society for Textual Scholarship conference in April 1985 was whether the Gabler *Ulysses* edition had relegated genuine *auctorial* variants to an 'inferior' position in the historical variation, rather than charting them in the synoptic text. Gabler defended the edition's principles of discrimination, but Kidd (in an as yet unpublished analysis) claimed that much of Joyce's 'intention' had been buried in the historical collation of the edition. The general relevance of the Joyce debate to this current article on Hoccleve and Middle English editing is that the editorial decision *where* to record certain variants has important implications for

synoptic or an historical apparatus can have significant political implications involving an editor's view of auctorial control over, and interest in, the transmission of the text – in other words, intentionality again.

On the Hoccleve edition, we take the position that we are recording only textual dissolution, not active resuscitation, in the life of the text, and that neither a synoptic nor a social text would be an appropriate construct from our apparatus. In other words, our attitude to collation approaches more closely the textological, remaniement school rather than the Gabler or McGann. This is based on the assumption that the *Regement* is a finished auctorial artefact in its earliest documentary form, and that the subsequent scribal involvement in transmission is more passive than active. A different persuasion would obviously result in a different status for collation and a different presentation of text. Theoretically, it could even provide the basis for a computer reconstruction of any eclectic version of the text, though (as I have already suggested) we do not believe that the degree of substantive variance warrants such extravagance.

What are the theoretical ramifications of the textual conditions of the Hoccleve corpus and the editorial treatment of this corpus? First, there is the problem of the 'presumptive authority of copy-text', or in more moral terms, what Greg calls the 'tyranny of the copy-text'.[42] In photographic facsimiles and even in diplomatic transcripts, this tyranny is, we assume, virtually absolute, and is carried over into 'best-text' editions, where the authority derived from provenance may be manifested in both codicological and palaeographic terms – again, the 'editorial death-wish'. The several editions of the poems contained in the Hoccleve holographs inevitably succumb to this presumption, as perhaps they ought, the major area of debate being how far these holographs can be deemed to represent the 'final' intentions of the author-scribe. The bibliographic and palaeographic features of the holographs confirm that they cannot be identified with what the geneticists call the 'avant-texte'[43] (anything predating an authorised publication – rough drafts, heavily revised foul papers, etc.). They are formally constructed 'finished' works, clearly intended for the public eye. Indeed, as John Burrow has demonstrated,[44] it is this 'finished' nature of, for example, the *Series* poems which provides them with their poetic

one's concept of the author's (or others') 'intention'. It is not merely a matter of typography and layout, for the conventional distinctions in such elements of a critical edition are the accepted 'codes' whereby editorial judgements are represented (and accepted by the reading public).

[42] For an account of 'the tyranny of copy-text' see Tanselle, 'Classical . . . Editing', 48 and fn. 33.

[43] For an account of the concept of '*avant-texte*', see Jean-Louis Lebrave, 'Rough Drafts: A Challenge to Uniformity in Editing', *TEXT* 3 (1986). For the history and current practice of genetic editing, see Louis Hay, 'Genetic Editing Past and Future', *TEXT* 3 (1986).

[44] Burrow, 'Autobiographical Poetry', 404, argues that it is 'the progress of rehabilitation in society' which is the subject of the *Series* poems. This rehabilitation would, of course, be incomplete if the sequence of poems was in some way 'unfinished'.

rationale – they are testimony to Hoccleve's having recovered from his madness and having produced public documents for public consumption – even though the subject matter is clearly highly personal. As finished documents the poems in the holographs do therefore represent not a dynamic text such as that possibly surviving in the *Troilus, The Legend of Good Women* 'Prologue' (or in later periods, *King Lear, Hamlet, The Rape of the Lock, The Prelude* or *The Waste Land*). This means that, unlike these other works, they are not susceptible to synoptic, genetic, or texto-logical presentation, but instead confirm perhaps the highest degree of presumptive authority in copy-text likely to occur in the editing of Middle English (i.e., beyond the pure diplomatic edition of a manuscript *qua* manuscript). This, at least, is a central part of the thesis underlying our employment of the accidentals of the holographs in the editing of the *Regement*: that the accidence of the morphology in the holographs is not a whimsical, experimental stage in the production of auctorial final intention, but is that final intention itself. Admittedly, the authority of copy-text is then used reflexively rather than directly, for the paradigms are significant not in the evidence they provide for consistency in the holographs, but for a putative consistency in the *Regement*. Paradoxically, therefore, the presumptive authority of copy-text in the holographs is used to undermine this same presumption in the *Regement*. To put it as bluntly as may be: it would hardly matter which of the complete manuscript witnesses we had delegated as copy-text for the editing of the *Regement*, for the presumptive authority of the copy-text is reduced in our edition to only one class in the Normalisation Model. Now, for convenience sake (to avoid a plethora of diacritics or an enormous mass of variants recorded in the accidentals apparatus), it is as well that we used Greg's criteria in the selection of copy-text, and that Arundel 38 functions remarkably well in this role. That is, less than one-third of the accidental forms in Arundel need normalisation by the external model, whereas for other witnesses, the proportion would be very much higher. If one of these other witnesses had, in despite of its lack of accidental (or substantive) authority, achieved some prominence as a textual vehicle (similar to that of, say, the Ellesmere manuscript of *The Canterbury Tales*), then an argument could be made for a diplomatic edition of this witness as embodying a specifically identifiable (and pre-sumably historically valuable) stage of textual transmission – a documentary form, in other words, of the *textus receptus*. But none of the *Regement* manuscripts has any such status, for even the so-called 'patronic' copies derive their status not merely from the act of presentation and possible enshrinement of the text, but from their having been copied during Hoccleve's lifetime and possibly under his supervision. In other words, nothing happens in the transmission of the Hoccleve text analogous to that freezing of an 'authorised' version attempted when Peisistratus decreed that approved texts of the three great Attic tragedians be placed in the

library at Athens. Textual dissolution (a well-behaved, gentlemanly dissolution, to be sure) continues below the apparent security of the 'patronic'
copies. These patronic copies (for our purposes, Arundel 38 and Harley
4866 only) represent, in any case, only one part of the 'divided authority'
invoked in the edition. At best, the patronics might be seen as containing a
presumptive authority in substantives (deriving from their genealogical and
historical position), but have no such authority in accidentals. As mentioned
earlier, Furnivall admitted the presence of 'northern forms' in his *apologia*
for Harley as copy-text, and these forms did not prevent him from
regarding Harley as (rightly) representing Hoccleve's substantive text with
some surety. As I have already suggested, Arundel might appear to be a
more convenient copy-text on both substantive and accidental grounds, but
finally it doesn't really matter.

The second theoretical problem is derived from the first. If there can be
a genuine divided authority in the editing of a Middle English work, what
status should we assign to the accidentals? In general, it is probably fair to
say that the predominant normalisation of accidentals previously practised
by medievalists has been undertaken with a view to creating a morphological
consistency in despite of both documentary and auctorial authority. Thus,
the smoothing of Old English forms to Wessex tenth century or the
reduction of scribal idiosyncrasies to the norm of South-East Midlands has
had a ready dialectal or palaeographic defence. On the other hand,
putative auctorial accidence has rarely been invoked – to my knowledge,
nobody has yet suggested that the Mercian 'symptoms' in the *Beowulf*
manuscript be used as a mechanism for a reconstruction of the complete
accidence (dialectal or otherwise) of the author. And why? Because both
auctorial intention and the meaning redolent in accidentals have until
recently been given comparatively short shrift in medieval studies. This
was one of the first criticisms made of both classicists and medievalists in
Tanselle's recent encyclopaedic survey of 'ancient' editing in *SB*,[45] and our
ready defence has always been that the documentary conditions forbid
such licence. Far better to acknowledge the limited authority either of the
diplomatic edition or of the recension to an archetype. Now that Kane and
Donaldson have blown the cover of the archetype in its claims as the

[45] Tanselle, 'Classical . . . Editing', *passim*, esp. p. 42, 'The editor is finally responsible for
establishing both substantives and accidentals, and to assume that scribal accidentals are too
far removed from the author's practice to be worth preserving is to ignore the connections
between accidentals and meaning. One may not in the end accept these accidentals, but the
question of what accidentals to include in a critical text must be faced. Authorial accidentals
in ancient texts may be more conjectural than in modern texts, but the attempt to approximate
them is not necessarily to be rejected in favour of standardised spelling and modernised
punctuation.' Tanselle's basic argument is stated in the last two sentences of the article
(p. 68), 'Editing ancient texts and editing modern ones are not simply related fields; they are
essentially the same field. The differences between them are in details; the similarities are in
fundamentals.'

earliest attainable stage in textual transmission, and now that we all seem
to be dissatisfied with the limitations of Manly–Rickert's 'O' prime, we
might be able to reassess our earlier theoretical constraints. It should be
fairly clear from the evidence suggested that even an author like Hoccleve
cared very much for the specific form in which his 'meaning' was embodied.
To deny this auctorial desire and to replace it by documentary rather than
auctorial intention has often had the result of placing medieval studies
outside the scope of some of the most significant textual debates of this
century. The ongoing struggle over intentionality waged among, for
example, Hancher, Tanselle, Mailloux, McLaverty, McGann and others[46]
is not one circumscribed by the documentary conditions of a particular
period. Thus, McGann's denial of the author's prerogative in the historical
evolution of the text might be documented in the nineteenth-century texts
he has worked on; but, as I have suggested earlier, a similar case could be
made from the Wycliffite tracts or the three versions of *Piers Plowman*.
McGann is consciously reacting against a hegemony that has not yet been
acknowledged in medieval studies – the Greg–Bowers concept of divided
authority and the defence of auctorial intention almost in despite of
documentary witness. I have argued elsewhere that McGann's attempt to
link Greg–Bowers intentionality with Lachmann genealogy is a decoy in
order to set his own ideology apart from all previous orthodoxies;[47] like
many of the contributors to this volume I do not therefore accept that
stemmatics is really as far as we can go in the reconstruction of intention,
and would hold that a 'social' school of textual criticism is invalid where
intention is recoverable, even a limited intention such as that attempted in
the holograph-less *Regement*.

That these contributors are facing such theoretical issues as intentionality
and geneticism is of great comfort to the editors of Hoccleve. Despite the
peculiar conditions of the Hoccleve texts, Hoccleveans are clearly not
alone in confronting questions that were perhaps unthinkable a few years
ago. Naturally, we believe that our solutions are the right ones, but I am in
any case grateful for the opportunity to have placed our edition and its
problems in the context of a larger circle of theoretical and practical
concerns.

[46] Michael Hancher, 'Three Kinds of Intention', *MLN* 87 (1972); Mailloux, op. cit.; Tanselle,
'The Editorial Problem of Final Authorial Intention', *Studies in Bibliography* 29 (1976),
167–211; James McLaverty, 'The Concept of Authorial Intention in Textual Criticism', *The
Library* Sixth Series, 6 (1984), 121–38; McGann, *Critique, passim* (esp. chaps. 3, 5, and 6),
and pp. 65–7 for his brief discussion of Bédier and Vinaver.
[47] Greetham, 'Normalisation', fn. 10. The case for denying McGann's linking of Greg and
Lachmann textual theory was developed in my paper given at the 1985 meeting of the South
Atlantic Modern Language Association at Atlanta ('Pre-Texts, Post-Texts, Inter-Texts').

APPENDIX A

Normalisation Model

Explanation: This is not a model illustrating the descending significance or the statistical incidence of actual forms, but rather a logical arrangement of 'levels' of normalisation, based upon the three major sources for producing the accidentals of the edited text – the HOCCLEX concordance (including a reverse lexicon, on which see below), the NORMLEX 'special' dictionary of normalised forms not extant in HOCCLEX, and the copy-text, BL MS Arundel 38. Furthermore, it is primarily a model for the likely editorial treatment of individual word-forms (or more properly word-form types), not for a system of accidence – either Hoccleve's or that of the scribe of Arundel. It is possible that such a system could be constructed from the evidence lying behind the model, but our unit of comparative data is *first* always the specific form as it occurs in a specific place or places in the text (i.e., only later, usually through NORMLEX or the reverse lexicon, is a formal morphological pattern extending beyond the immediate evidence of HOCCLEX transferred to the edited text). Similarly, the model – as it reflects our editorial method – is not a lexical study *per se*; that is, it is concerned with the morphology of the word as it occurs in the text, and not with its lexical identity or history. This is an important consideration in interpreting the model, for while a particular *form* of a word might not exist in one column, the word itself (in a related form) could very well be extant. This explains the apparent anomaly of level 12, where there is no entry in either the HOCCLEX or the COPY-TEXT columns, and yet there is a 100% entry in the NORMLEX column: i.e., the particular form (say, a third-person singular of a regular verb) happens not to exist in the texts from which HOCCLEX is derived, and the copy-text is either very ambiguous in its preferred forms for this verb in this specific inflected form, or uses an inflection which does not appear in HOCCLEX for this verb, or perhaps not for *any* verb. None the less, it would be possible to construct the appropriate preferred Hocclevean inflection from HOCCLEX and to read that, without ambiguity, into NORMLEX – in an example of the occasional employment of the general principles of accidence as a secondary editorial activity, based on the evidence of HOCCLEX and NORMLEX together. Anomalies such as this notwithstanding, the model still functions primarily as a record of the specific form in the specific word, not of the putative degree of consistency in the idiolect as a whole. In fact, as is readily seen, an entry appears in the NORMLEX column *only* when there is no entry in the HOCCLEX column; that is, recourse to NORMLEX is taken only when a highly conservative use of HOCCLEX will not produce a well-attested form for the specific inflection (or root) needed. The 100% HOCCLEX forms would be automatically read into NORMLEX but would not need to be cited in editorial work, hence their not recurring in the NORMLEX column. This simply confirms the relatively greater authority of HOCCLEX over NORMLEX (even though, in this case, they carry identical data, so that no choice has to be made between them). The entire procedure is, of course, merely another (post-classical) occurrence of the basic principle of 'analogy' as defined by the Alexandrian librarians, editors, and grammarians. One final *caveat*: since we have not yet created a complete concordance of all copy-text forms to parallel HOCCLEX for the holographs, any statistics cited in the COPY-TEXT column are inevitably less firm (but also less significant for a critical as opposed to a diplomatic edition) than those for the HOCCLEX. Frankly, we are not convinced that such a concordance would be of any great value editorially (although it could be of use to palaeographers, philologists, and dialecticians). For although Arundel happens to obey Gregian requirements for copy-text as regards its accidentals, it is essentially being used as a vehicle to present comparative data for the recognition and, where necessary, the construction, of auctorial intentions.

	HOCCLEX	NORMLEX	COPY-TEXT	EDITED TEXT
1.	100% usage	–	= 100% usage	HOCCLEX[1] & COPY-TEXT
2.	100% usage	–	= high usage	HOCCLEX[2]
3.	100% usage	–	= indifferent	HOCCLEX[3]
4.	100% usage	–	= low usage	HOCCLEX[4]
5.	100% usage	–	–	HOCCLEX[5]
6.	90%–99% usage	–	= 100% usage	HOCCLEX[6]
7.	1%–90% usage	–	= 100% usage	HOCCLEX[7] or COPY-TEXT
8.	–	100% usage	= 100% usage	NORMLEX[8]
9.	–	100% usage	= high usage	NORMLEX[9]
10.	–	100% usage	= indifferent	NORMLEX[10]
11.	–	100% usage	= low usage	NORMLEX[11]
12.	–	100% usage	–	NORMLEX[12]
13.	–	–	= 100% usage	COPY-TEXT[13]
14.	indifferent	indifferent	indifferent	COPY-TEXT[14] or HOCCLEX or NORMLEX

NOTES:

[1] The well-attested forms in HOCCLEX parallel *exactly* the same forms in the copy-text. In practice, this level accounts for, perhaps, 50% of all cases in the normalisation procedures, thereby confirming Arundel's status as copy-text on Gregian criteria as well as its function as base text on 'classical' principles.

[2] While copy-text might occasionally use a variant form, it clearly prefers the same form that is *consistently* used in HOCCLEX.

[3] Copy-text does show the form used in HOCCLEX, but as an 'indifferent' variant, in comparison to the consistent usage in HOCCLEX.

[4] While copy-text clearly prefers a form other than that in HOCCLEX, the holograph usage is still absolutely invariable.

[5] Even where the form does not exist in copy-text, the holograph preference is unambiguous. Usually, of course, the HOCCLEX form would therefore not occur in the edited text at all, except perhaps in circumstances where the scribal inflection seemed an error (e.g., in number, agreement, etc.), when the form derived from HOCCLEX would take precedence.

[6] Note that the required 'level' of evidentiary support in HOCCLEX is higher than in the corresponding entry for copy-text (line 2 of model). This reflects the editorial desire to represent auctorial (as opposed to scribal) choice with greater surety, and, in general, not to admit HOCCLEX (or NORMLEX) forms as paradigms unless there is either a clear 'blank entry' in the copy-text data or a statistically and morphologically well-attested norm in the great majority of auctorial or auctorially-derived forms.

[7] Given the general assumptions (regarding auctorial and scribal usage) under which the normalisation model is constructed, this level should be very rare (and in fact turns out to be so), but could contain occasional anomalies. If one were using orthodox base-text theory (or copy-text theory in its usual restriction to the features of a single text), then the 100% usage form in copy-text would clearly support an unambiguous preference, albeit scribal, or at least not *demonstrably* auctorial. If the copy-text form is therefore *highly* atypical as measured against the HOCCLEX extant patterns (say, less than a 25% concurrence with HOCCLEX), then great care would obviously be needed in establishing preferred auctorial usage. Thus, although this level, particularly towards the lower statistical end just cited, occurs infrequently in the normalisation (perhaps once every 500 lines), it is by far the most problematical. Note, furthermore, that we had originally employed the same series of discriminations for HOCCLEX (high, indifferent, low) in this category as in levels 2–4 and 9–11 for copy-text. However, given our general principle that a demonstrable consistency of usage in HOCCLEX

is necessary for normalisation of copy-text to proceed, anything under a 90% usage (particularly as measured in this category against a 100% usage in copy-text) seemed possibly suspect and might therefore lead to a selection of copy-text over HOCCLEX, as the model indicates. Therefore, a single category representing this level of indeterminacy, rare though it be, is a more honest response to the statistical conditions than a three-tier breakdown would be.

[8] While the required form does not exist in the holographs, it would be easy to create it by morphological extension. This required form corresponds exactly with the form in copy-text, and would merely confirm a conservative reading of copy-text by reference to NORMLEX.

[9] Copy-text preference would again confirm the form created by morphological extension in NORMLEX. Since this form is at least *derivable* from auctorial usage in HOCCLEX and supported by the majority readings in copy-text, its consistency would be employed throughout the normalisation of the copy-text variants.

[10] An indifferent variant in copy-text, but with the NORMLEX form established as a consistent and unambiguous derivative from HOCCLEX.

[11] A logical extension of the previous two levels, where despite the statistical evidence of the copy-text, a minority form in the copy-text would be preferred since it would be derivable unambiguously from NORMLEX (and therefore from HOCCLEX). Note that the 'presumptive authority' of copy-text would be employed, not in cases like levels 9-11 (where the authority of the consistent *external* evidence – i.e., NORMLEX – is paramount), but in cases where the 'indifference' of the copy-text scribe would be matched by a similar (in incidence, if not always in exact type) indifference in HOCCLEX.

[12] The normalised form is not extant in the copy-text (the scribe presumably preferring *other* variants of the same basic word) or in HOCCLEX (presumably because of the lack of concurrence of the two lexicons). The form could, however, be fully supported by NORMLEX in evidence drawn from related forms in HOCCLEX. This is therefore a level which logically proceeds quite straightforwardly from the previous three, where the normalised form was gradually having its statistical base in copy-text reduced. Note that, while the statistical base might appear to have vanished, in fact this could conceal a very high level of authority for morphological extension. As suggested above, this level could describe cases where a particular word happens not to occur in the holographs (and therefore does not turn up in the HOCCLEX column), but does occur in the copy-text, in, however, a form recognisably different from the clear auctorial preference that could be established in NORMLEX if the word *had* been used in the holographs. Say, for example, Hoccleve had happened not to use the word (ModE) *though* in the holographs, but it did show in the copy-text. We can establish from HOCCLEX that a) he never used a 'ʒ' and that b) he never used a 'þ' except in the contracted form *þᵗ* = *þat*, (ModE *that*), and that therefore a copy-text form of *þouʒ* would be an *impossibility* in HOCCLEX. The normalised form, based on 100% usage *patterns* in HOCCLEX, would be perhaps *though* or *thogh*. Thus the form (if it represented a choice between an initial 'þ' and 'th', or a final 'ʒ' and 'gh') could merit the 100% level in NORMLEX, while not occurring in HOCCLEX or copy-text in the form created by NORMLEX and used in the edited text.

[13] This would cover very few cases, and would be most prominent in nonce-words, often proper nouns, which for obvious reasons would often not be replicated in HOCCLEX. The 100% in the copy-text column, therefore, would often represent in actual incidence a very small number, usually a single occurrence – for the scribe of Arundel, while closer to Hoccleve's usage than the other copyists, does not share his author's passion for orthodoxy in orthography to the same degree.

[14] Again, a very rare level, where NORMLEX would not be capable of creating a consistent reliable form by morphological extension, but, on the contrary, several forms which would mirror the apparent indifference in HOCCLEX. In such cases, we would invoke the principle of copy-text as residual authority, as long as the forms showing in copy-text reflected putative auctorial choices. If the *type*, but not ratio (or incidence) of indifferent forms in copy-text were dissimilar to those in HOCCLEX and NORMLEX, then presumably the use of these *latter* forms would have to be considered. However, since this does not seem to appear in the editing of the *Regement*, the case is included here only as a logical completion of the statistical types cited, and an additional testament to the conservative principles upon which the normalisation proceeds.

(Reprinted from *Studies in Bibliography* 38 (1985), 131–4, by permission.)

Flow-chart of Accidentals Normalisation

The flow-chart (fig. 2) is a simplification of the normalisation process, and does not include every stage that an editor might have to follow in creating a normalised text. For example, the 'create NORMLEX' box could very well involve the consultation of the reverse lexicon, as could the 'check attestation' boxes. But in general, it does chart the stages fairly realistically. This is the process generally followed:

1. The editor first looks up the A (copy-text) form in HOCCLEX (i.e., the lexicon based on the Hoccleve holograph); if the A-form is found in HOCCLEX *exactly*, then the editor checks its attestation (i.e., how many times that form occurs in the holographs, being careful to compare its incidence with that of other, possibly variant forms). Once the attestation is checked, the editor then consults the Normalisation Model (Appendix A) to see if the statistics compiled support the use of the HOCCLEX form (e.g., whether it has 100% incidence, etc.). Note that the HOCCLEX form may, of course, be identical to the A-form (in fact, in roughly 60 per cent of cases, it probably will be), but that if the incidence supports the HOCCLEX form, it is theoretically *that* form which is being used, not that of copy-text. At this stage, it does not really matter whether the editor has normalised (by substituting HOCCLEX for copy-text), but only whether the attestation of the form in HOCCLEX confirms it as an auctorial usage. This form is then added to the NORMLEX file, which will ultimately consist of all well-attested Hocclevean forms used in the *Regement*, no matter where they come from (HOCCLEX, copy-text, or other forms already in NORMLEX).
2. If the A-form is not found exactly in HOCCLEX, the editor then checks for other variant forms under which it might appear (e.g., initial long or short 's' variants). If a variant is found, and if it is well-attested (as opposed to the copy-text form, which presumably does not exist in HOCCLEX), then the editor proceeds as above, adding the HOCCLEX form to NORMLEX and using it in the edited text. If neither the original A-form *nor* any variant is found in HOCCLEX, the editor then consults NORMLEX to see if a form exists there. Obviously, if a form *is* found in NORMLEX, it will have been created from earlier NORMLEX variants – maybe by the use of the reverse lexicon – and will not represent a form extant in HOCCLEX, which has already been checked.
3. Having found a suitable form in NORMLEX, the editor then consults the Normalisation Model to see if it is usable. Logically, if it has been entered into NORMLEX correctly, then it *will* be usable, but it is as well if the appropriate-ness of the form is considered. For example, a suffix created in NORMLEX for a polysyllabic word *might* not be suitable as the ending of a monosyllabic word. However, given that the NORMLEX form is indeed usable, we simply employ it in the edited text in place of the A-form. Where the *exact* form as it occurs in NORMLEX cannot be used, the editor then considers whether a NORMLEX form based upon those already extant can be created. If it can (again, possibly using the reverse lexicon), this form is then added to the NORMLEX dictionary, its appropriateness is checked on the Normalisation Model, and it is used in the edited text.
4. If a NORMLEX form cannot be created (and if the form has not already been found in NORMLEX), the copy-text form is then used, in an example of the status of copy-text as residual authority. Copy-text would also be used if, for some reason, we were to discover that the forms already extant or just created in

NORMLEX cannot be used in this particular case. As mentioned earlier, this should not occur if all has gone properly in the creation of NORMLEX, but the situation is plotted on the flow-chart since it is at least a theoretical possibility. Note that this situation (the non-use of NORMLEX and the reliance on copy-text) will not be the *only* cases where copy-text is used – as might appear from the flow-chart. In practice, the great majority of HOCCLEX forms will in fact also be represented by copy-text, but in these examples, copy-text does not carry the authority for the form, HOCCLEX does.

Here is a single line of normalisation illustrating the process: Copy-text reads

What why3t that inly penſyf is I trowe

1. *What*: The form is well-attested in HOCCLEX (156 incidences), and there are no variant forms which offer it any competition. With an apparent 100 per cent incidence, therefore, the form is confirmed by the Normalisation Model and we use it in the edited text.
2. *why3t*: The form does not exist in HOCCLEX (the *yogh* is sufficient to prevent that), so we search for variants, beginning with those closest to the A-form. HOCCLEX turns up, for example, *whyt* twice, but on reference to the text, it appears that these forms = 'white' not 'wight' and cannot therefore be cited in the evidence. We then turn to forms in *wi-* and come up with *wight*, with a very high attestation (62 times), reinforced by two additional occurrences of similar *wi-* forms (*wighte* and *wightes*). There are no rival *wyght* forms in HOCCLEX. We have therefore found a suitable variant in HOCCLEX, one which the Normalisation Model confirms as usable, and we therefore use this variant, record its attestation, and add it to NORMLEX (as we had already done for *what*).
3. *that*: This form is well-attested in HOCCLEX, with 118 occurrences, and no variants with initial *th-*. Hoccleve's *preferred* form is the contraction þᵗ, with 1303 occurrences; however, since the *that* form is also clearly the auctorial preference for the expanded version, it should be used in cases like this. We therefore enter *that* into NORMLEX, and use the HOCCLEX (and copy-text) form in the edited version.
4. *inly*: This occurs only once in HOCCLEX, so its attestation is not high enough to make us very secure. However, there are 970 occurrences of *in* in HOCCLEX, and many others of compound words beginning with *in*. This compares with only 5 occurrences of *ynne*, 1 of *ynnynge* (and 0 for *yn*). The first element in *inly* would therefore seem to be well-supported. Similarly, there are in HOCCLEX no well-attested variants on *-ly*, and thus, while the compound itself occurs only once in this form in HOCCLEX, there is no competition from any other form and the copy-text form is retained. We use HOCCLEX (which, as remarked above, happens to be the copy-text form as well), and add it to NORMLEX.
   penſyf: The word does not exist in HOCCLEX, nor is there any plausible variant for this form. We must therefore use NORMLEX, if possible. The only problem might be in the suffix *-yf*, for the root *penſ-* would seem to be a fairly standard morpheme, the only likely variant being the long/short 's' (the former represented in the print-out of HOCCLEX and the reverse lexicon by '2'). We therefore go to the reverse lexicon. Suffix forms in *-yf* are listed thus:

2349 FY22ECXE
3641 FYL
3362 FYNK
4817 FYR

        551 FYRT2
        4957 FYRTS
        2925 FYT2AH
        1601 FYTATROFNOC
        3905 FYTOM
        1353 FYTYAC
        5777 FYW

The *-yf* suffix is therefore fairly well attested. The variant in *-if* produces the following list:

        3208 FI
        2348 FI22ECXE
        991 FILLIAB
        491 FIT2
        4951 FITS
        1302 FITYAC

There are no variants in, for example, *-ffe* or *-ff*. Thus, the *penſyf* is clearly a *possible* Hocclevean usage, and this is partially confirmed by the *hastyf* and *confortatyf* readings in the reverse lexicon (i.e., adjectival forms where the *-yf* is a genuine suffix, unlike, say, *knyf* or *lyf*). The form *excessyf* is, of course, more ambiguous, for the variant *excessif* also exists; it would therefore be improper for us to create a *general* NORMLEX suffix usage for *-yf* based on the evidence of the reverse lexicon, but we can certainly say that the *penſyf* form is arguably auctorial. Note incidentally, that this run through the reverse lexicon does confirm that *-ffe* and *-ff* are both very unlikely 'Hocclevean' forms. We therefore compile a list of such 'negative' paradigms based upon our work on HOCCLEX and NORMLEX, and this list of 'impossible' forms obviously saves time in subsequent consultation of the lexicon, and can be employed in cases of genuine copy-text indifference elsewhere.

6. *is*: This is a very well-attested form in HOCCLEX (749 occurrences), and there are no likely variants (e.g., in *ys*). We therefore use HOCCLEX/copy-text, and add the form to NORMLEX.
7. *I*: The *I* is certainly well attested (with 640 occurrences), although the rival form *Y* does also exist (with 348 occurrences). Add *I* to NORMLEX, but also add the variant *Y*.
8. *trowe*: This is a well-attested form in HOCCLEX (13/0 occurrences). Add it to NORMLEX and use in the edited text.

The final edited line therefore reads as follows:

What wight that inly penſyf is I trowe

and the accidentals apparatus would be:

1] *wight* (62 + 2/0) A *whyȝt*

That is, we do not record in the apparatus the statistics supporting the *retention* of A-forms, only those supporting the normalisation. The other statistics (e.g., on *that*, *is*, etc.) are, of course, recorded by each editor as each entry is made into NORMLEX, but these are cited only in the textual notes, introduction, or glossary.

*PROBLEMS OF 'BEST TEXT' EDITING AND THE HENGWRT MANUSCRIPT OF *THE CANTERBURY TALES*

Ralph Hanna III

The problem my title suggests is twofold. First of all, why should one prepare a 'best-text edition' of a literary work? Second, in the specific instance of *The Canterbury Tales*, what claims should be accorded to the Hengwrt manuscript – National Library of Wales Peniarth 392 – in such an edition? To a certain extent, these questions are intertwined – or at least, how you choose to answer the first question conditions how you can answer the second: after all, even in the confines of the individual lemma, and even in the confines of an eclectic scholarly edition, individual manuscripts do not possess absolute value for textual purposes, only what I would call contextual value.[1]

About defining 'best text editing', there are, I think, minimal problems. Such an edition chooses one copy of the work as qualitatively superior to all others and follows that copy's readings with greater or less pertinacity. However, the basis for such a choice remains uncertain: presumably one can only determine a 'best text' to edit by the rather circular procedure of some editorial activity, at least trial collations of a part. This circularity eventually approaches absurdity, since once a 'best' version has been chosen, a printed collation is, at least theoretically, supererogatory. Most usually, only when the 'best' or base manuscript is palpably impossible are collations truly necessary: they exist to defend a change to the reading of other, necessarily 'wusser' texts. ('Best texts' are only such in the aggregate whereas editors, alas, must attend to individual lemmata.)[2]

The initial difficulty, then, requiring discussion is: what is a 'best text' edition for? I begin with the fact that editions are composed to communicate

---

*In the past year my thinking about the text of *The Canterbury Tales* has been especially stimulated by lengthy conversations with Joseph A. Dane and Larry D. Benson. I have also been aided by constructive suggestions about this paper made by my colleague Robert N. Essick.
[1] Cf. Rosamund Allen, *King Horn* (New York: Garland, 1984), p. 28: 'Only variants, not manuscripts, have value. Moreover they have value only in relation to each other.'
[2] This bind, what Walter W. Greg called 'the tyranny of copy text' (see *Studies in Bibliography* 3 (1950–51), 26), is amusingly described by E. Talbot Donaldson, 'The Psychology of Editors of Middle English Texts', in *Speaking of Chaucer* (New York: Norton, 1972), pp. 102–18, at pp. 113–16.

texts, and the fundamental choice of editorial technique is not based on some property inherent in the materials edited but on the communication which the editor intends to effect. That is, editorial technique isn't God-given or absolute but a fact about audience or about critical perspective. There is no one way to edit any text but a multiplicity of possible editions, limited only by the audiences with the money to purchase copies or the scholar's ingenuity in discovering contexts into which the work might be placed. Thus, one can have scholarly editions with full variant apparatus, as well as student editions constructed on a variety of methods; but one can also have editions of the work on a perfectly diplomatic basis, with or without the rest of some single manuscript in which the work appears, or, for example, in the case of classical and patristic texts, editions of late medieval recensions, demonstrably scribal products but still of interest. In each case, the choice of method and contents reflects a particular sense of audience needs.

So the question can be rephrased: what audience (alternatively, what perspective on the work) requires a 'best text' edition? Here, rather than address a multiplicity of possible practical rationales for 'best text' editions, I want to discuss two purely theoretical claims for 'best text' editing which I think have been quietly but persistently present in recent efforts at 'authorising' the Hengwrt manuscript. These I can rephrase in terms of my argument as suggesting that the audience editors ought most to consider is the original audience of the poem; in following a 'best text', editors seek to place the modern audience in the position of that Ur-audience. This choice can be theoretised in two ways: either as a mystified nostalgia for the supposedly simplified position of the medieval reader or, in reverse, as a statement about the overly sophisticated habits of modern eclectic editors. Neither view is, to me, factually compelling.

I separate these views, even though their end results are the same, because they involve rather different suppositions about texts and their purposes. The nostalgic view in effect argues that medieval readers read literary texts from single manuscripts; consequently, providing the reader with the 'best manuscript' gives him at least as good a text as any medieval reader had, and, probably, so the argument runs, gives him better, since most medieval readers didn't have the 'best' manuscript. In contrast, the second view acknowledges (and repudiates) the power of modern editorial methods for constructing texts; it adopts an apparently conservative view in which the creation of a non-medieval text corrected on the basis of all manuscripts is viewed as a historical speculation. In opposition, it offers apparently hard fact, the 'best text' which survives – an object with its worst excrescences – obvious errors – trimmed.

The first view falls rather easily, I should think. It is not clear that either medieval readers or scribes really were limited to single manuscripts. Copying or reading, especially of materials in Middle English, was, even in the fifteenth century, something of a fanatic's occupation; consequently, texts often got copied and read *because* people knew them already.[3] The evidence for this, generally inseparable from apparently non-genetic transmission of readings, is memorial contamination of a scribe's actual archetype with readings which he recalls from other versions of the text he has heard or read. The same thing presumably occurred with readers. In addition, both scribes and readers were probably adept at running correction of their texts, simply on the basis of *Sprachgefühl* (we do the same thing every morning with our *Times*, London or Los Angeles).[4] Readers thus weren't limited to the manuscript before them but could in fact conjecture a better one; a good many Chaucerian readings not in Hengwrt, Ellesmere, or MSS of that ilk (D 117 *wright* comes to mind) are the result of such procedures.[5] Finally, this view confuses two things that are distinct (leaving aside the question of authorial version*s*) – the text read by the audience and the text intended for them by the author.

The second, conservative view requires that the reader not accept a modern construct, for which there is no evidence of medieval existence. Rather than allowing a textual version for which there is no positive evidence, it offers apparently hard fact. I think, though, that Rosamund Allen has nailed this view effectively: she argues perspicaciously that such an assertion of the single manuscript, rather than the critical edition, is the ultimately eclectic editorial act, inasmuch as it accepts, more or less non-critically, all the decisions of a single mind.[6] That this mind happens to

---

[3] This is, after all, what the 'bespoke trade' in books which typified medieval production means – that readers sought works they specifically desired, and thus, very likely, knew in some detail. Even a copyist like Robert Thornton, who surely came upon many texts by accident, just as surely sought copies of specific works. Moreover, his situation was far less exceptional in one important respect than it often appears: a great many manuscripts were copied by their owners, often professional writers (as Thornton wasn't), for their own private use.

[4] The scrupulousness of modern, as opposed to medieval, proofreading tends to reduce the force and impact of many examples. But compare: '[He] just got up and walked out, leaving me with this Danny person, who had just finished his goddamnest training' (Armistead Maupin, *Tales of the City* (London: Corgi, 1984), p. 21). This nonsense can be cleared up by reading 'goddamn est training', i.e. *erhard seminar training*, a psychological self-improvement system.

[5] Such corrected readings do not occur very often, perhaps once every four hundred lines. *wright*, of course, was suggested by Donaldson, '*Canterbury Tales*, D 117: A Critical Edition', *Speculum* 40 (1965), 626–33 (reprinted, *Speaking of Chaucer*, pp. 119–30). The reading has been printed in Donaldson's *Chaucer's Poetry* (2nd edn; New York: Ronald, 1975) and R. A. Pratt's *The Tales of Canterbury* (Boston: Houghton, 1974). It will appear in the forthcoming third edition of F. N. Robinson's *Works*. Many such readings have achieved the status of convention, for example *Merchant's Tale* E 2230 'Ethna' (in Ha5 Ps only, in an extremely complicated context); for discussion and full variants, see John M. Manly and Edith Rickert, eds., *The Text of the Canterbury Tales*, 8 vols. (Chicago: Univ. of Chicago Press, 1940), III: 477–8, VI: 483. In contrast, some persuasive examples have yet to be printed by any editor, for example, *Parson's Tale* 869 'centesimus fructus, secundum Jeronimum, *Contra Jovinianum*' (in Ha4 only; all others stop at 'fructus').

[6] *King Horn*, p. 99.

be five hundred years closer to the text than a modern editor does not diminish the fact of that mind's uniqueness, nor does it vouch for its taste and skill at every potential lemma.

I am afraid that this second view in particular has been responsible for much of the recent Hengwrtisation of the *Canterbury Tales*. The arguments of Norman Blake and of a good many *Variorum* editors from Norman come down to an assertion of the Hengwrt scribe's unique gifts as a transmitter of Chaucer's text, an assertion which renders *modern* eclecticism unnecessary. In contrast, Donald Baker, apparently speaking for the staff of the *Variorum* itself, argues cogently for a 'best text' presentation on the basis of an expected audience's use of the Oklahoma edition.[7] I'm quite willing to accept this logic, so far as it goes: that an edition variorum requires some form of reference system; that such a reference system should be modestly authoritative yet still free of the idiosyncrasies which mark (or mar?) past editions; that a manuscript provides one such source; that Hengwrt, as very likely the oldest and surely one of the most faithful sources for the poem, provides a particularly happy source.

But what of Blake and those who share his point of view? Their claims seem to me to confuse the 'best text' with something else, a 'perfect text'. Unlike Rosalind Field, in her thoughtful scrutiny of the individual variants (in a paper given at the conference but not published here), Blake and some Variorum editors seem to me to assert what is to be proved (a polite way of saying that they consistently, if not relentlessly, practise *petitio principii*, rather than textual criticism). That is, they frequently seem in the rhetorical position of arguing, 'This is the Hengwrt reading; therefore it is Chaucer's reading,' rather than asking 'Which reading here seems most likely to be Chaucerian?' What are required at this time, I think, are extensive efforts like Field's at a balanced measurement of Hengwrt's value in determining Chaucer's text.

At least one indication of a limitation in Hengwrt as a reproduction of Chaucer clearly has to do with its tale order. The state of the manuscript seems to me best explained as the result of procedures which I have elsewhere called 'codicising' and which have been discussed in slightly different contexts by Pam Robinson and Jeremy Griffiths.[8] That is, the

---

[7] *A Variorum Edition . . . Volume I . . . A Facsimile and Transcription of the Hengwrt Manuscript* (Norman: Univ. of Oklahoma, 1979), p. xvii. This view should be contrasted with N. F. Blake's arguments that Hengwrt descends uniquely from Chaucer's holograph and is thus anterior to all other manuscripts of the *Tales*; see 'The Relationship between the Hengwrt and Ellesmere Manuscripts of *The Canterbury Tales*', *Essays and Studies* 32 (1979), 1–18; and the edition, *The Canterbury Tales* (London: Arnold, 1980), esp. pp. 3–13. A somewhat different, but categorical, defence of Hengwrt is provided, *A Variorum Edition . . . Volume II, Part 9: The Nun's Priest's Tale*, pp. 4, 97.

[8] P. R. Robinson, 'The "Booklet": A Self-Contained Unit in Composite Manuscripts', *Codicologica* 3 (1980), 46–69, makes the important point that manuscripts frequently do not represent a single act of production; Griffiths's Oxford dissertation examines in-production shifts of plan in several *Canterbury Tales* manuscripts.

scribe at no point seems to have had settled ideas as to what the overall shape of *The Canterbury Tales* (and thus of his manuscript) was. The text came to him as a sequence of *membra disjecta*, perhaps from different sources; and the scribe was aware at various points only of linkages to other units or of their absence. As a result, he occasionally had to extemporise – including such efforts as rewriting links which came to him late so as to minimise difficulties in the tale order he'd adopted and adjusting quire size to handle some blocks of material (a long quire to handle late supply of *The Second Nun's Tale* – in the probably Chaucerian order following the Franklin). And of course, his supply was subject to complete breakdown: the scribe never received *The Canon's Yeoman's Tale, The Merchant's Prologue,* or the expanded *Nun's Priest's Prologue.* (The absence of this last, with some other omissions, may imply that Hengwrt represents an antique, and perhaps unrevised, version of Chaucer's text.) On other occasions, timing may have prevented the scribe from ordering materials as he would have preferred: Fragment D appears to be stuck in at a convenient break in the series of booklets which comprise the manuscript – the proper position after B1 was now in the middle of a consecutively written quire (and booklet).

I emphasise these facts, well-known as they are,[9] because of what they suggest about the scribe's personality. Blake correctly began his efforts at asserting the value of Hengwrt as a 'perfect text' with a defence of its tale order (a defence which I clearly find unconvincing) because he must have seen that the flat codicological facts were damning. Some of the straits to which the scribe was driven in concocting a tale order reveal him as no better than he should have been – a person who took refuge in silent deviousness when he found himself in a tight corner. In short, it would be hard to believe in his impartiality as a noble and faithful transmitter of the text were one to have to accept the codicological data straight.

I don't think Blake should have worried: the text that the scribe was given to transmit was superior, by far, to the manner in which he received it. This quality shows up in a rather widely dispersed group of superior substantive readings, where Hengwrt often parts company from such manuscripts as Ellesmere, Gg.iv.27, and Harley 7334. A pot-pourri from *The Knight's Tale*[10] would include such readings as:

A 980   The mynotaur which þat he *wan* (El Gg Ha4 *slough*) in Crete

A 992   The bones of hir *freendes* (El Ha4 *housbondes*) þat were slayn

---

[9] They are copiously and carefully demonstrated by A. I. Doyle and M. B. Parkes, in the 'Paleographical Introduction' to *Variorum Volume I*, pp. xix–xlix.

[10] I have tried to choose readings from early in the *Tales*, but my lists are neither comprehensive nor comparable; they thus should not be taken as indicating any ratio of right to wrong lections.

or

A 1039   I noot which was the *fairer* (El Gg Ha4 *fyner*) of hem two.

At the same time, although probably in fewer instances, Hg certainly errs against right readings in such texts; examples would include:

A 60   At many a noble *aryve* (so Gg Ha4; Hg El *armee*) hadde he be

A 637–8   And whan that he wel dronken hadde the wyn,
            Thanne wolde he speke no word but Latyn (Hg *om.*, an eyeskip)[11]

or

A 3110   In al the *route* (Hg *compaignie*) nas ther yong ne oold.

For many other equally substantive but less dramatic readings similar, divided results also obtain; these readings include a large number of variants difficult to resolve – alternation between different prepositions and demonstratives (and especially archetypal *o* variously interpreted as *of*, *on*, or *or*), between historical present and usual narrative past, between conjunction and conjunction + *that*, among parataxis with *and*/hypotaxis/ no connective, among *wel*/*ful*/zero. Again, although many of the readings are debatable and of minor effect, Hg is probably marginally superior to El.

In these readings I describe Hengwrt's superiority as marginal, and it must be recognised that many of the claims for Hengwrt's superiority rest upon faith, not demonstration. A litany of Hengwrt defenders has been that Manly–Rickert's monumental textual effort testified to the value of Hengwrt, because those editors for long spaces of the *Tales* found themselves printing as Chaucer's text the text of Hengwrt. Several points need here to be made. First, in printing Hengwrt frequently Manly–Rickert were also printing Ellesmere, for the two manuscripts differ from one another with considerably less frequency than most other manuscript pairs in the *Canterbury Tales*.[12]

Second, where these two copies vary, a situation in which Manly–Rickert often argued that Ellesmere had been editorially sophisticated,[13] especially in metrical terms, it is not clear that Manly–Rickert's adherence to Hengwrt offers any support for those who believe Hengwrt a 'best text' because uniquely replicating Chaucer's holograph. Manly–Rickert were making no effort to print Chaucer's holograph; they wanted only to present O1, 'the archetype of all surviving manuscripts', a text at some undefined remove from the holograph and one which they were certain contained

---

[11] Eyeskip omissions seem a tendency one can ascribe to the Hengwrt copyist; other early examples occur at A 2779–82, 3155–6, 3721–2 (also *om.* by Gg Ha4, coincidentally).
[12] Cf. the tabular presentation of manuscript variation in *Variorum* volumes, at II, 9: 93, for example.
[13] See Manly–Rickert, *Text* I: 150.

errors. Simply to note four early examples, Manly–Rickert print Hengwrt as the reading of O1 in situations where they flatly believe the manuscript erroneous at:

A 430 And Discorides and *Rusus* (El *Risus*, Gg *Rufiis*; *Rufus* correct)

A 1906 And on the *westward* (also El; *gate westward* correct) in memorie

A 2874 Vpon his *handes his* (El *handes hadde he*, Ha4 *handes were*) gloues white

and

A 2999 Al mowe they tho dayes *abregge* (El Gg Ha4 *wel abregge*).[14]

One should also be aware that such bizarreries occur because of Manly–Rickert's method. That is, the text they print was created, not by examining direction of variation, but by traditional nineteenth-century recension. Manly–Rickert grouped manuscripts by shared errors, used these errors to create stemmata (usually varying with the individual tale), and then sought to use majority rule (as determined by stemmatic form) to find readings of O1, the archetype. Given the difficulties with recension as an editorial tool which have become increasingly apparent (and which might have been so to Manly–Rickert), it is hard to repose absolute faith in a text based upon the results of recension. In recent years, it has become increasingly difficult, thanks to George Kane's and Blake's devastating analyses of the vagaries of Manly–Rickert's practice.[15] That the Chicago edition often printed Hengwrt should not, in itself, induce anyone to see Hengwrt as a 'best text' guide to what Chaucer wrote.

This seems to me particularly true of one subject which has become vexed of late, achieving considerable prominence in the *Variorum*, for example – Chaucer's metre. Hengwrt is marginally rougher than Ellesmere, more prone not to offer hendecasyllables but headless and Lydgatian lines (either clashed stresses or preserved -e at the caesura). *Variorum* editors have invoked in defence of these Hengwrt forms the fact that Manly and Rickert printed many lines extant in varying metrical versions in Hengwrt form. And such Hengwrt variants underlie Manly–Rickert's argument that Ellesmere has been edited to achieve smoother lines.

Variorum practice has been to seize lovingly upon the deviant lines of Hengwrt as examples of Chaucer's variousness, editorialised out in Ellesmere. This has the effect of calling in question, for example, virtually every *eek*, *ful*, and *wel* in the corpus – since they typically vary with *eek*, etc.

[14] See the explanatory notes in Manly–Rickert, *Text* III: 424, 430–31, 435, and 437, respectively.
[15] Kane, 'John M. Manly and Edith Rickert', in Paul G. Ruggiers, ed., *Editing Chaucer: The Great Tradition* (Norman: Pilgrim, 1984), pp. 207–29; and Blake, 'The Editorial Assumptions in the Manly–Rickert Edition of *The Canterbury Tales*', *English Studies* 64 (1983), 385–400.

omitted, the omission then creating a non-iambic metrical pattern.[16] (Ironically, Hengwrt, along with Ha4, includes such a possibly scribal *eek* early on at A 217 to avoid the headless '*And with* worthy wommen of the town'.)

To such conclusions, two objections may be lodged. First, insofar as *Variorum* practice depends upon Manly–Rickert's, the claim that these earlier editors did not believe that Chaucer wrote a fundamentally hendecasyllabic line rests on only cursory study of the Chicago edition. Many non-hendecasyllabic lines which Manly and Rickert printed they believed erroneous.[17] Second, the argument that smooth Ellesmere lines are non-Chaucerian must face substantial historical objections. The only model for such a line was Chaucer himself, no other examples having preceded him in English. Scribes would have been accustomed to headless lines and those with clashing stresses from the native four-stress tradition. *Variorum* editors thus offer the incongruous argument that the Ellesmere scribe (among others) was more progressively Chaucerian than Chaucer.

Though I have no doubts at all that Chaucer's metrical practice was more various than editions like Robinson's suggest, I begin to doubt the wisdom of elevating metrical diversity to an editorial principle. I am further certain that the corollary debunking of Ellesmere is wrong. Rather than editorialising, many of its readings are correct and many others attributable to normal scribal procedures.

To conclude: I think one can welcome the Hengwrt controversy. It has obviously made Chaucerian textual studies a much more contentious and exciting place to be. As one who hopes that acrimonious sparks provide scintillae of holy wisdom, I believe that such a situation is to be desired. But although one can venerate wisdom, one probably shouldn't venerate overmuch the tools that only lead to it. Thus Hengwrt, although an extremely valuable witness to the text of the *Canterbury Tales*, deserves a more searching examination on a variant-by-variant basis than it has yet received.

[16] In discussion, John Burrow suggested that Chaucer clearly envisions lines based on fixed syllable count in his caution that 'som vers' may 'fayle in a sillable' (*House of Fame* 1098). The modern editorial tendency to value irregularities seems entirely predictable from a literary taste which prefers Wyatt and Donne's 'conversational directness' and wrenched accent to Jonson's easy (and no less conversational) regularity.

[17] Frequently Manly–Rickert's explanatory notes betray a certain malease about deviant forms, and the language of the notes implies that they essentially believed in a hendecasyllabic Chaucerian line. See among many examples which might be cited, *Text* III: 425 (A 660), 427 (A 876), 428 (A 1095), 430 (A 1900), 433 (A 2420), and cf. 429 (A 1376). But contrast *Text* III: 421 (A 1), 423 (A 217), where Manly–Rickert insist that Chaucer's versification is more various than earlier editors (Skeat, the Globe, Koch, Robinson's first edition) had been willing to admit.

THE HOCCLEVE HOLOGRAPHS AND HOCCLEVE'S METRICAL PRACTICE [1]

Judith A. Jefferson

The study of the prosody of Hoccleve's 'worthi maister', Chaucer, has been hampered by the difficulty of determining from the manuscript evidence what represents Chaucer's own intention (as regards the use of final -*es* or punctuation marks, for example) and what is simply the result of scribal omissions or additions. Early Chaucerian scholars, being convinced that Chaucer was the initiator of the English pentameter line, felt free to emend the text *metri causa* in accordance with that belief,[2] but some more recent scholars, such as Southworth and Ian Robinson,[3] have questioned the assumptions which underly this practice, offering their own alternative versions of Chaucer's metre, and, despite the vigorous rebuttals of these views offered by Donaldson and Samuels,[4] there has since been less unquestioning belief in the Chaucerian iambic pentameter line.

From one point of view, however, the study of Hoccleve's prosody is considerably less complicated than any similar study of the prosody of Chaucer. There are three holograph manuscripts of Hoccleve's works: Durham University Cosin V.III.9, and two Huntington Library manuscripts, HM 111 and HM 744.[5] Between them, these manuscripts contain all the works to be found in the EETS edition of the Minor Poems, all in

[1] This article is a short account of certain aspects of Hoccleve's metrical practice. I expect to be able to provide a more comprehensive account, including, for example, more information on the rhythms of Hoccleve's poetry, at a later date.

[2] See, for example, T. Tyrwhitt, 'Essays on the Language and Versification of Chaucer' in Tyrwhitt, ed., *The Canterbury Tales* (2nd edn. Oxford, 1978), Vol. 1, 57. For comments on the effect emended texts, and in particular that of F. N. Robinson, have had on expectations of Chaucer's language and metre, see N. Blake, ed., *The Canterbury Tales* (London, 1980), 12.

[3] See J. G. Southworth, 'Chaucer's Final -E in Rhyme', *PMLA*, 62 (1947), 910–35, continued in *PMLA*, 64 (1949), 601–10; *Verses of Cadence, an Introduction to the Prosody of Chaucer and his Followers* (Oxford, 1954); *The Prosody of Chaucer and his Followers*, Supplementary Chapters to Verses of Cadence (Oxford, 1962); and I. Robinson, *Chaucer's Prosody: A Study of the Middle English Verse Tradition* (Cambridge, 1971).

[4] See E. T. Donaldson, 'Chaucer's Final -E', *PMLA*, 63 (1948), 1101–24, and *PMLA*, 64 (1949), 609; and M. L. Samuels, 'Chaucerian Final -E', *N&Q*, 217 (1972), 445–8.

[5] For identification of the MSS as holographs see H. C. Schulz, 'Thomas Hoccleve, Scribe', *Speculum*, 21 (1937), 71–81. For further evidence of Hoccleve's scribal activities see A. I. Doyle and M. B. Parkes, 'The production of copies of the *Canterbury Tales* and the *Confessio Amantis* in the early fifteenth century', in M. B. Parkes and A. G. Watson, eds., *Medieval Scribes, Manuscripts and Libraries; Essays presented to N. R. Ker* (London, 1978), 163–210.

Hoccleve's own hand, except for the first 665 lines of the *Series*, up to and including line 252 of the *Dialogue*, where the scribe was John Stowe.[6] This, of course, eliminates many of the problems of possible scribal corruption, since although Hoccleve, even when copying his own works, would be bound to make errors, they would not be the sort of errors which resulted from a lack of knowledge of the author's language or intention.

The arguments about late medieval prosody can be divided conveniently into two separate groups: arguments about syllable number and arguments about stress, and I have been dealing with these separately, beginning with the question of the syllable count. I have been able to look at the Durham manuscript in Durham, but for the Huntington manuscript I have had to rely on microfilm. I have been very fortunate in that I have been able to make use of a copy of the computer tape of the text of the holograph manuscripts which is being used for the normalisation of accidentals in the forthcoming edition of Hoccleve's *Regement of Princes*.[7]

In order to obtain as clear a view of Hoccleve's practice as possible, I began my own consideration of the syllable count by looking first at those lines where the controversy over the possible pronunciation of final -*e* does not arise, that is those lines which have no internal final -*e*.[8] Thirty-five per cent of the lines in the holograph manuscripts are found to fit into this category. If we discount feminine rhymes, which for the purpose of this discussion can be considered to be extra-metrical, we find that the vast majority of these lines, ninety-eight per cent in fact, have ten syllables, a

---

[6] *Hoccleve's Works, the Minor Poems*, ed. F. J. Furnivall & I. Gollancz, revised J. Mitchell & A. I. Doyle, EETS ES 61 and 73 (one Vol.) (1970). *The Series* is the name given by E. P. Hammond to the linked group of poems which appear as items XXI–XXIV in the EETS edition of the *Minor Poems*, cf. E. P. Hammond, ed., *English Verse between Chaucer and Surrey* (2nd edn. New York, 1965), 69.

[7] I am very grateful to the Editors of the *Regement of Princes*, and in particular to Peter P. Farley of Adelphi University, who has been responsible for the computer part of the Hoccleve edition, for making this tape available to me. For analysis of the material I have used the Oxford Concordance Program written by Susan Hockey and Ian Marriott (Oxford, 1980), which provides facilities such as concordance and reverse concordance (i.e. with the words listed in order of their endings). For most purposes other than possibly the study of punctuation, the single-line unit appears to provide an adequate context.

[8] In order to isolate these lines, it has been necessary to determine how to treat the various bars, loops and flourishes used by Hoccleve which might possibly be considered to be abbreviations for final -*e*, i.e. the loops on final *k*, *f*, *g*, and *t*, and the bars on *gh*, *ght*, *ssh* and *ll*, the flourish on *r* and a small tail which is occasionally found on final *d*. Basically, the flourishes which consist of little loops, as well as the tail on the end of the *d* and the bars through *ssh*, *gh*, and *ght*, have been considered to be otiose, both on grounds of grammatical evidence (such flourishes and bars appear in positions where Hoccleve does not normally show evidence of using final -*e*, for example on nouns derived from Old English masculine and neuter nouns without ending, e.g. *folk* I 63, *theef* III 52, *thing* XXI 255, etc.) and on grounds of distribution (for example the bar through *gh* and *ght* is almost invariable while *k* appears almost always *either* with flourish *or* with final -*e* so that *k* plus flourish seems to be in contrast with -*ke* and not equivalent to it). (For references see below note 16.) The flourish on *r* and the bar through *ll* have however been treated as indicating final -*e*.

very high proportion and one which must at least suggest that Hoccleve intended to write decasyllabic verse.[9]

Moving on, then, to consider Hoccleve's use of final -*e*, it is clearly important to determine to what extent this conforms to the rules of etymology and of historical grammar. The opponents of the iambic pentameter view of Chaucerian poetry, for instance, have been much exercised over what they see as unacceptable inconsistency in the use of such -*es*. Ian Robinson, for example, claims that, with as 'widely permissive' a rule for the pronunciation of final -*e* as that put forward by E. T. Donaldson 'it might well be that any longish line of fourteenth-century verse could be read as pentameter'.[10] In fact, however, Hoccleve's use of final -*e* is extremely regular, and there is certainly no evidence of wholesale inconsistency of the type which might suggest that such -*es* had become meaningless because unsounded. In general, non-inflexional -*es* have their origin in an ending to be found in the parent word, the major exception to this being nouns of Old English origin which belonged to certain feminine declensions, where the use of final -*e* has been extended from the oblique cases.[11] Variation in Hoccleve's use of non-inflexional -*e* is extremely rare although certain polysyllabic words do show evidence of forms both with and without -*e*, presumably as a result of changes in the degree of stress born by the penultimate syllable, and there are a few variations which appear to be used solely for the purpose of rhyme.[12]

There is a little more variation in the use of inflexional -*es* and we shall look at this more closely in a moment. All inflexional -*es* are regular, however, except, as Charlotte Babcock has pointed out, for the extension of the use of final -*e* from the singular imperative of the weak conjugations

---

[9] There are of course other problems in determining the syllable count quite apart from the question of whether or not the final -*e* was pronounced. I have allowed variation in the syllable count of particular words with a particular spelling only where this appears to be position dependent. For instance, the adjective *gracious* appears to be disyllabic when it immediately precedes its noun (IX 23, etc.) but trisyllabic where it follows its noun (XII 17, etc.). Though such variations may often support an iambic rhythm, I see no reason for assuming that they were a purely poetic phenomenon.

[10] I. Robinson, op. cit., 90–91.

[11] Southworth (*Verses of Cadence*, 23) suggests that many Chaucerian final -*es* were inorganic and unsounded and added merely to denote the length of the preceding vowel in accordance with the practice of Norman scribes. Much of his evidence for this is drawn from nouns with inorganic final -*e*. His explanation, however, leaves a much larger proportion of the evidence unaccounted for than does the traditional explanation. For a detailed response to Southworth's arguments see Donaldson, arts. cit. For suggestions as to the origin of unetymological final -*e* where it appears on OE masculine and neuter nouns, etc., see R. B. McJimsey, *Chaucer's Irregular -E* (New York, 1942).

[12] E.g. *maner* (XXIII 155, XXIV 620), beside *maneere* (XXII 570, XXIII 431, etc.), *acate* (III 181) beside *thacat* (XVIII 100) (both in rhyme), *dart* (GIII 20) beside *darte* (XXIII 575) in rhyme, *weye* (VIII 11, XVI 3, etc.) in rhyme beside usual *wey/way*. The adjective *long* appears occasionally with final -*e* in expressions stating extent of time, possibly as a result of confusion with its adverbial use for the same purpose (e.g. II 237). Some apparent variations in noun ending are in fact petrified datives, e.g. *take on hoonde* (XXI 520).

to the singular imperative of the strong, a change which arises from a perfectly reasonable cause: the gradual loss of distinctions which were present in earlier Middle English.[13] Inflexions which have generally been *lost* are the plural inflexion in the preterite of strong verbs, and the final -*e* on the preterite singular of weak verbs, though this latter is retained where such preterites have been subject to syncope or contraction, in which case it provides a means of distinguishing between the preterite and the past participle.[14]

There is, then, no historical or etymological reason for supposing that Hoccleve's final -*es* could not have been pronounced, although it is true that his very restricted use of the definite inflexion makes it impossible to draw from his practice in this respect the particularly strong support *for* pronunciation which M. L. Samuels obtains from the more extensive use of this inflexion in Chaucer's poetry.[15] Further, from the metrical evidence, Hoccleve's practice as far as rhyme at least is concerned very definitely suggests that final -*e* was pronounced. Hoccleve almost invariably rhymes words ending in final -*e* with other words ending in final -*e*. In the whole of the Hoccleve holographs there is only one exception to this practice (*hye me* rhyming with *tyme* (III 126 & 128)[16] where the -*e* in question is internal to the rhyme rather than final.[17] Moreover, comparison of lines with and without internal final -*e* provides further evidence in favour of pronunciation. For example, if we compare the two types of line as they occur in the poem *The Complaint of the Virgin* (HM 111 ff. 3a–7b) we find that of the 79 lines without internal final -*e* all except one, i.e. 98.7 per cent, are decasyllabic. If final -*e* is pronounced, except where elided, then the lines *with* internal final -*e* follow a similar pattern: out of 125 lines, 4 have only 9 syllables, 1 possibly 11, and the remainder, i.e. 96 per cent, have the usual 10. If, however, final -*e* is not pronounced, then the syllabic pattern for these lines is completely different and 67 lines, 53.6 per cent, have nine syllables or less.

---

[13] See C. F. Babcock, 'A study of the Metrical Use of the Inflectional -E in Middle English, With Particular Reference to Chaucer and Lydgate' *PMLA* 29 (1914), 59–92.

[14] E.g. *deemed* pret sg. (XXIV 577), *made* pret. sg. (II 187, 305, 306, etc.) *maad* past part. (II 17, 410, 413).

[15] Art. cit. Samuels' argument is that scribes could not have used the definite inflexion as thoroughly and consistently as they did unless they understood it, i.e. unless it was current in contemporary speech. Hoccleve's use of the definite inflexion, however, is rather restricted, being mainly confined to certain common adjectives (*good*, *old*, etc.) in particular traditional phrases, especially certain forms of address and expressions connected with religion (*O goode god* XXIV 138, *the foule feend* XVIII 155, etc.) and it therefore seems likely that the definite inflexion was no longer a functional form.

[16] For the convenience of readers, references are to the EETS edition of the *Minor Poems*. Poems edited by Gollancz have references prefixed by the letter G.

[17] Note that Hoccleve uses an irregular imperative form of the same verb in order to facilitate rhyme: *hy the* rhyming with *swythe* (XXIV 328–9) cf. *hye thee* (XXII 415, etc.). For a detailed account of Hoccleve's rhyming practice see E. Vollmer, 'Sprache und Reime des Londoners Hoccleve', *Anglia* 21 (1899), 201–21.

The strongest argument, however, in favour of the decasyllabic line and therefore of the pronunciation of final -*e* comes from the quite clear evidence provided by the holograph manuscripts that Hoccleve made use of a variety of stratagems, made choices from amongst the options available to him in order to maintain his decasyllabic line. Such choices can be categorised as follows:

1. *Optional elision of unstressed vowels*

The final -*e* of the definite article, for example can be elided before a vowel where this is necessary for the syllable count. It is noticeable that Hoccleve takes care that his intentions in this respect shall be quite clear to his reader and where he wishes such an -*e* to be elided he omits it in writing. This pattern is probably most evident in the *Tale of Jereslaus' Wife* where we find *themperice(s)* (5 times) beside *the emperice(s)* (7 times), *themperour(es)* (3 times) beside *the emperour(es)* (11 times), and *therl(es)* (twice) beside *the erl(es)* (8 times), in all but one instance in accordance with the demands of the syllable count.[18] For example, Hoccleve writes:

> Every night / wher lay *therl* and the Contesse   XXII 310

beside

> Shee with *the Erl* and his wyf / was doun born   XXII 425

The infinitive prefix *to* and the object pronoun *me* can be treated in a similar manner, and in these cases, too, Hoccleve takes care to make his intentions clear to his reader.

2. *The Optional use of pleonastic þat*

Optional use of pleonastic *þat* can provide variation in the syllable count of a large number of conjunctions and relatives. The holograph manuscripts, for instance, contain 187 examples of the use of the plain conjunction *as* beside 64 examples of *as þat*. In all but five cases, this choice results in a clear decasyllabic line, in two of the five remaining lines the use of *as þat* increases the count from eight to nine syllables, in two cases the syllable count could be restored by the replacement of the more common form *as* by the less common form *as þat*, and one case is doubtful.[19] Similarly, there

[18] *themperice(s)*: XXII 198, 352, 400 (11 syllables, see below under *the erl(es)*), 709, 948; *the emperice(s)*: XXII 143, 338, 389, 702, 786, 807, 814; *themperour(es)*: XXII 212, 804, 841; *the emperour(es)*: XXII 106, 135, 250, 389, 729, 744, 768, 806, 816, 818, 930; *therl(es)*: XXII 310, 339; *the erl(es)*: XXII 286, 288, 333, 400 (11 syllables), 425, 701, 853, 857. It is noticeable that in the one instance where emendation might be required in order to maintain the syllable count this would call for the replacement of the more common and orthographically more regular form by that which is less common.
[19] *as*: I 55, I 92, I 132, II 126 (only 9 syllables if final -*e* of *folwe* elided, though I think this unlikely given that the following syllable *it* appears in rhyme), II 154, II 179, II 186, II 331, II 352, II 371, II 377, II 383, II 387, II 431, II 442, II 464, II 494, III 10, III 30, III 39, etc.; *as þat*: I 108, I 222, II 60, II 174, II 212, II 434, II 511, III 85, III 182, III 192, III 226, III 354, III 411, III 437, III 442 (9 syllables), VII 99, VIII 3, XI 7, XVI 24, XVII 65, etc.

are 27 examples of *syn* beside 10 examples of *syn þat* and 102 examples of the plain conjunction *if* beside 38 examples of *if þat*, in all but one instance in accordance with the demands of the syllable count.[20] *til/til þat, which/ which þat, lest/lest þat, or/or þat, for/for þat, whan/whan þat, how/how þat* are used in a similar manner. A good example of Hoccleve's practice in this respect is to be found in XXIII 246–7:

> And now *as* fisshes been with hookes kaght
> And *as þat* briddes / been take in a snare

Some conjunctions present additional possibilities. For example, the conjunction *but* meaning 'unless' can appear as *but, but if* or *but if þat* while the conjunction *thogh* can appear as *thogh, althogh, thogh þat* or *althogh þat* and Hoccleve makes systematic use of these alternatives, too, for the maintenance of his syllable count.

3. *Variation in the form of adverbs*

Variation of this type for the purpose of syllable count is not particularly common, but the category does contain one very clear example of the way in which Hoccleve can make use of such alternatives when available:

> *Fro whenne* / blessid sone of god / *fro whenne*
> Descendid is thy greet humilitee
> *Whens* comth the loue / we feele in thee brenne
> *Fro whens* eek is procedid thy pitee
>
>   GII 29–32

It is worth noting that the use of *fro whenne* with written *-e* as an alternative to *fro whens* implies that Hoccleve expected final *-e* to be pronounced, and further examples of this kind will be dealt with below. Similar, if not particularly frequent, use is made of the alternatives *thens/thennes, hens/hennes* and *hennes forward/hens forward/hens foorth/ hennes foorth*.[21]

---

[20] *syn*: I 65, I 83, I 89, I 176, II 71, II 103, III 99, III 383, X 61, X 92, XII 12, XIV 4, XXI 677, XXI 708, XXI 727, XXII 44, XXII 199, XXII 638, XXIII 62, XXIII 774, etc.; *syn þat*: I 188, III 337, XIII 6, XXI 288, XXIII 215, GII 66, GV 20, GVI 15, GIX 27, GX 21; *if*: I 102, I 118, I 141, I 233, II 2, II 49, II 74, II 111, II 115, II 134, II 141, II 161, II 201, II 262, II 263, II 326, II 340, II 377, II 441, II 476, etc.; *if þat*: II 182, II 206, II 351, II 362, II 394, II 402, II 457, III 17, III 173, III 245, VII 60, IX 46, XVI 22, XXI 358, XXI 458, XXI 686, XXI 787, XXII 153, XXII 157, XXII 297, etc.

[21] *thens*: XXI 570, XXII 483, XXII 883 (probably only 9 syllables), XXIII 694, XXIV 253, XXIV 456, XXIV 498, XXIV 563; *thennes*: XXII 51; *fro thennes*: XXII 42; *hens*: I 228, XXII 45, XXII 205, XXII 415, XXII 571, XXIII 51, XXIII 95, XXIII 106, XXIII 392, XXIII 574, XXIII 577, XXIII 684, XXIII 916, XXIII 928, XXIII 933, XXIV 137, GVII 77, GVII 87; *hennes*: XVIII 8, XXIII 136, XXIII 183; *hens foorth*: XXII 165, XXII 727, XXIII 642, XXIII 650, XXIII 772, XXIV 364, GVII 39; *hens forward*: XXIII 770; *hennes foorth*: II 69, III 49; *hennes forward*: I 184, II 127.

4. *Varying Forms of Verbal Inflexion*

i) Before a consonant the usual ending of the imperative plural is *-eth*, but before a vowel/weak *h*, where the reduction of the ending to *-e* would result in elision and therefore in a change in the syllable count, *-eth* is used 10 times and *-e* 19 times, resulting in each instance in a decasyllabic line,[22] for example:

> Be to your liges also sheeld & wal
> *Keepe* and *deffende* hem from aduersitee
> Hir wele and wo / in your grace lyth al
> *Gouerneth* hem in lawe and equitee
>
> IV 17–20

ii) *Plurals in -e/-en*

With the exception of the preterite plurals of strong verbs which normally have no ending, the indicative plurals of lexical verbs which appear before a consonant normally end in *-en*.[23] Once again, however, where there is the possibility of elision, the alternatives *-e* and *-en* are systematically used for the purpose of maintaining the syllable count, *-e* being used 85 times and *-en* 42 times,[24] for example:

> Also yee *holden* ageyn pilgrimages   II 393

beside

> What / al is nat worth *þat* yee *clappe* & muse   II 396

iii) *Past Participle in ø/y-, -e/-en*

Before a consonant, the usual ending for the past participles of strong verbs is *-en*, but before a vowel *-e* is used 42 times and *-en* 34 times in accordance with the demands of the syllable count,[25] for example:

> Whos kerf nat *fownden* is / whan past is shee   XXIII 203

---

[22] *-e* ending before vowel/*h*: II 303, III 288, IV 9, IV 11, IV 12, IV 23, IV 34, V & VI 31, V & VI 36, V & VI 42, V & VI 59, X 140, XVII 59, XXIV 399, XXIV 621, XXIV 641, GVIII 418, CVIII 445, GVIII 468; *-eth* ending before vowel/*h*: I 132, I 228, II 447, IV 20, XIII 27, XVII 60, XVII 64, XXII 120, XXIV 663, GVIII 389.

[23] With non-lexical verbs, this is not necessarily the case. The indicative plural of the verb *willen*, for example, appears only once with an *-en* ending (GVIII 463).

[24] *-e* ending before vowel/*h*: I 99, I 204, I 238, II 13, II 154, II 300, II 317, II 337, II 339, II 372, II 396, II 465, II 501, III 158, III 230, III 242, III 246, III 282, III 322, III 325, etc.; *-en* ending before vowel/*h*: I 228, II 86, II 311, II 323, II 327, II 393, II 425, III 26, III 141, III 143, III 242, III 354, V & VI 24, VII 51, VIII 44, XVII 68, XXI 421, XXI 578, XXI 777, XXII 495, etc. In two instances (XXI 276 and XXII 693) the use of *-en* may still give less than the usual ten syllables.

[25] *-en* ending before vowel/*h*: II 102, II 482, III 29, III 165, III 396, VII 7, IX 7, X 43, XIII 35, XVII 4, XXI 327, XXI 468, XXI 549, XXII 1, XXII 84, XXII 422, XXII 517, XXII 743, XXII 956, XXIII 118, etc.; *-e* ending before vowel/*h*: I 61, I 155, I 189, II 7, II 161, II 437, II 441, III 75, III 109, III 214, IV 27, VIII 10, XI 6, XVII 67, XXI 585, XXI 672, XXI 774, XXII 122, XXII 304, XXII 317, etc.

beside

No preef *fownde* is / of the cours of his flight   XXIII 205

For weak verbs and for certain irregular verbs like 'to do', this type of variation is not an option, but all past participles have the possibility of the use of the *y*- prefix, and Hoccleve employs this in 30 cases in the holograph manuscripts where an extra syllable is needed,[26] for example:

Whan *þat* thow hast thus *doon* / than aftirward   IX 37
And hath *ydoon* of tyme yore ago   IX 58

iv) *Infinitives in for to/to/φ, -e/-en*

Variation in the form of the prefix to the infinitive is one of Hoccleve's favourite methods of controlling the syllable count. For example, infinitives acting as clausal subjects of complements (often occurring in constructions where there is an additional anticipatory subject, *it*), and infinitives following certain verbs such as *gan*, *shapen* or *lyken*, can appear with the prefixes *for to* or *to* or with no prefix at all, verbs such as *dredden* or the impersonal verb *listen* can appear with the prefix *to* or with no prefix, and infinitives expressing purpose can appear with *to* or *for to*.[27] There is a clear example of Hoccleve's use of such alternatives in ll. 187–8 of the *Letter to Cupid*:

Men *to seye* of wommen wel / it is best
And nat *for to despise* hem ne depraue

Infinitives in *-en* are found occasionally in conjunction with one of these

---

[26] *-y* prefix used to provide an extra syllable: II 510, III 94, III 184. III 197, III 203, III 391, IX 58, X 78 (NB *ymakid* cf. *ymaad* II 203), X 100, XXI 393, XXI 515, XXI 726, XXII 424, XXII 429, XXII 626, XXII 720, XXII 791, XXII 792, XXII 850, XXII 928, etc.

[27] Infinitives appearing as subjects or complements, a) with no prefix: XVII 6, XVII 18, XXI 392, XXI 745, XXII 647, XXII 784, XXIII 481, XXIII 485, XXIII 597, XXIII 761, XXIII 847, XXIV 36, XXIV 143, XXIV 194, XXIV 296, GVIII 66, GVIII 175, GVIII 237; b) with prefix *to*: II 409, III 151, III 208, III 312, XVII 7, XVIII 17, XVIII 77, XXI 292, XXI 496 (9 syllables), XXI 603, XXI 728, XXI 746, XXII 45, XXII 722, XXIII 43, XXIII 98, XXIV 199, GIV 19, GVIII 65, GVIII 187; c) with *for to*: II 401, II 459, X 62, XVIII 19, XXI 553, XXI 682, GV 123, GVIII 188, GVIII 374.
Infinitives following *gan*, a) with no prefix: X 114, XXII 17, XXII 241, XXII 350, XXII 352, XXII 528, XXII 691, XXII 705, XXIII 89, XXIV 175, XXIV 360, XXIV 380, XXIV 423, XXIV 476, XXIV 550, XXIV 644, XXIV 661, XXIV 662; b) with prefix *to*: XXI 543, XXII 656, XXIV 346; c) with prefix *for to*: XXIV 232. The use of *gan* at all of course affects the syllable count, though it is most often used also as a means of enabling the subsequent infinitive to appear in rhyme.
Infinitives following *listen*, a) with no prefix: II 34, II 186, II 201, II 206, II 262, III 84, III 120, III 234, VII 10, VII 28, XVII 67, XVIII 160, XXI 358, XXI 455, XXI 465, XXI 678, XXII 159, XXII 297, XXII 442, XXII 921, etc.; b) with prefix *to*: VII 96, X 94, XVII 37, XXI 414, XXI 743, GV 42, GVIII 27, GVIII 138.
Infinitives expressing purpose, a) with prefix *to*: II 310, II 388, II 462, III 144, III 152, III 420, VII 76, X 21, XVII 12, XVIII 56, XVIII 93, XVIII 95, XXI 349, XXI 444, XXI 548, XXI 609, XXI 801, XXII 32, XXII 437, XXII 607, etc.; b) with prefix *for to*: II 308 (9 syllables), III 100, VII 43, VII 95, VII 106, X 47, XVIII 66, XXII 109, XXIII 52, GI 82, GV 4 (11 syllables), GVII 104, GVIII 287.

prefixes when they are needed to provide an additional syllable before a vowel (for example *for to eten* GIII 51) and possibly occasionally as variations in support of the iambic rhythm (for example, *to knowen* instead of *for to knowe* III 331), but they are mainly used where the infinitive in question follows an auxiliary verb, that is where no variation in prefix use is possible. Following the verb *may*, for example, there are 44 instances of infinitives followed by a vowel, 36 of which end in *-e* and 8 in *-en*, in every case in accordance with the demands of the syllable count,[28] for example:

> *þat* we *may maken* our confessioun   GI 51

beside

> As *þat may lyke* vn to thy Deitee   GI 55

It should be noted that the distribution of the *-e* and *-en* endings of the infinitive very firmly suggests that Hoccleve expected final *-e* to be pronounced (except where elided). With one exception (*armen* GVIII 135) the *-en* ending is never used before a consonant, whereas it is used 39 times before a vowel in positions where an extra syllable is necessary in order to maintain the syllable count (although in one instance this results in only nine syllables).[29] The implication must be that before a consonant the *-en* variation was of no use to Hoccleve since, given that final *-e* was already syllabic, it would have made no difference to his syllable count.

Other variations in the Hoccleve holographs present even more direct evidence in favour of the pronunciation of final *-e* since in these cases optional final *-e* is used where necessary to provide an additional syllable:

1. *Varying Forms of Verbal Inflexion*

i) *had/hadde*
The usual form of the preterite of the verb *haven* for both lexical and auxiliary verbs, singular and plural, indicative and subjunctive, is *had*, but Hoccleve writes *hadde* occasionally before a vowel and in 12 cases before a consonant in positions where pronunciation of final *-e* is necessary to maintain the syllable count,[30] for example:

---

[28] Infinitives following *may*, a) in *-en*: I 198, II 342, XXI 394, GI 51, GVIII 31, GVIII 53, GVIII 119, GVIII 200; b) in *-e*: I 87, I 100, I 183, I 193, II 55, II 264, III 6, IV 3, XXI 294, XXI 315, XXI 445, XXI 509, XXI 618, XXII 398, XXII 533, XXII 738, XXII 774, XXIII 47, XXIII 119, XXIII 133, etc.

[29] Infinitives with *-en* endings: I 45, I 198, I 202, II 342, III 92, III 176, III 208, III 288, III 331, X 55, XXI 394, XXI 434, XXI 453, XXI 605 (9 syllables), XXI 707, XXII 598, XXII 603, XXII 658, XXII 838, XXII 32, etc.

[30] *hadde*: I 104, III 186, XVIII 7, XXII 716, XXIII 492, XXIII 517, XXIV 86, XXIV 237, XXIV 278, XXIV 326, GI 35, GI 42; *had*: I 118, II 210, II 433, III 132, III 151, III 294, III 313, V & VI 17, VII 83, XXI 382, XXI 430, XXI 486, XXI 585, XXI 783, XXII 191, XXII 317, XXII 348, XXII 349, XXII 383, XXII 390, etc.

And whan shee ther*e* in / *hadde* been a whyle   XXIV 237

Whan shee *had* preid / an hidous storm aroos   XXII 910

ii) *han/haue*
Before a consonant, the usual form of the infinitive and the present plural
of the verb *haven*, whether used as a lexical or an auxiliary verb, is *han*, but
haue occurs in 13 cases where an additional syllable is necessary in order to
maintain the syllable count (in one case giving only nine syllables)[31] for
example:

For men sholde *haue* noon othir deemynge   XXII 347

Men sholde of hem *han* dominacioun /   XXI 734

iii) *-yng/ynge*
Final *-e* as an ending to both present participles and gerunds is optional.
Before a consonant, there are 37 forms with *-e* and 26 forms without *-e* and
in all but one instance this pattern supports the syllable count,[32] for
example:

Thy *louyng* charitee nat list desdeyne   GII 40

beside

In the world / so *louynge* tendrenesse   XXII 394

It is perhaps worth pointing out that overall there does not appear to be
any relationship between retention of final *-e* and possible variation in the
stress pattern to support an iambic metre.[33]

iv) *Variations which occur only occasionally*
The plural form of the verb *shall* appears once as *shole* (XXII 283) instead
of the usual *shuln*, the infinitive *seye* is used occasionally before a consonant instead of *seyn* (e.g. II 227), and there is one example of the past
participle *bore* appearing before a consonant (XXIV 294) beside two
examples of *born* (GVIII 404, XXIII 215).

---

[31] *haue* pl.: XVII 4, XXI 672, GVIII 201; *haue* inf.: XXI 633, XXI 706, XXII 99, XXII 202,
XXII 347, XXII 407, XXII 867, XXIII 384 (9 syllables), XXIII 635, GIII 61.
[32] *-yng* (present part): I 77 (9 syllables), III 44, II 260, VII 4 (9 syllables but clearly requiring
emendation), X 27, XXIII 86, XXIII 519, XXIV 205, GI 67, GI 95, GII 40, GII 62, GIII 19,
GIII 20, GIII 24, GV 45, GVIII 19, GVIII 116, GVIII 140, GIX 12; *-yng* (gerunds): X 16,
XXIV 357, GVIII 122, GVIII 219, GVIII 358; *-ynge* (present part.): II 67, II 353, VIII 45, XV
22, XVIII 9, XXII 277, XXII 362, XXII 394, XXII 877, XXIII 493, XXIII 764, XXIII 784,
XXIII 803, XXIV 338, XXIV 505, XXIV 544, XXIV 671, GII 3, GIII 65, GIV 26, GV 26,
GVIII 379; *-ynge* (gerund): I 128, III 385, VII 71, IX 46, X 73, XXII 775, XXII 808, XXII 914,
XXIII 269, XXIII 587, XXIII 681, XXIV 161, GIV 49, GV 97, GV 101.
[33] This ties in with the findings of Halle and Keyser as regards Chaucer's metre: M. Halle and
S. J. Keyser, *English Stress, Its Form, Its Growth and Its Role in Verse* (New York, 1971), 105,
especially note 11.

2. Variation in the Form of Adverbs and Conjunctions

i) than/thanne

Before a vowel, *thanne* is the more usual form of the adverb, but before a consonant *than* is more common, *thanne* being used only six times, in each instance in accordance with the demands of the syllable count,[34] for example:

> And *thanne* shee spak / and seide in this wyse   XXII 772

beside

> To his brothir / *than* spak this Emperour   XXII 778

Cf. also *whanne* (XVIII 8) beside usual *whan*.

ii) before/beforn

Before a consonant, the adverb *beforn* occurs seven times, and the adverb *before* three times, on each occasion in accordance with the demands of the syllable count,[35] for example:

> Whidir *beforn*/shee bad him for to go   XXII 457

> Goon / but *before* dressith him hir man   XXII 514

3. Variation in the inflexion of adjectives, possessive pronouns, etc.

None of these variations occurs very frequently. The plural form of the adjective *greet* appears before a consonant once with final -*e* (XXIII 442) and once without (III 362),[36] the adjective *best* preceded by the definite article appears before a consonant twice with and twice without final -*e* (II 346, II 437, GVIII 412, XXIII 477), the adjective *second* appears before a consonant once with and twice without final -*e* (GVII 50, XXIV 527, XXIV 530), the plural of the possessive pronoun *your* normally has no ending (II 277, 281, 324, etc.) but appears once before a consonant with final -*e* (XXIII 715), and there may be some variation in the use of the plural -*e* inflexion on the relative pronoun *which* (see *which* without -*e* XXI 670, though loss of -*e* here may simply be due to the degree of separation between the relative and its preceding noun).

[34] *thanne*: XXII 541, XXII 571, XXII 772, XXII 852, XXIII 617, XXIII 790; *than*: II 12, II 396, IX 33, XXII 582, XXII 694, XXII 778, XXII 886, XXIII 169, XXIII 400, XXIII 477, XXIV 59, GVII 61, etc.
[35] *beforn*: XXII 457, XXII 846, XXIV 230, XXIV 279, XXIV 325, XXIV 367, XXIV 402; *before*: GI 132, XXII 514, XXII 703.
[36] And NB l. 13 of the poem *How to Learn to Die* (XXIII in the EETS edition), where the Durham MS (f. 52b) has 'Sotil matires right profownde', etc. beside HM 744 (f. 53a) 'Sotile materes profounde', etc.

The systematic use of these variants for the maintenance of the syllable count very definitely suggests that final -*e* was pronounced, although it is perhaps worth pointing out that in the hierarchy of devices used by Hoccleve for this purpose the optional use of final -*e* does not appear very high up on the list, and with the exception of the examples mentioned in note 12 above does not normally involve non-inflexional -*e*. Compared to such devices as the optional use of pleonastic *þat*, for example, variation in the use of final -*e* as a metrical device is extremely rare. There is no evidence, for example, of variation in the use of final -*e* as an inflexion in auxiliary verbs other than in those cases listed under '1' above. The one other apparent such variation to appear in the EETS edition of the *Minor Poems* (*wol* instead of the usual *wole* for the third person singular of the verb *willen*, XXI 394) appears to be a mistranscription of *wel*. It is noticeable in fact that where there is a variation in Hoccleve's use of final -*e* the usual pattern is for Hoccleve to revert occasionally to a more old-fashioned form, to go back, for example, to using an inflected form where the inflexion would normally have been lost, rather than to adopt the opposite device of dropping a final -*e* which he would normally use. There is certainly no evidence that written final -*es* appearing before a consonant were not normally expected to be pronounced. Lines with too *many* syllables within the Hoccleve holographs are in fact extremely rare.[37]

Hoccleve's verse, then, very definitely appears to be decasyllabic. The question then arises as to whether it was purely syllabic or whether it had some additional organisation based, for example, on a recurrent beat, whether this be the five-beat line of iambic pentameter, or the four-beat line, composed of two balanced half-lines, or on some other principle. My

---

[37] There is, however, a certain amount of evidence that final -*e* may not always have been elided before a vowel, e.g. where such an -*e* occurs as part of a formal term of address as in XXIV 183: 'O reuerent *sire* / vnto whom quod shee'. Emphatic or contrastive stress and certain junctures, e.g. those in lists, may have a similar effect.

A major class of exceptions to the rule that final -*e* is invariably pronounced before a consonant is to be found in words ending in -*re* where the syllable immediately preceding final -*e* bears weak stress. In such cases it appears that final -*e* is not normally pronounced. Words of this type include *wher(e)*, *ther(e)* and *her(e)* ('here'), as well as the pronouns *hir(e)* ('her' or 'their'), *your(e)* and *our(e)*. It is not always possible to tell from the orthography whether Hoccleve meant final -*e* to be pronounced in such cases, especially where the word ends in *r* plus flourish (an ending which is used extensively before a vowel where it would not of course imply pronounced final -*e* and somewhat less frequently before a consonant). As a general rule, however, and following the pattern of those words which have either written -*e* or no ending, pronunciation or lack of it appears to depend on the stress borne by the word in question, e.g. genitive *hir(e)* does not normally have pronounced final -*e* and nor does existential *ther(e)*, nor do the adverbs *ther(e)*, *her(e)*, *wher(e)* when they appear in compounds. Where such words bear stronger sentence stress, however, they often do take -*e*, e.g.:

> His be the shame / as it by reson oghte
> And vn to here / thank perpetuel   GVIII 75–6

where *here* is in contrast with *his*. Such variation, therefore, is not strictly a *metrical* device, though the demands of the metre may indicate to the reader the degree of emphasis which Hoccleve wishes to place on the word in question.

investigations into these various possibilities are not by any means complete, but there are certain questions, particularly with regard to iambic penta- meter, which need to be addressed. One is the question of whether adherence to his syllabics or to the rhythmic beat was uppermost in Hoccleve's mind, and there is, I think, a certain amount of evidence that his syllable count was more important to him. There are, for example, a number of lines in the Hoccleve holographs where a rhythmically four-beat line could be changed into a perfectly regular iambic pentameter by the use of one of the alternatives employed by Hoccleve to maintain his syllable count, but Hoccleve appears to be unwilling to do this where it would increase the number of syllables beyond the usual ten. So, for example, we have,

> Weepeth and crieth as lowde *as* yee may   I 132

where we could have

> Weepeth and crieth as lowde *as þat* yee may

> Han artid me *speke* as I spoken haue   III 396

where we could have

> Han artid me *to speke* as I spoken haue

> Lete on me flowe / *to pourge* my blame   XVIII 93

where we could have

> Lete on me flowe / *for to pourge* my blame

> Let al this passe / ther cam *to* the port   XXII 498

where we could have

> Let al this passe / ther cam *vn to* the port

> Our sharpe strokes *how* sore they smyte   GVIII 244

where we could have

> Our sharpe strokes *how* sore *þat* they smyte

It is true that emendation of these lines by the use of one of these variants might appear to be simply an extension of the type of emendation which might very well be suggested for the maintenance of the syllable count, but whereas such emendation for the purpose of syllable count could be seen in terms of extending a practice (the systematic use of alternatives) for which there is ample evidence in the Hoccleve holographs, there is no evidence for the use of such alternatives for the maintenance of rhythmic patterns where this would interfere with the syllable count. Lines with too many syllables are, as I have said, unusual in the Hoccleve holographs and none of them, as far as I can tell, is of this type.

Within the confines of the syllable count, however, there is evidence that choices were made in order to support a regular iambic rhythm. For instance, the choice of *for to* rather than *before* to provide the necessary extra syllable in l. 457 of the *Tale of Jereslaus' Wife* (quoted above p. 105) is a choice made apparently for rhythmic purposes, and the *-en* form of the infinitive has been chosen on occasion in preference to a form with *to* or *for to* for similar reasons, for example:

> *To knowen* of a goddes pryuetee   III 331[38]

though there are, on the other hand, almost as many occasions where this device could have been employed and has not been.[39] It is of course true that, having chosen to write a decasyllabic line with a fixed beat on the rhyming syllable, Hoccleve would be likely to write a high proportion of iambic pentameters since the other choice open to him (apart from the occasional six-beat line) would be lines with a particularly insistent rhythm: four-beat lines with two or more trisyllabic feet, of the 'Ladybird, ladybird fly away home' variety.[40] The rhythm of such lines has an obvious tendency to override the sense and would clearly not be suitable for the type of poetry which Hoccleve wishes to write. A high percentage of iambic pentameters would not therefore necessarily imply that Hoccleve thought of himself as being confined exclusively to five-beat lines or that all other lines were evidence either of ineptness or error.

How strictly Hoccleve felt he had to stick to a five-beat rhythm has obvious implications for the problem of variable stress. This problem is of a different kind from the question of whether or not a final *-e* was pronounced since it requires constant decisions by the reader. If the reader is constantly going to have to alter the stress patterns of words in order to accommodate the metre then the metre itself must be clear to him. For example, a line such as

> And our taklynge brast / and the ship claf   XXII 915

could be made into a perfectly acceptable iambic pentameter by stressing *taklynge* on the second syllable, but it seems unlikely that the reader would take this step when the three lines which have immediately preceded it,

> And shortly / of this for to speke and telle
> The wynd ful sore / in the sail bleew & haf
> And the wawes began to bolne & swelle

---

[38] And III 92, III 208, III 288, XXIV 536, GVIII 294, GVIII 307, GVIII 416.

[39] See X 62, XXI 359, XXIV 369, GVII 11, GVIII 374.

[40] For the dangers which the iambic pentameter runs of slipping into a four-beat, trisyllabic rhythm and methods adopted to avoid this see Fitzroy Pyle, 'The Rhythms of the English Heroic Line: an Essay in Empirical Analysis', *Hermathena*, 53 (1939), 100–26, and 'Pyrrhic and Spondee: Speech Stress and Metrical Accent in English Five Foot Iambic Verse Structure', *Hermathena*, 107 (1968), 49–74. For the insistence of the four-beat rhythm as opposed to the five-beat see D. Attridge, *The Rhythms of English Poetry* (London and New York, 1982), especially 124ff. For the insistence of the triple metre see ibid., 100–101 and 122, note 7.

although they are all *possible* iambic pentameters, could so easily them-selves slip into a four-beat rhythm. One of the problems with Hoccleve's prosody is the number of lines which do rather tend to teeter on the brink of the four-beat. For example, between four and five per cent of lines without problems of variable stress begin with two weakly-stressed syllables and a strongly stressed syllable, lines such as

And to brynge it aboute he faste wroghte   XXII 75

or

And as blyue in hir wombe gan they frete   XXIV 661

There are lines like

And causith al fruyt for to wexe & sprynge   XIII 5

where, in normal pronunciation, *al* would have a degree of stress sub-ordinate to that of *fruyt*, thus giving a four-beat line with triple rhythm, or lines resembling those with weak initial syllable which require the promo-tion of a weak syllable after a pause, for example:

Now shal be doon / *þat* I longe haue ment   XXII 203

In a strictly iambic context, all such lines would be read as iambic pentameters, but given that a large proportion of Hoccleve's lines require pressure from the metre anyway because of the demands of variable stress, the question must arise as to whether the number of unequivocally iambic pentameter lines is sufficient for the iambic pattern to be always absolutely clear to the reader.[41]

[41] I would like to thank Professor John Burrow for his continual help and encouragement, Dr A. I. Doyle for advice given when I consulted the Durham manuscript, and Professor Derek Pearsall for inviting me to give this paper.

THEORIES AND PRACTICES IN THE EDITING OF THE CHESTER CYCLE PLAY-MANUSCRIPTS

David Mills

1. *Materials and Editions*[1]

The changing character of Chester's three-day Whitsun Plays and the extraordinary endeavours of the city fathers to make those plays acceptable to local and national objectors during the sixteenth century are reflected in the various contemporary civic and guild records and in the two versions of the Banns to the Plays – Pre- and Post-Reformation respectively – that have survived. Yet despite the revisions and the attempted defences, Chester's sixteenth-century Whitsun Plays, which are first mentioned in 1422 as a Corpus Christi Play, had their last, and most controversial, performance over a four-day period at Midsummer, 1575.

Such was the local interest in the plays that the text of Chester's 'mystery cycle' remains today the most extensively attested of all the English cycles. Three manuscripts of individual plays survive – the Manchester fragment of *The Resurrection* (M), the Peniarth *Antichrist* (P), and the Coopers' *Trial and Flagellation of Christ* (C). And five manuscripts contain versions of the whole series of plays – Huntington 2 (Hm), Additional 10305 (A), Harley 2013 (R), Bodley 175 (B) and Harley 2124 (H). It is possible – but by no means certain – that MSS M and P date from the period of the cycle's performance. The other six, including the five cyclic manuscripts, all signed and dated by their scribes, are copies made between 1591 and 1607, long after the suppression of the cycle.

When R. M. Lumiansky and I began to prepare a new edition of the plays in the mid-1960s, we were aware of at least three possible meanings for the phrase 'The Chester Cycle'. First, there was the hidden, practical

[1] See R. M. Lumiansky and David Mills, *The Chester Mystery Cycle: Essays and Documents. With an essay, 'Music in the Cycle' by Richard Rastall* (hereafter, Lumiansky–Mills) (Chapel Hill, 1983): Essay 4, 'Development of the Cycle' and 5, 'Documents Providing External Evidence'; also Lawrence M. Clopper, 'The History and Development of the Chester Cycle', *MP* 75 (1978), 219–46 and *Records of Early English Drama: Chester* (Toronto, 1979). For cycle-text and descriptions of the manuscripts, see *The Chester Mystery Cycle*, edited by R. M. Lumiansky and David Mills (EETS ss. 3, London, 1974), Vol. I, *Text* from which all quotations are taken. There is one copy of the Pre-Reformation Banns – BL Harley 2150, of 1540; and there are four copies of the Post-Reformation Banns – two prefacing cycle-manuscripts R and B and two others in the Chester City Archive CX/3 and BL Harley 1944 versions of Rogers's *Breviary of Chester History* of 1609f.

performing cycle, constantly changing between 'some time before 1422' and 1575. Then there was whatever immediate hidden version or versions lay behind the extant manuscripts as exemplar(s). And finally there were the extant manuscripts themselves, no longer reflections of a living acting tradition but books, literary texts put together by their scribes for reasons very different from those that inspired the writers of the living plays.

We were, additionally, conscious of the ways in which previous editors and textual critics had handled these problems. The earliest editors, beginning in 1818 with J. H. Markland's edition of *The Flood* and *The Massacre of the Innocents* for the Roxburghe Club, were concerned primarily with introducing a readership to a text, not with the niceties of textual scholarship.[2] Indeed, Thomas Wright, who in 1843 and 1847 published the first edition of the full cycle for the Shakespeare Society, cheerfully asserted: 'All the transcripts, made by persons who were not well acquainted with the language of the original MS from which they copied or with palaeography in general, are full of errors, which could only be partially eradicated by a careful collation of them, a work of so much labour that it would hardly be repaid by the result.' Instead he transcribed A (1592) with corrections occasionally from R (1600) and H(1607).[3] In so doing, he evaded the difficulties which beset the next four scholars who engaged the complex problems of Chester's manuscripts.

The first EETS edition of the play, begun by Hermann Deimling and completed after his death by a 'Dr. Matthews' of whom nothing further is known, was a thorough and scholarly work dogged by misfortune.[4] In 1831 J. P. Collier, in his *History of English Dramatic Poetry and Annals of the Stage* (II. 227–9), had revealed the existence of a previously unknown manuscript of the cycle, now Hm 2, written in 1591. In his introduction, Deimling describes his unsuccessful attempts to trace this manuscript in preparing his edition, and the first volume of his text – published in 1892 and ending in mid-sentence, on a comma, at Play 13, line 282 – drew only upon the four later manuscripts. Though the Matthews continuation of 1916 collated all five manuscripts and, in prefatory lists, added 1591 variants for vol. I, the result was unsatisfactory and we shall never know if Deimling's initial choice of base manuscript would have been different had Hm 2 been available to him.

[2] J. H. Markland, *Chester Mysteries: De Deluvio Noe. De Occisione Innocentium* (Roxburghe Club, 1818); J. P. Collier, *Five Miracle Plays or Scriptural Dramas* (London, 1836: 'Antichrist'); J. P. Collier, *The Advent of Antichrist. A Miracle Play. Now First Printed from the Duke of Devonshire's Manuscript* (London, 1836); W. Marriott, *A Collection of English Miracle Plays or Mysteries* (Basel, 1838: 'Deluge' and 'Antichrist').
[3] T. Wright, *The Chester Plays* (Shakespeare Society, 1843 and 1847), p. xx.
[4] Hermann Deimling and Dr Matthews, *The Chester Plays* vol. I (EETS es. 62, London, 1892) and vol. II (EETS es. 115, London, 1916). Professor Korshin has recently proposed an identification of 'Dr Matthews' with the American scholar Albert Matthews which will appear in volume 2 of our edition (at press).

Deimling rightly drew attention to the fact that H (1607) differed in many significant readings from the other manuscripts which he called 'The Group' and to which we can now add Hm 2. He also identified A and R, both by the same scribe, George Bellin, as a sub-group, with R drawing upon the earlier A but also upon some other source.[5] His analysis led him to the conclusion that H offered 'the best text' linguistically and also, it can be inferred, 'as deviating less from the original form of the Chester Plays'.[6] To the curious postulate that the latest manuscript attested the earliest tradition were added two unfortunate editorial consequences – that the base text contained more unsupported readings than any other manuscript; and that, since it lacked some extended passages found in 'the Group' (which Deimling regarded as 'something like ornamental flourishes about an old and original nucleus'[7]), the variants at the foot of the page include from time to time extended sections of text for the reader to piece into the H-version.

The edition pointed the issues which were debated by our two immediate editorial predecessors, W. W. Greg and F. M. Salter.[8] Each was concerned with the status of Hm 2; and in 1935 each focused his discussion on one of the single-play manuscripts not available to Deimling-Greg, on that of the Peniarth *Antichrist* (P), and Salter on George Bellin's 1599 copy of *The Trial and Flagellation of Christ* (C) made for and still owned by the Coopers' Company of Chester, one of the guilds responsible for that play's performance. Greg held that all extant manuscripts descended from a common text, Chester's Civic Register or 'Regynall', of the fifteenth century, mediated through a series of lost intermediaries. After P, H remained closest to the Register, but Greg preferred the linguistic conservatism of Hm as base for a cycle-edition. Salter argued rather that each

---

[5] See further, R. M. Lumiansky and David Mills 'The Five Cyclic Manuscripts of the Chester Cycle of Mystery Plays: A Statistical Survey of Variant Readings', *LSE* n.s. 7 (1974), 95–107. Of particular relevance here are

(i) Readings found in one manuscript against readings common to the other four:
Hm – 447; A – 718; R – 467; B – 930; H – 1949.

(ii) Readings shared by two manuscripts against readings common to the other three:
HmA – 23; HmR – 22; HmB – 101; HmH – 109;
AR – 767; AB – 24; AH – 28;
RB – 30; RH – 35;
BH – 175.

The figures suggest the high number of unique forms in H and the close relationship of George Bellin's two manuscripts, A and R.

[6] Deimling, pp. xviii, xxviii.

[7] Deimling, pp. xxviii–xxix.

[8] W. W. Greg, *The Play of Antichrist from the Chester Cycle* (Oxford, 1935); see also his second lecture on 'Bibliographical and Textual Problems of the English Miracle Cycles', *The Library*, v (1914), 168–205, and his Appendix, pp. 74–83, to Salter's edition of 'The Trial', following. F. M. Salter, 'The "Trial and Flagellation": A New Manuscript', in *The Trial and Flagellation with Other Studies in the Chester Cycle* (Malone Society Studies, 1935) edited by W. W. Greg.

play had its own unique textual history. Divergencies among manuscripts owed more to scribal practice than to lost intermediaries and were evidence of the condition of the common exemplar from which the cyclic scribes all worked, particularly in the case of unique forms or shared forms in B and H. Hm again was accepted as the best basis for an edition.

2. *The Destabilising of the Cycle-text*

These textual studies obviously beg the usual editorial problems of base text, emendation, etc. They also raise two special issues of immediate concern to the editors of play-cycles but, I think, of much wider potential importance. First, what do we understand by 'The Chester Cycle'? And, second, what were the scribes of the cyclic manuscripts trying to produce? Let me take first the more 'philosophical' problem about the definition of 'a cycle'.

There are five reasons for postulating the existence of a lost but definitive exemplar of the Chester Cycle. First, it is standard editorial practice to assume some sort of authorised, if not actually authorial, version of a text which may have been subsequently corrupted in transmission. But while this is a useful and not unreasonable postulate for a literary text it is more difficult to sustain for a civic cycle whose text was subject to constant circumstantial modification and modernisation. To cite a few instances from the Chester records – the Pre-Reformation Banns mention a play of *The Assumption of the Virgin* not found in the later Banns or extant texts;[9] the Post-Reformation Banns describe a role for Antichrist's Doctor not found in our manuscripts;[10] the play-list in MS Harley 2150 asserts the control of the city council over guild-responsibility[11] and text, while in 1575 the mayor Sir John Savage is authorised to take expert advice to 'reform' the text[12] and the Smiths offered two versions of their play, 'to take the best'.[13] There was a process of deliberate change. Either one postulates a whole series of authoritatively determined 'cycles' or one assumes a single 'cycle' in a constant state of flux – effectively, an incomplete work that never perfects itself, like the *Canterbury Tales*. Its final state, in 1575 or whenever, would represent a cessation of change rather than a completion of form.

The second reason for postulating a definitive exemplar is that the defence of the cycle in the Post-Reformation Banns, probably attached to

---

[9] The two versions of the Banns are in Lumiansky–Mills as Documents 20 (a) and (b). All line references relate to that edition. See Early Banns, 128–31.
[10] Late Banns, 172–8.
[11] Lumiansky–Mills, Doc. 18(c).
[12] Lumiansky–Mills, Doc. 15(a).
[13] Lumiansky–Mills, Doc. 17(b) (ii), p. 245.

the Register,[14] predicates just such a text. The basis for the defence is that the cycle is a coherent and functional genre originating in the mind of a single author, like a literary text. The location of the cycle's origins in the mind of a literary and didactic innovator serves to establish the antiquity of the customary cycle-performances as well as the relevance of its innovating purpose. The civic initiative for organising the guilds to perform the cycle is attributed in these Banns to Sir John Arnewaye – popularly, but unhistorically, believed to be Chester's first mayor. The authorship of the new cycle is attributed to the late thirteenth–early fourteenth-century monk-historian Randle Higden, of St. Werburgh's Abbey, Chester, author of the influential Latin history entitled *Polychronicon*.[15] His plan was to bring the true Scriptures to the people in their own language, an evangelising purpose totally consistent with Protestant concerns. Hence the Banns seek to separate this consciously constructed text from, at one extreme, popish superstitious cycles of the type found elsewhere and 'rightly' proscribed by the Church of England authorities, and, at the other, the empty vanities of the professional stage no less 'appropriately' condemned by the local Puritan community.[16] Among the evidence for this long tradition is the strange, antiquated language used. R. M. Lumiansky and I – like others before us – have pointed out the chronological and factual inconsistencies in the Banns account; but the significance of this form of defence is its necessary shift in emphasis away from the notion of textual instability and towards something more like the situation obtaining with literary texts.[17]

Hence the text itself ostensibly provides a third reason for postulating the existence of a definitive exemplar. Out of the 1476 stanzas in Hm 2, 1117 are of the same form, the so-called 'Chester' stanza, and many others are simply variants of it.[18] This is a remarkable metrical consistency by the standard of our other extant cycles but not by the standard of literary narratives or verse histories. Moreover, the cycle, as has often been noted, has remarkable tonal consistency, recurring cross-references and links, a sustained thematic coherence that is maintained by the device of 'sign', and an overall frame for the action – it is self-consciously unified.[19] And throughout it shows the recurring influence of another vernacular work in

---

[14] David Mills, ' "In This Storye Consistethe Oure Chefe Faithe": The Problems of Chester's Play(s) of the Passion', *LSE* 16 (1985), 326–8.

[15] On Higden, see DNB; Lumiansky–Mills, p. 168; Late Banns, 1–27.

[16] Late Banns, 35–48 and 190–213. I have argued this case more fully in ' "None had the like nor the like darste set out": the City of Chester and its Mystery Cycle', *Staging the Chester Cycle: Lectures given on the Occasion of the Production of the Cycle at Leeds in 1983*, ed. David Mills (Leeds (at Press)), pp. 1–16.

[17] See F. M. Salter, *Medieval Drama in Chester* (Toronto, 1955), pp. 37–41.

[18] Lumiansky–Mills, Appendix: Stanza-forms in the Cycle, pp. 311–18.

[19] See John J. McGavin, 'Sign and Transition: The *Purification* Play in Chester', *LSE* n.s. 11 (1980), 90–104.

verse composed in Chester, the fifteenth-century *Stanzaic Life of Christ*. The *Life* is extant in three manuscripts and was evidently familiar in Cheshire. It draws upon both *Legenda Aurea* and Higden's *Polychronicon*, thereby lending some plausibility to the claims for Higden's authorship made in the Banns. It could have been incorporated for that reason.[20]

Such consistency is clear enough – indeed, it explains why we preferred *The Chester Mystery Cycle* to Deimling's *The Chester Plays* as the title of our edition. The problem is to understand and evaluate it. An important example is Play 5, *Of Moses and Balaam and Balak*, in which 'the Group and H diverge so extensively as to offer two related but quite different plays'.[21] Combining critical and textual concerns, Deimling supported H as offering a more coherent play and one closer to 'the older dramatic version'. The Group, however, has at the end of the play lines which invite the audience to the next day's performance of the next play in the manuscripts, *The Nativity* (Play 6):

> Nowe, worthye syrs both great and smale,
> here have wee shewed this storye before;
> and yf hit bee pleasinge to you all,
> tomorrowe nexte yee shall have more.
> Preyenge you all, both east and west
> where that yee goe, to speake the best.
> The byrth of Christe, feare and honest,
> here shall yee see; and fare yee well.
>
> (Play 5, 448–55)

H lacks these lines and we have no other indication of a division whereby a day's performance ended at Play 5 rather than the Play 9 of the play-lists. As Balak prepares to leave near the end, moreover, the Group has a long speech, not in H, which is introduced in the manuscripts by a side-note: 'Here Balaham speaketh to Balaack, "Abyde a while"' (Play 5, 335+SD). It is hard to regard this as a stage-direction: perhaps it is a cue to actor or producer, but that too seems unlikely: more probably it is indicative of a textual transition meaning 'At this place in the text comes Balaham's speech beginning "Abyde a while"'. Here, as elsewhere in the cycle, the text seems to offer us different ways of continuing appropriate to different circumstances – not one cycle, but several, none without some authority.[22]

---

[20] For text and manuscripts (BL Additional 38666, BL Harley 2250 and 3909) and parallels with the cycle, see *A Stanzaic Life of Christ*, edited by Frances A. Foster (EETS os. 166, London 1926). R. H. Wilson, 'The *Stanzaic Life of Christ* and the Chester Plays', *SP* 28 (1931), 413–32, points further parallels between the work and the cycle.

[21] See David Mills, 'The Two Versions of Chester Play V: Balaam and Balak', in Beryl Rowland (ed.), *Chaucer and Middle English Studies in Honour of Rossell Hope Robbins* (London, 1974), 366–71.

[22] See David Mills, 'Stage Directions in the Manuscripts of the Chester Mystery Cycle', *METh* 3 (1981), 45–51; and Lumiansky–Mills, pp. 28–32.

'Different' means not 'older' or 'better', but simply 'other'.

There is also evidence of similar alternative variants within the common text of the Group. For example, in Balak's speech of self-introduction, found in all five manuscripts (Hm 2, Play 5, 96–167), the Group includes a passage of forty lines (124–63) that are not in H. Balak, the Moabite King, is worried at the presence on his borders of the seemingly invincible Israelites, but recognises that, since God is with Moses, he cannot repulse them in open conflict; he will therefore proceed more subtly, using the special powers of the Gentile soothsayer, Balaam:

> Whosoever Balaham blesseth, iwys,
> blessed that man sothlye is;
> whosoever he cursys fareth amyse,
> such name over all hath hee.
>
> (120–23)

But instead of carrying out this plan, he suddenly reverts to his earlier, rejected, threats of direct vengeance:

> But yett I truste venged to bee
> with dynte of sword or pollicye . . .
>
> (124–5)

He invokes his pagan gods (113–47); he recalls – to the shame of those gods – the episode of the Exodus (148–55 – not, incidentally, played in the cycle) and urges them to use their numerical superiority against the one Jewish God (156–63). Logically, tonally, even syntactically, this passage does not connect with the preceding lines. Metrically, it intervenes between two halves of a Chester stanza, the quatrain of 120–23 above being completed at 164–7 below, with its logically connective *therefore*:

> Therefore goe fetche hym, batchelere,
> that he may curse these people heare.
> For sycker on them in no manere
> may we not wroken be.

Obviously the passage should not be where it is – but it offers a plausible characterisation of Balak as a pagan heretic, wilfully resisting divinely revealed truth, and hence as a conventional ranting tyrant. Though this picture is not that of the politic pagan that emerges in the H-version of the play, it does have much in common with the King in the Group-version whose death – together with his treacherous helper, Balaam – is described at the end of that play in terms of the just vengeance of God. And this tyrant-figure also seems more appropriate to his description in the Pre-Reformation Banns as 'that fears and mightie kyng'.

Two minor comments may be added in passing. First, the idea of 'authorised texts for different occasions' is not restricted to cycle performances. The *Shepherds' Play*, for example, was frequently extracted for independent production before visiting dignitaries – the last occasion being in 1577 at the High Cross before Lord Derby. The play in the Group includes an episode after the three Shepherds and their servant Trowle have presented their gifts in which their boys also offer gifts; internal evidence in the text further suggests that this episode was itself expanded from three boys to four at some stage.[23] Deimling regards the scene, absent in H, as not 'genuine' – but its expanded version offers more participation (probably for the Cathedral choirboys) and a more elaborate and extended performance, and it is reasonable to postulate that independent production of the play would offer opportunity for such elaboration. Second, the idea of a unified cycle is a late development. At Play 16 line 10 the Group reads *thy postie powere*, where H reads *powere* – correctly since the word is fixed by rhymes with *here*, *cleare*, *were*, *prayere* and *dangere*.

> Condemne not oure matter where groosse wordes you heare
> which importe at this daye smale sence or understandinge –
> as sometymes 'postie', 'bewtye', 'in good manner' or 'in feare' . . .

say the Post-Reformation Banns in defence of the cycle's textual antiquity. In Play 16 line 10 someone had substituted an archaism to the detriment of rhyme and the margin correction of *powere* has been incorporated into the text of 'the Group' in error instead of being substituted for *postie*, as in H.

The fourth argument for the definitive exemplar arises from the literary concerns just discussed. It is that critics have tended to discuss cycles as if they manifest a literary genre accessible by literary theories which address their structural coherence and thematic wholeness. To destabilise the notion of a cycle-text is simultaneously to challenge that critical basis. A cycle, as I see it, is a street of plays, each with its own history, each constantly being modified by its occupants. Here or there one is demolished or replaced by a new structure, partly but not wholly constrained by the surrounding structures. Salter recognised such a possibility in claiming a unique textual history for each play, though I would not wish that to imply that an editor should undertake a restoration which, though attractive, produces a street that never before existed. In the past a dramatic 'borough-engineer' might always stroll down the street, dismantling or replacing dangerous bits or strengthening weak points; such may have been the role of the 'Wakefield Master' in Towneley or the 'York Realist' in York. But at Chester it is as if the whole cycle has been redesigned at one time as a functional precinct, full of straight lines and contrived vistas, imposing a clear shape upon an earlier, probably looser, anthology of plays in order to explain and defend it. To propose, as I do, an emphasis upon a

---

[23] Lumiansky–Mills, p. 34. For independent performances of plays at Chester, see Lumiansky–Mills Docs 16(b), 16(c), 16(d), 16(m).

text as a record of change is to privilege historical process and functional flexibility over literary form and evaluation – a view that from the standpoint of literary criticism may seem somewhat radical.

The fifth and final argument for the definitive exemplar lies in the character of the extant manuscripts themselves. We possess only one civic exemplar, that of York, which bears on its pages the evidence of continuing textual modification. Both Towneley and N-Town in their different ways aspire to be books, seeking some kind of visible formality and decorative value at the hands of their scribes. The evident literary intention of their copying inevitably raises questions about their value as evidence of practical dramatic performance. At Chester, the intentions of the scribes were to create books, not acting texts, and in so doing they were compelled to make decisions about the alterations and the alternatives present in their copy-text. Two factors governed those decisions – what they could decipher, and what kind of book they wished to write. And since the latter brings me to my second special issue, I will give just one example of the first, the problem of decipherment.

In Play 20, lines 145–8, Hm reads:

> And that the wycked may eychone   145
> knowe and see all one
> howe worthelye they forgive
> that blysse that lasteth aye   148

The variants for these lines are:

145	may] *om* B, men H
	after wycked, maye *cancelled* B.
146	knowe] maye know BH
	one] and one H.
147	forgive] forgone ARBH.
148	aye] ever AR.

BH found *maye* to the left of *knowe* while HmAR locate it after *wycked*. The most probable explanation of the confusion is that *maye* was set in the left margin of the exemplar in a position indeterminate between 145 and 146, perhaps also with an obscured insertion-mark or/and a cancellation in those lines. Having decided to assign *maye* to 146, BH must then decide what to do about 145. Miller, the H-scribe, recognises that – in the absence of *maye* – the metre of 145 requires a monosyllable, and supplies *men*; Bedford ignores the metrical consideration and leaves the line deficient by his omission. HmAR, by assigning *may* to 145, create a metrically regular line, leaving 146 deficient. Is *men* 145 H Miller's invention or was it in the text and regarded as cancelled by HmARB? Or did the text originally have the auxiliary verb *mon* after *wycked* which later became the source of the

confusion? Such questions are unanswerable, but they indicate the probability here, as in almost all cases, that manuscript-variants in the cycle-texts
arise because the scribes reach different solutions to the obscurities of their
common exemplar as they try to make sense of its readings.

3. *The Books of the Scribes*

Edward Gregorie, the Hm-scribe, styles himself 'scholler at Bunbury' and
under the direction of the Puritan minister Richard Roe was one of the
guardians of the church who copied and signed the accounts in 1606–9.[24]
George Bellin, the scribe of A, C and R, was an ironmonger who acted as
scribe to the guilds of the Cappers and Pinners, the Coopers and the
Ironmongers, as well as being clerk to Holy Trinity Church, Chester, till
his death in 1624. Well connected by marriage, he knew the Chester
antiquarians David Rogers and Randle Holme; his commonplace-book,
with pious verses and prayers, survives.[25] William Bedford, scribe of B in
1604, was clerk to the Brewers' Guild from post-1606 to his death in 1622
(when Bellin succeeded him at a considerably higher wage). James Miller,
the one named scribe of the three in H, was precentor at Chester Cathedral
from pre-1584/85 and rector of St Michael's, Chester, from 1605 until his
death in 1618. His will mentions his Latin books of divinity; his music and
song books, his school-books, and 'all the rest of my English bookes,
Historyes, Chronicles and Divinity'.[26]

These scribal biographies are, I think, significant in establishing the
scholarly aspirations of Gregorie and the scholarly credentials of Miller.
Gregorie is a conservative scribe, evidently trying to reproduce the old
forms before him and not afraid to leave a gap where he cannot decipher.
Miller is a restorer, intelligently steering his way through the variants of the
exemplar and emending according to clear principles of rhyme and metre,
so that many of his unique variants are changes in word-order or the
introduction of additional syllables. The lay-out of every page was pre-
planned and ruled by Miller – he is more a restorative editor than a scribe –
and like all such should be treated with extreme suspicion. But both
Gregorie and Miller offer different ways of reading and organising the

[24] On Gregorie, see David Mills, 'Edward Gregorie – a "Bunbury scholar"', *REED Newsletter* (1982) No. 1, 49–50.

[25] On Bellin, see F. M. Salter, 'The Banns of the Chester Plays', *RES* 15 (1939), 436–7 and fn. 2 to those pages. Bellin's commonplace book is BL Harley 1937: it contains a note: 'Received of Mr Thomas harvy the 22nd September 1601 iis & iid in parte of payment for his Children scoole hyer from michaellmas to Christmas next cominge due to me at Christmas nexte'. [*bracketed to right* iis iiis]. This may indicate that Bellin offered tuition to the children of Chester aldermen.

[26] On Miller, see David Mills, *The Chester Mystery Cycle: A facsimile of BL MS Harley 2124* (Leeds, 1984) p. viii and 'James Miller: the Will of a Chester Scribe', *REED Newsletter* 9: 1 (1984), 11–13.

Register into a coherent form. Because they do so from different viewpoints, one manuscript offers a control to set against the other, and with the exception of Wright, modern editors have selected one of these two for base text, with a preference for Gregorie's conservatism.

The two guild-scribes approach the Register with less scholarly scrupulousness and less concern for consistency, though both wished to possess their own copies of the cycle. Moreover, Bellin, having written A – which, since he still had access to it eight years later, may be assumed to be his personal copy – seems to have accepted a commission to write R which required greater accuracy. Unsupported readings from either scribe cannot be trusted. Bellin, a bad Latinist at all times, is repeatedly cavalier in his text, omitting, censoring and substituting – his substitution of *ever* for *aye* at Play 20, line 148 above in rhyme-position is a recurring specific example and characteristic of his general approach. Bedford, a more slapdash penman, scrawls and blots his way across his unruled pages, but still seeks to write what he believes he sees. His manuscript is a mimesis of his mind in action – writing automatically, then re-reading and excising, over and over again – with little appreciation of the choices the Register offers him. Bedford offers glimpses of the condition of the exemplar because he does work so automatically, albeit carelessly, and B therefore can offer clues to the possible origins of divergent readings in Hm and H.

These four scribes evidently wished to make a lasting record of what they believed to be the ancient text of Chester's traditional civic plays – a text whose survival was threatened because the performance of the plays was prohibited. Inevitably, each scribe offers an idiosyncratic reading of the Register that takes into account its co-existing alternatives, and its obscurities, corrections and modernisations, augmented by the scribe's own concern with semantics, syntax and metre, his willingness to 'emend', his own accuracy and his sense of stylistic propriety. Each scribe fixes the material in a form accessible to contemporary study. Editors need to be conscious of these determining factors in interpreting the evidence of the text provided by the extant manuscripts. But they can recognise that variations within and among the manuscripts give clues to the condition and contents of the lost Register, revealing it to be a practical working document, itself part of a continuous process of change and adaptation. Perhaps behind it lie other cycles, other working documents, whose texts cannot now be retrieved. This situation is evidently different from that usually proposed for medieval literary texts or for printed play-texts for the sixteenth-century stage, where something as definitive as 'the poem' or 'the play' (and, of course, 'the poet(s)' or 'the playwright(s)') can plausibly be postulated as a starting point.[27]

---

[27] See further Alexandra F. Johnston, 'The *York Cycle* and the *Chester Cycle*: What do the records tell us?' which I read after this paper was completed. I am grateful to Professor Johnston for allowing me to read her paper in proof.

Postscript

It was considerations of convenience that led us to adopt Gregorie's conservative Hm 2 as the base text for our edition. Its inclusiveness and its high proportion of supported readings afforded us the means to present the whole cycle with all its variants clearly for the readers' evaluation. To that presentation, however, we have felt it essential to add further analyses, to alert the reader to the diversities within the extant text, to assert its instability, and to explore the critical consequences of those facts.

THE VALUE OF EDITING THE *CLERK'S TALE* FOR THE *VARIORUM CHAUCER*

Charlotte C. Morse

To make grandiose claims for my own edition-in-progress[1] would be foolish: no editorial project, however well-conceived and well-executed, can satisfy every scholar's desire and every reader's curiosity. Moreover, the decisions and guidelines governing a general project or series are not usually of the editor's own devising. I am aware of at least some of the controversy the Variorum Chaucer has aroused, but to date I have generally found the guidelines sensible and flexible. Individual editors of the Canterbury volumes have introduced refinements in presentation or procedures as they have seemed necessary or helpful. I think particularly of the form of the textual introduction in these volumes, for which Derek Pearsall established the model in his final draft of the *Nun's Priest's Tale*.

What value there is in editing the Variorum *Clerk's Tale* cannot be addressed in isolation from the larger project. Briefly, I believe that the principal value of the Variorum lies in the notes and introductory matter, textual and critical. Editors of the Variorum *Canterbury Tales* will be considerably less able to hide their evidence and the basis for their decisions than is common in editions of the tales: this comparative openness is the great strength of the edition.

An audience with some notion of the history of a large project may be less disappointed in it, may even appreciate the practical decisions that must be taken for any progress at all to occur. Most large projects, and the Variorum was no exception, proceed at first with maddening slowness, as I learned while working on the staff of Research Grants in the National Endowment for the Humanities. Any large project that comes to fruition must have some individual(s) willing to persist in directing the project often through rather dark hours, especially likely after the first enthusiasm

---

[1] Textual data and analysis in this essay derive from my forthcoming edition of the *Clerk's Tale* for the Variorum Chaucer series. For the Variorum and hence for this discussion, the main edition of Chaucer's *Tales* is that of John M. Manly and Edith Rickert, *The Text of the Canterbury Tales: Studied on the Basis of all Known Manuscripts*, 8 vols. (Chicago and London, 1940). I have benefited from conversations with John Burrow, Paul Ruggiers, Larry Benson, Ralph Hanna, and A. S. G. Edwards. My greatest debt as a Variorum editor is to Derek Pearsall, who gave me a copy of his final draft for the edition of the *Nun's Priest's Tale* at the same time as he submitted it to Paul Ruggiers, the General Editor of the Variorum Chaucer.

dissipates and the need for meticulous and tedious planning, experimentation, and decision-making begins. To survive, such a project must also respond to some serious need(s) of the participants or the audience or both.

At the time when the Variorum project was taking shape, there were three major Chaucer projects in planning stages. Besides the Variorum, there was talk of a third edition of Robinson's Chaucer and of a Nelson Chaucer. A new edition of Robinson, under Larry Benson's general editorship, will soon appear. The Nelson Chaucer, involving Derek Brewer, Talbot Donaldson, Denton Fox, and John Burrow, among others, was to be a multi-volume, critical edition of Chaucer's works, annotated, but it collapsed on commercial grounds. Paul Ruggiers, whose persistent pursuit of the Variorum is now bearing fruit, once thought of the Variorum *Canterbury Tales*, with which the Variorum was to begin, not as an edition, but as a review of scholarship and criticism, on the model of Merritt Hughes's commentary on Milton. Once Ruggiers and his advisors abandoned such a plan, the decision to make a new text based on the Hengwrt manuscript followed, though not without some consideration of the use of an already existing text. There were theoretical problems with the choice of any available text, however, quite apart from rights to such texts, and so Ruggiers committed the Variorum to being a new edition of the *Tales* as well as a commentary.

These discussions and decisions of the 1960s and early 1970s reflected changing conditions within university studies of literature. The post-World War II growth of universities, particularly in North America, was finally stabilising. The veterans and the baby-boomers who had so absorbed the resources, enthusiasm and energies of university faculties, which had grown to meet the demand, were becoming the past. Critical interpretation had seemed urgent to that broader post-war audience, and so the new critical approach to literary texts emanating from Yale and the methods of allegorical interpretation emanating from UNC-Chapel Hill PhD's generated ever more essays on Chaucer's works and made it difficult for scholars to command their field as they had done for PhD examinations in the 1950s and earlier. North Americans were just beginning to recover, on a significant scale, an interest in manuscript studies that World War II had disrupted. Older Americans and many British scholars understood the importance of editorial work and recognised that the Manly–Rickert edition of the *Canterbury Tales,* monumental as it is, needed renewed scrutiny from a generation not intimidated by reverence for the two American scholars nor inclined to ignore or dismiss them.

The need for reassessment of and for control over the burgeoning secondary literature drove the beginning stages of all the new projects. They were conceived in the empiricist tradition of Anglo-American scholarship, appropriate to editorial work. Yet the Variorum will add something beyond empiricism, something of the spirit guiding modern literary studies, because the Variorum requires that the same editor put into question the object of study, namely the text, and reflect self-consciously over the history of its interpretation. The lack of certainty, which was so difficult for our predecessors to bear, but which is so much a part of the Chaucerian tradition, should be easier to admit in the current climate of literary studies. The history of the influence or reception of Chaucer's texts has not received broad attention. To attend to this history leads to a far more acute self-consciousness about the audience, which includes us, than we have yet experienced in Chaucer studies.

Having the luxury of a much fuller scope for treatment than Benson can afford in Robinson 3, the Variorum editor must sometimes find himself experiencing a defamiliarisation of the text, as he realises that there has been no note for some item that invites explanation or comment. How much editors add is a matter of discretion, but at least in some cases there will be significantly new notes, and that will be particularly true for textual notes. Readers of the Variorum should be able to share the editor's sense of defamiliarisation and, as a result, should be able to identify items that still ask for comment. When I belatedly began to study Chaucer, having begun my literary endeavours in Renaissance studies, I found the notes so comparatively inadequate that I assumed that I had somehow, out of idleness, missed an important edition of Chaucer. The Variorum promises more adequate notes.

One of the more controversial decisions of the Variorum was to edit from a small number of important manuscripts, chosen to represent the major families of manuscripts disclosed by Manly–Rickert in their analysis of a corpus of variants based on all the manuscripts. Critics contend that such a selection cannot test Manly–Rickert's results. This criticism, while of course partly true, is a good deal less compelling than it may appear. What the variorum will not test is Manly–Rickert's classification of manuscripts, though it may indicate where such classifications are doubtful or inadequate, since editors are referring to the full Manly–Rickert corpus of variant in making editorial decisions and notes. The greatest uncertainties lie in the large group of *d* manuscripts, which have not proved important in establishing the modern text of Chaucer's work.

How accurate Manly–Rickert were in recording variants matters greatly, as George Kane has most recently said.[2] Before the Nelson Chaucer collapsed, John Burrow had checked the reliability of Manly–Rickert's corpus of variants to see whether it could be used as the basis for the Nelson edition. He concluded that the improvements he or anyone else might make were too marginal to undertake. The University of Chicago

---

[2] 'John M. Manly (1865–1940) and Edith Rickert (1871–1938)', in *Editing Chaucer: The Great Tradition*, ed. Paul G. Ruggiers (Norman, Oklahoma, 1984), 207–29.

has deposited its rotographs of Chaucer's manuscripts and the cards on which the Manly–Rickert project recorded variants with the Variorum in Oklahoma. Ruggiers reports that, in vetting the texts that have come through, he has found the cards to be of an even higher level of accuracy than the published corpus of variants, mistakes having crept in occasionally in the process of moving from the card to typescript. Moreover, the cards record all the manuscripts having the reading Manly–Rickert accepted, information that is sometimes quite helpful but that can only be worked out very laboriously from their published work. Variorum editors note all differences from Manly–Rickert's corpus of variants, but users of the Variorum should understand that a substantial portion of those differences arise from slightly different guidelines for recognising variants; difference does not necessarily or usually, in my experience, imply a mistake in Manly–Rickert.

Manly–Rickert's informative descriptions of manuscripts have long earned them praise and rarely seem in need of major correction. Their corpus of variants also appears to be highly reliable. Their text generally follows the Hengwrt manuscript and has encouraged a mid-twentieth-century preference for Hengwrt over Ellesmere (Ellesmere, however, reportedly gained favour with Pratt in his revisions of the *Canterbury Tales* for Robinson 3).[3] The inadequacy of Manly–Rickert's textual notes is obvious; presumably they were racing against death to finish their work and the notes lost. Or perhaps, as Ruggiers has suggested to me, Manly intentionally avoided explanations where none could in factual terms be adduced. Whatever their attitude towards notes, Rickert was dead before the edition was finished and Manly died a few months after publication in 1940. Their death and the war muted criticism of their work. Both J. Burke Severs and Germaine Dempster could have been more forthright in their criticism of the Manly–Rickert theory of early versions of the Canterbury

---

[3] The main alternative to Hengwrt (now Peniarth 392, National Library of Wales, Aberystwyth) is Ellesmere. In usually following Hengwrt, the Variorum will generally coincide with the editorial judgement of Manly–Rickert, except in cases where we know or suspect that they reckoned a Hengwrt reading to belong to O^1 but not to O, where O is the author's original and O^1 the hypothetical ancestor of all manuscript texts (a hypothesis that George Kane notes is unsustainable). The most radical proponent of Hengwrt is Norman Blake; see especially his edition, *The Canterbury Tales* (London, 1980), and 'The Relationship Between the Hengwrt and the Ellesmere Manuscripts of the *Canterbury Tales*', *Essays and Studies*, 32 (1979), 1–18. For other editions heavily reliant on Hengwrt, see E. Talbot Donaldson, *Chaucer's Poetry: An Anthology for the Modern Reader* (New York, 1958); and Robert A. Pratt, *The Tales of Canterbury, Complete* (Boston, 1974). Walter W. Skeat relied heavily on Ellesmere in his 1894 (Oxford) edition of the *Canterbury Tales* as did Kenneth Sisam in a school edition of the *Clerk's Tale* (Oxford, 1923) and as did F. C. Robinson but to a lesser degree in his editions of Chaucer's *Works* (Boston, 1933, 1957). The so-called Robinson 3, under the general editorship of Larry Benson, will reportedly rely heavily on Ellesmere; see also Benson's reply to Blake's 1979 article: 'The Order of *The Canterbury Tales*', *Studies in the Age of Chaucer*, 3 (1981), 77–120.

tales discernible in the manuscripts. The *Clerk's Tale* offers a major test of this theory, which it fails, as I will explain later in this essay.

Variorum editors are using Hengwrt as their base manuscript, a decision that seems sensible in the light of its evident authority (editing without a base manuscript in a case such as the *Canterbury Tales* makes no sense to me, though I have heard it suggested). Editors are free to emend but encouraged to consider hard the need to do so. To be sure, most editors in this century have thought the choice between Hengwrt or Ellesmere as base manuscript to be a narrow one, as it is in the *Clerk's Tale* and as we might expect it to be where the textual quality of several extant manuscripts is high. There are only 91 readings over which the modern editions collated for the Variorum disagree in the *Clerk's Prologue and Tale*, 56 of these involving Ellesmere. None of the alternatives affects the meaning of the text very much, some not at all. The scribe of Ellesmere, as fifteenth-century scribes generally did, tended to regularise Chaucer's text, and so did editors at the end of the last century. Early modern editors embraced regularity because the rules by which regularity could be determined had just been worked out and regularity was fashionable. It decisively laid to rest the old and embarrassing charge that Chaucer's poetry was rough, which like Matthew Arnold's charge that Chaucer's poetry lacks high seriousness was a charge that seemed to make Chaucer less than a great poet. But of the 91 alternative readings in the *Clerk's Tale*, over 50 make equally acceptable sense and only 16 involve metre.

Given the nature of the readings which constitute the area of controversy in the *Clerk's Prologue and Tale*, the choice between Hengwrt and Ellesmere as base text approaches the arbitrary. Whichever text you suppose more closely represents Chaucer's *modus scribendi* is the text you will choose, but the choice is *a priori*, based mostly on attitudes to metrical regularity. Metrically, the differences in the *Clerk's Tale* come down to one headless line in Hengwrt, one Lydgate line and a quasi-Lydgate line in Hengwrt, one case of no elision in Hengwrt where the same vowel ends one word and begins the next, and one instance involving distaste for elision in Ellesmere.[4] As for other disputed readings, does Hengwrt's avoidance of haphazard shifts between present and preterite tenses (6 instances) represent Chaucer's practice?[5] How do we choose between one idiom and another, usually a choice between prepositions, such as *of* or *for*, *in* or *on*, in expressions where either is idiomatic (10 instances)?[6] Or how about 4 variations between *this* and *the*, 2 between *this* and *his*?[7]

---

[4] For variations between Hengwrt and Ellesmere, see *The Canterbury Tales: A Facsimile and Transcription of the Hengwrt Manuscript, with Variants from the Ellesmere Manuscript*, ed. Paul G. Ruggiers (Norman, Oklahoma, 1979): *ClPT* 136; 420, 685; 511 (43 may be similar); 537.

[5] Ibid., *ClPT* 78, 424, 450, 579, 687, 1085.

[6] Ibid., *ClPT* 56, 96, 118, 257, 522, 551, 653, 895, 941, 1172.

[7] Ibid., *ClPT* 316, 342, 445, 859, 582, 587.

The case for choosing Hengwrt over Ellesmere isn't overwhelmingly strong, but Hengwrt is in a few instances less editorialised than Ellesmere, and this seems to be a consistent pattern, beyond the *Clerk's Prologue and Tale*. Thus, the choice of Manly–Rickert, Donaldson, and Pratt (1974) has run to Hengwrt. The palaeographical evidence that puts Hengwrt probably earlier than Ellesmere, both the work of one scribe who in the intervening period copied Gower, also tends to favour Hengwrt, but that evidence cannot be conclusive.[8] Priority does not necessarily mean superiority.

There is, of course, the possibility that Chaucer or his scribe had copied out the *Clerk's Prologue and Tale* more than once; that Hengwrt and Ellesmere descend from two authentic but slightly different copies; and that we are not dealing with premeditated but with casual revision by Chaucer or by a scribe he supervised.

The most interesting result of my textual work is my rejection of Manly–Ricket's theory of early versions of the *Canterbury Tales* in the case of the *Clerk's Tale*.[9] I believe Manly and Rickert fell upon this theory in a desperate attempt to justify the stupefying amount of work they were doing in collating and classifying all the Chaucer manuscripts. To discover that in almost all situations, only a few manuscripts had any textual authority, and that the authority of several was so consistent that one could make a good text without the rest of the evidence must have been discouraging. Given the climate in which they worked, reasons for ignoring the implications of their discovery seemed good.

The history of the theory of revision in the *Clerk's Tale* can be briefly told. As knowledge of Chaucer's manuscripts accumulated in the twentieth century, scholars focused on the textual differences in what I call the end-pieces of the *Clerk's Tale*, and it is these differences that led some of Manly–Rickert's predecessors and contemporaries to presume or infer an early version of the *Clerk's Tale*. Thomas Tyrwhitt in 1775 set up the modern speculation when he relegated the Host Stanza to a footnote, suggesting that Chaucer had cancelled it, an idea he probably derived from Harley 7334's probably accidental lack of the Host Stanza (Tyrwhitt set higher store by Harley 7334 than editors since Thomas Wright, 1847–51, have done).[10] At the beginning of this century, as more manuscript evidence became available, Eleanor Hammond elaborated a theory of the development of the *Clerk's Tale* that foreshadows Carleton Brown's and

---

[8] Ibid., 'Palaeographical Introduction' by A. I. Doyle and M. B. Parkes, and their article, 'The Production of Copies of the *Canterbury Tales* and the *Confessio Amantis* in the Early Fifteenth Century', *Medieval Scribes, Manuscripts, and Libraries: Essays Presented to N. R. Ker*, ed. M. B. Parkes and Andrew G. Watson (London, 1978), 163–210, esp. 170–74. See also Manly–Rickert, I, 266–83, and II, 477–9 (Hg), and I, 148–59 (El) for descriptions of Hengwrt and Ellesmere.

[9] Manly–Rickert, II, 495–518.

[10] See George R. Keiser, 'Revision in Group E of the *Canterbury Tales*', *Manuscripta*, 17 (1973), 159–77.

Manly–Rickert's.[11] The manuscripts that omit the Wife of Bath stanza, 1170–76, 'For which heere, for the wyves love of Bathe', also place the fourth stanza of the envoy in sixth and last position (i.e., lines 1195–1200 follow 1212). Most omit the Host Stanza and lack the Clerk–Merchant link, 1213–44.

It is easy enough to understand how the theory of the early version grew. You can perhaps imagine Manly and Rickert's excitement as the classification of manuscripts relegated all those with the peculiar features I mention to one group textually. They form Manly–Rickert's large group d (d^*) for the *Clerk's Tale*. This group is textually inferior to the independent manuscripts as well as to Cambridge Dd.4.24 and it does not have any very early extant members. Nevertheless, Manly–Rickert perused d^* manuscripts for signs that their text derived from an early version of Chaucer's translation. They came up with thirty lines in the *Clerk's Tale* where the variants seemed to them good enough to be early versions of the lines rather than the results of scribal variation.

Bear in mind, however, that J. Burke Severs did not publish his work on the sources of the *Clerk's Tale* until after the Manly–Rickert edition appeared, by which time both Manly and Rickert were dead. Before Severs, some scholars believed that Chaucer had used a French version of the Griselda as well as Petrarch's Latin, but the French in question was identified with Philippe de Mézières's translation. Although Elie Golenistcheff-Koutouzoff recognised the existence of an anonymous French translation in his 1933 study and included a text of it,[12] his book seems not to have come to Manly or Rickert's attention. Consequently, they could not test the supposed early lines against the French text that in 1942 Severs would definitively show Chaucer had used.[13] Severs himself conservatively tested 13 of Rickert's lines against the French in a 1946 article and eliminated 8 of them.[14] The case for all of them is weak. All of the lines in question can be accounted for as scribal variation.

Once the case for an extant early version of the tale of Griselda evaporates, the vagaries of manuscript transmission adequately account for the state of the d^* manuscripts with respect to the end-pieces of the *Clerk's Tale;* both Severs and Dempster proposed such vagaries. He shows the d^* Envoy to be scribal. She rejects the theory that the d^* manuscripts reflect an early version of the *Clerk's Tale*; she also rejects Manly–Rickert's

---

[11] Hammond, *Chaucer: A Bibliographical Manual* (New York, 1908), pp. 243–57; Brown, 'The Evolution of the Canterbury "Marriage Group"', *PMLA*, 48 (1933), 1041–59, and 'Author's Revision in the *Canterbury Tales*', *PMLA*, 57 (1942), 29–50; and n. 9, above.

[12] *L'Histoire de Griseldis en France au XIVe et au XVe Siècle* (Paris, 1933).

[13] *The Literary Relationships of Chaucer's Clerkes Tale*, Yale Studies in English, 96 (New Haven, 1942); Severs published the texts of Chaucer's Latin and French sources a year earlier, in *Sources and Analogues of Chaucer's Canterbury Tales*, ed. W. F. Bryan and Germaine Dempster (Chicago, 1941).

[14] 'Did Chaucer Revise the *Clerk's Tale*?', *Speculum*, 21 (1946), 295–302.

notion that many of the manuscripts of the *Canterbury Tales* derive from early or even pre-*Canterbury Tales* versions of the tales.[15] It is not so easy to test the evidence in tales that are not translations, a condition that makes the failure of the theory with respect to the *Clerk's Tale* a very damaging failure.

In summary: Tyrwhitt's supposition that Chaucer must have intended to cancel the Host Stanza loses force because there is no manuscript evidence for it, while the manuscripts with the best texts include it, always in final position, after the Envoy. There is also no good manuscript evidence of an early version of Chaucer's *Clerk's Tale* and no manuscript evidence of stages in accommodating the translation of Griselda to the *Canterbury Tales*. There may have been an early version of the *Clerk's Tale*. There may have been stages in its accommodation to the *Canterbury Tales*. Chaucer may have intended to cancel the Host Stanza. But we don't know and we can't know, because the manuscripts offer no evidence. We can only spin theories.

Some theories are better than others, and some ought to be resisted for lack of information. A Variorum editor has the first whack at articulating what the state of a given Chaucer text is, but should also be supplying users of the edition with information upon which to make informed judgements and build convincing theories. The openness with which Variorum editors must address their evidence constitutes the greatest value these editions will hold for readers. A lesser but humbling value will be the revelation of changing fashions in Chaucer studies – for example, the culture-bounded-ness implicit in what once seemed utterly objective judgements or constant interpretive issues – the latter a subject for another day.

---

[15] Severs, 'Did Chaucer Rearrange the Clerk's Envoy?', *Modern Language Notes*, 69 (1954), 472–8; Dempster, 'A Period in the Development of the *Canterbury Tales* Marriage Group and of Blocks B² and C', *PMLA*, 68 (1953), 1142–59; 'Manly's Conception of the Early History of the *Canterbury Tales*', *PMLA* 61 (1946), 379–415; 'A Chapter in the Manuscript History of the *Canterbury Tales*', *PMLA*, 63 (1948), 456–84; 'The Fifteenth Century Editors of the *Canterbury Tales* and the Problem of Tale Order', *PMLA*, 64 (1949), 1123–42.

POET AND SCRIBE IN THE MANUSCRIPTS OF GOWER'S *CONFESSIO AMANTIS*

Peter Nicholson

The *Confessio Amantis* belongs to the small group of Middle English poems that survive in a large number of manuscripts: we have fifty-one complete or nearly complete copies at latest count, plus a number of fragments.[1] And the general quality of these manuscripts, both in costliness of production and in the overall uniformity of the text, is unusually high. Even some of the poorest among them, as Macaulay observed, would rank with the best copies of some of Chaucer's works, and second only to the very best manuscripts of the *Canterbury Tales*.[2] Unfortunately we still do not know exactly how so many manuscripts of such high quality were produced. Macaulay judged that Gower himself must have had some hand in their production and attributed the best of these copies to Gower's own scriptorium,[3] a belief that received even fuller elaboration from John Hurt Fisher.[4] More recently, however, their conclusions have been brought into question by A. I. Doyle and Malcolm Parkes.[5] In examining the work of the five scribes who collaborated on Trinity College Cambridge MS R.3.2, Doyle and Parkes have drawn a picture of commercial copying beyond the poet's own control that is quite different from Macaulay's and Fisher's. Equally important, they provide a model for how much we can still learn from the manuscripts themselves about the complicated circumstances of their production.

The question of Gower's own role in the copying of these manuscripts has some obvious implications for the study of his text, for the *Confessio*

---

[1] For a complete list see the forthcoming *Descriptive Catalogue of the Manuscripts of the Works of John Gower*, ed. Derek Pearsall, Jeremy Griffiths, and Kate Harris.

[2] G. C. Macaulay, ed., *The Complete Works of John Gower* (Oxford, 1899–1902), II, clxvii. Volumes II and III of this edition, containing the *Confessio Amantis*, are identical to *The English Works of John Gower*, EETS, e.s. 81–2 (London, 1900–1901).

[3] Macaulay, II, cxxx, clxvii; and more explicitly in the notes to his chapter on Gower in *The Cambridge History of English Literature*, II, *The End of the Middle Ages*, ed. A. W. Ward and A. R. Waller (Cambridge, 1908), p. 512.

[4] *John Gower: Moral Philosopher and Friend of Chaucer* (New York, 1963), pp. 92–3, 101, 116–17, 303–6.

[5] A. I. Doyle and M. B. Parkes, 'The Production of Copies of the *Canterbury Tales* and the *Confessio Amantis* in the early fifteenth century', in M. B. Parkes and A. G. Watson, eds., *Medieval Scribes, Manuscripts, & Libraries: Essays presented to N. R. Ker* (London, 1978), pp. 163–210, especially p. 200, n. 98.

survives in a number of different forms. Gower evidently changed his mind about his poem: we have alternative versions of both the prologue and the epilogue, dedicating the *Confessio* either to Richard II or to his successor; and there are some miscellaneous passages of varying length in some of the middle books of the poem that appear to be authorial but that occur in varying combinations in the copies that we have.[6] We also have one manuscript in which the revised passages at beginning and end have been written over erasure or on new leaves substituted for old, and other copies that appear to be derived from exemplars that were revised in the same way. Macaulay believed that all of these changes were due to the author himself, and that each of the different forms in which the poem survives marks a different stage in the poet's own revision. He thus divided the manuscripts into groups according to the degree of correction and revision that he found, identifying three principal versions that he called 'recensions', and also labelling different stages of revision within 'recension one' and 'recension two'. He then defined his main task as editor as the choice of which of all these different authorial versions best represented Gower's final intention for his poem.

Macaulay's decision on this matter, along with his entire notion of authorial revision and 'recension', has since become enshrined in virtually all of the commentary and textual criticism of the *Confessio*. His is an attractive view, to be sure, especially since it makes the task of editing so much simpler. But particularly because of the evidence that some of the most important manuscripts were altered after they were written, it does depend upon that underlying assumption that the poet himself controlled the form in which his work appeared and that he had a direct hand in the preparation of these copies. One part of Macaulay's account can be challenged on textual grounds alone: I have argued elsewhere that the variations that we find among the manuscripts of 'recension one' are more easily attributed to scribal error than to authorial revision, thus casting even more doubt on Gower's direct supervision of the copying.[7] Some similar problems on the relationship between the poet and his scribes arise with Macaulay's notion of authorial 'recensions', problems which have even more serious consequences for the study of the text. His account raises two questions in particular: first, what we can honestly determine about the poet's supervision of the copying without simply begging the question of the authority of some of the early copies; and second, the exact relation between the different forms in which the poem is now preserved and the process of the poet's own revision, particularly as it concerns his 'final intention'.

---

[6] See Macaulay, II, cxxvii–cxxxviii.
[7] Peter Nicholson, 'Gower's Revisions in the *Confessio Amantis*', *Chaucer Review*, 19 (1984), 123–43.

For both questions it is necessary to look at two manuscripts particularly closely, the 'Fairfax' copy, Bodley Fairfax 3, and the 'Stafford' copy, now Huntington Ellesmere 26 A 17. These two are among the earliest manuscripts of the *Confessio* in any form; they are the two that are most often suspected of having been supervised by the poet; and most importantly they are the earliest known copies of Macaulay's recensions 'two' and 'three', and the origins of the different 'recensions' are inseparable from the peculiar history of these two manuscripts. Of these the best known is certainly Bodley Fairfax 3 since Macaulay used it as the base manuscript for his edition. Macaulay was attracted to Fairfax because of its high quality, which is not in dispute; because of the clear evidence of its revision – this is the copy in which the old prologue and epilogue have been removed and new versions inserted in later hands; and because he dated its final revision later than the completion of Stafford. Thus he labelled the group that it belongs to as the last of the three 'recensions', and he presented Fairfax as the best representative of Gower's 'final judgment as to the form of his work' (II, cxxxvii).

The fact that at least three different hands were involved in its production is an indication, however, of some of the complexity of its history and of the difficulty of seeing it quite as simply as Macaulay did. Fairfax is indeed a very interesting book, but principally because of the number of different layers to its history, a succession of alterations and additions appearing in this manuscript at different times that serve finally to distinguish 'recension three' from the other versions of the poem. Some of these changes can perhaps be ascribed to Gower, and others almost certainly can not. Because of the central importance that the manuscript has assumed it is rather important to distinguish these different layers; and when we do, Fairfax provides a particularly good demonstration of the problems involved in determining precisely how the different surviving forms of the *Confessio Amantis* first evolved.

To begin with the work of the original scribe: Fairfax began its life, before any thought was given to changing the prologue and epilogue, as merely another copy of what we now call 'recension one'. It was a careful and deluxe copy, which may have something to do with its later history; and it did have a small number of peculiarities which are discussed below. Textually, however, it simply remains to be shown that it was superior to other good copies of either 'recension one' or 'recension two'. We have a small number of very early manuscripts of the different 'recensions', four of which (three of 'recension one',[8] plus Stafford) are particularly close to Fairfax. The best evidence of the textual quality of all of these is provided by their general uniformity, and thus Fairfax is most clearly authoritative

---

[8] Oxford, Bodley 902 (Macaulay's *A*); Cambridge, St John's College MS B 12 (*J*); and Cambridge University Library MS Mm.2.21 (*M*); see Macaulay, II, cxxxii, cxxxviii–cxl.

only when it is supported by the others. In the places where it differs its authority is not at all clear, and there is a great danger of creating an illusion of superiority simply by labelling it as a copy of 'recension three'. By Macaulay's own account,[9] which is fully supported by the evidence of the textual notes in his edition, all other 'third recension' copies derive either directly or indirectly from Fairfax itself, and thus all the instances in the first scribe's hand in which 'recension three' differs from 'recension one' represent variants arising in only a single manuscript as opposed to the other independent copies to which it is most closely related. The number of such variants is not very large. There are some 300–400 Fairfax readings, most of them admittedly quite trivial, that Macaulay himself rejected in his edition.[10] There are a smaller number of instances in which he retained a reading from Fairfax that was not supported by other independent copies, and of these several are questionable at best, and none is demonstrably superior to the reading in the other manuscripts.[11] The variants that are found in Fairfax are in fact no different in kind from the unique readings found in the other early copies. There is no necessary reason to attribute any of these directly to the author; instead, some of the characteristics of what we now call 'recension three' appear to be merely scribal variants of the most conventional sort.

There are a few other peculiarities in Fairfax that are a bit more significant than these because they create somewhat greater differences between 'recension three' and 'recension one', and because they raise a little more clearly the problem of the relationship between the poet and his scribes. There are a small number of passages in the Prologue and Book I, amounting to forty-two lines altogether, that do not appear in other early 'first recension' copies; and there are also an unusually large number of corrections over erasure. The corrections, which occur at the rate of about one per folio, would appear to provide the best evidence that Gower himself oversaw this copy.[12] Though there may be an unusual amount of

---

[9] Macaulay, II, cxxxv–cxxxvii, clx–clxv.

[10] Some typical examples of rejected readings, all from Book I: 130, 227, 234, 266, 281, 293, 294, 335, 349, 355, 374, 377, 397, 454, 458, 584.

[11] For example: Prol. 267; I, 160, 232, 294, 582 *mar.*, 1966, 2511, 2796 *mar.*, 2801; II, 1133, 1285, 1809, 2369, 2733, 3204 *mar.*; III, 355, 2207 *mar.*, 2248, 2436, 2478; IV, 30, 1519 *mar.*; V, 2162, 2690, 4717, 4739, 5035, 6046; VI, 531; VIII, 994, 1836, 2098, 2653. There are also many instances (e.g. I, 2179) in which Macaulay retains a questionable reading from Fairfax that also has other independent support. In the absence of a complete collation of all of these copies it is impossible to say which departs from the generally attested reading least often.

[12] As examples of the frequency of correction, erasures occur at the following places in Book I: 75–9, 132, 222–7, 365, 444, 446, 448, 474, 525, 625, 897, 920, 925, 944, 1077, 1436, 1572, 1696, 1801, 2051, 2066, 2193, 2213, 2313, 2315–16, 2330, 2507, 2622, 2644, 2705, 2713–14, 2973, 3069, 3423. There are also several other less certain instances. At I, 625 the scribe rubbed so hard that he made a hole in the page, taking out the *g* in *singe* (I, 495) on the other side. On the corrections see also Macaulay, II, clix.

rewriting in Fairfax, however, rewriting over erasure is not at all uncommon, even in manuscripts of no authority whatever.[13] In nearly all instances, moreover, the rewritten passages in Fairfax are supported by the other manuscripts of the poem to which it is most closely related, and therefore indicate nothing other than the scribe's own correction from his exemplar. The more important instances are those in which the rewritten passage is not supported by independent copies because they might provide evidence of actual revision, but these are very few: three single words (Prol. 336; VII, 1640 *ver.* 4; 1984 *ver.* 2), two of them in Latin and all well within the capacity of a scribe; and three couplets (I, 2713–14; IV, 1321–2; and IV, 1361–2) in which the scribe has rewritten most but not all of the two lines. One of these is the passage in the tale of Rosiphelee that was made famous, as an instance of Gower's revision, by C. S. Lewis:[14]

> The beautee faye upon hir face,
> Non erthely thing it may desface.
>
> (IV, 1321–2)

It is very difficult to assess this revision without knowing exactly what was originally written underneath. There is nothing at all unique about it, however, for we have dozens of other examples of short passages rewritten by scribes after some sort of damage to the text.[15] If this were not Fairfax we would conclude that in these instances too the scribe was attempting to repair a flaw, especially since in all three couplets a portion of the underlying text has been retained. It is perhaps rash both to disagree with Lewis and to attribute the two most famous lines in the entire poem to a nameless scribe, but we simply lack any evidence that they were dictated by the poet.

The other additions to the text, the forty-two lines in the Prologue and Book I, were not written over erasure and therefore raise different questions about Gower's role, but the six separate passages that were added are not of identical significance. Four of the six (Prol. 495–8, 579–84; I, 1405–6, 2267–74) have no effect whatever on the sense – in two cases, in fact, they are merely padded expansions of shorter passages that occur in the other manuscripts – and they illustrate instead one of the problems that the scribes faced when copying the poem, the necessity of making some provision for the initials of various sizes that break up the text. All four occur at the end of one of Genius' moral discussions, and all serve only to make it possible to place the large three- or four-line initial that begins the next section at the very top of the following column.[16] If

[13] British Library MS Harley 3490 (Macaulay's H_1), for instance, a very late copy of 'recension one', also contains numerous erasures.
[14] C. S. Lewis, *The Allegory of Love* (London, 1936), p. 204.
[15] See the list in my essay on 'Gower's Revisions', pp. 134–5 and p. 142, nn. 45–8.
[16] There may have been a similar insertion in Stafford; see note 33, below.

Gower himself took so close an interest in the preparation of Fairfax that he troubled over the placement of the initials then he might also have been responsible for the many corrections. But since these additional passages are in the original scribe's hand and are not written over erasure, we would have to imagine Gower looking directly over the scribe's shoulder as he wrote. It is more likely that the scribe copied these passages from his exemplar, which requires, however, both that he was following its column arrangement exactly, and that the exemplar had illuminations of precisely the same size as those in Fairfax at the beginning of the Prologue and Book I. Since it is not likely that the author's copy had illuminations of any sort, the scribe's exemplar thus brings us no closer to Gower himself. It is thus easiest to believe that these passages were added by either an editor or a scribe, and it is quite possible that they were original to Fairfax itself.[17]

The other two insertions are not so easily accounted for. The more important is a passage of sixteen lines that has been added to the tale of Narcissus (I, 2343–58) which is of notably better quality than the other insertions. Interestingly enough, the new text does have an effect upon the layout, for with the insertion the tale now occupies precisely one manuscript page, beginning with the large initial in the upper left-hand corner of f. 21. If this long passage were added only for the layout then it would be equally difficult to attribute to the poet since he could not have foreseen exactly where on the page the tale would begin. The very length of the passage suggests a different purpose and that it is indeed authoritative, but it is still not clear how it came to be inserted into this copy. On the very next page there is another four-line insertion into the penitent's response (I, 2369–72) that makes no significant addition to the sense but that cannot be explained in terms of layout or the placement of initials. If these two passages are genuinely authorial then they must have been present in the scribe's exemplar, and indeed represent either an earlier or a revised stage in the history of the text. In that, they pose the most interesting problem of all, for they belong in the same category as the similar additional passages in Books V and VII that characterise 'recension two'.[18] What is most striking about these passages is that no one manuscript contains them all: the most significant revisions of the text occur separately and in copies that are evidently independent of one another. The variations represent either authorial alterations occurring at different times, or scribal access to

---

[17] The situation is complicated by the presence of the last of these passages (I, 2267–74), plus the two additions to the tale of Narcissus discussed below, in Harley 3490 (H_1), a late and not very reliable copy of 'recension one' with sporadic affinities to Fairfax. See Macaulay, II, cxxxiii, cxlii–cxliii. There are several textual differences in the passages in question, and the additions in H_1 are without any effect on the layout of the page. The relation between these two manuscripts is still not clear. H_1 may be a mixed copy, deriving in part from Fairfax itself before it was transformed, or it may indicate that Fairfax itself is derived from an earlier exemplar with these additions.

[18] See note 26, below.

different portions of a revised exemplar. If Gower himself was responsible for the different selection of passages in each copy we still do not know in what order the differing versions first occurred: even the dates of the manuscripts, if they were known precisely, would provide no certainty since any copy might have come from an intermediary source. And if the alterations were instead chosen by the scribes from the author's papers, then no single manuscript represents the poem exactly as Gower left it. The manuscripts provide proof that the text of the poem evolved, but no evidence on the precise steps in that evolution.

There is thus an enormous amount of uncertainty both about the origin of Fairfax and about its relation to the poet's copy, but for that reason it illustrates some of the most important problems in the textual history of the poem. It also suggests two important observations: first that an individual manuscript may contain variations that are due only to the special circumstances of its production; and second, that the text itself has a history apart from the manuscripts in which it is now contained. Now this is the manuscript, with its altered 'recension one' text and its scribal additions and alterations, that was later transformed by the substitution of the new prologue and epilogue. There is no apparent link between this revision and the earlier changes, but the alteration raises very much the same sorts of problems, concerning the nature and origin of the newly added passages, and exactly who was responsible for the substitution.

There is no reason to think that either the new prologue or the new epilogue was composed especially for Fairfax. Both bear dates, in the text or the margin, that place them in the early 1390s, when Gower may have first presented a copy of the poem to Henry of Lancaster, later Henry IV.[19] The epilogue, moreover, bears evidence of more than a single layer of composition. One of the changes is the removal of the compliment to Chaucer that precedes the final prayer (VIII, 2941–70). In rewriting it, Gower very carefully substituted a passage of exactly the same number of lines, suggesting that when he did so he did not wish to disturb the main body of the epilogue that follows. We cannot tell, of course, whether it was the Ricardian epilogue or the Lancastrian version at that point; only that the two changes seem to have been made at different times. One of the more interesting parts of the textual history of the poem takes place, therefore, well before the transformation of Fairfax. The Fairfax scribes inherited these passages fully written sometime after Henry's accession. They recognised the timeliness of the new dedication, and by this time Chaucer himself may no longer have been alive, making the compliment to him somewhat moot. The decision was made to bring the manuscript that had been prepared at such great cost up to date, and the scribes did so: by

---

[19] Prol. 23–4 *mar.*, 25; VIII, 2973–4 *mar.* On the circumstances of the presentation see my article on 'The Dedications of Gower's *Confessio Amantis*', *Mediaevalia*, forthcoming.

substituting the new beginning and end; by adding some marginal notes to the events referred to in the prologue; by adding some of Gower's shorter works, in Latin and French, at the end of the book; and by providing an updated colophon.[20]

The most intriguing aspect of this revision is that both scribes are thought to have worked on other manuscripts of Gower. The first, who did most of the revised epilogue, is also credited with the Trentham MS (now British Library Add. 59495) which contains, among other works, our only copy of the *Cinquante Ballades*. This scribe can be recognised not only from his hand but also from his orthography, which differs from Gower's in several obvious regards.[21] The other, who finished the epilogue and made all of the other additions, worked with several other copyists on at least four manuscripts of the *Vox Clamantis*, which needed even more badly to be updated once Henry IV came to the throne.[22] The work of these scribes certainly indicates a closeness to Gower and some sort of access to good exemplars of his work. Gower's authorship of the revised prologue and epilogue has never been in question, however. What is in question is whether the Fairfax manuscript, transformed as it is, represents Gower's own fixed and final intention for his poem, and in that regard the scribal evidence is simply not very helpful. We still do not know enough about the scribes who produced the revised copies of the *Vox Clamantis*. They appear to have been much more closely organised than the group studied by Doyle and Parkes, but all four manuscripts of the *Vox* on which they collaborated contain some unmistakable allusion to the poet's death,[23] making it necessary to believe that someone other than Gower supervised their work, at least at its completion; and there are still some very complicated problems in the textual history of the poem similar to those in the *Confessio* that are not made simpler by our knowledge of the association of these scribes.[24] Fairfax, of course, might well have been revised before Gower's death, but even so Gower's supervision of these scribes is

[20] Macaulay, II, clvii–clviii.

[21] See Macaulay, I, lxxix; III, 548, 550–51. Macaulay's judgement on the identity of the scribes is accepted by M. L. Samuels and J. J. Smith, 'The Language of Gower', *Neuphilologische Mitteilungen*, 82 (1981), 295.

[22] See the description of the *Vox Clamantis* manuscripts in Macaulay, IV, lx–lxv.

[23] Of the four early manuscripts of the *Vox*: *G* contains a drawing of the poet's tomb with verses on his death (printed by Macaulay, IV, 367); *C* and *H* bear a shorter but similar request for prayers for his soul (IV, 367); all three of these refer to the life of the poet in the past tense ('Dum vixit') in the title to 'O Deus Immense' (IV, 362); *C*, *H*, and also *S* bear a colophon that contains the words 'dum vixit' (IV, 360). Macaulay (IV, 419) believed that the words 'dum vixit' might have been written by Gower himself, but see Doyle and Parkes, pp. 163–4, n. 3.

[24] No two of these manuscripts are precisely alike either in contents or arrangement, and though the same scribes can be found working in all four, their tasks differed from one copy to another, suggesting that there was no consistent direction of the revision and frustrating any attempt to decide which of these best represents Gower's final intention for the *Vox Clamantis*.

no more certain than it is in the case of the Latin manuscripts, especially since his own blindness evidently followed very closely upon Henry's accession.[25] There are indications, moreover, that even if Gower himself was the editor, he intended something much less than a wholesale revision of the poem. For in 'updating' Fairfax the scribes used passages that had been written at least seven to ten years before, rather than inserting a new dedication to the king; and the alterations occur only at the very beginning and at the very end, the two places obviously most convenient for the scribe. What we have, then, is not an entirely new edition of the poem but simply the refurbishing of a valuable commercial product, given the new political circumstances of the early 1400s. Rather like the short passages that were added for the sake of the following initial, the transformation has all the character of a unique accommodation made for this particular manuscript at the particular time that it was revised.

What we now call the 'third recension', then, is merely the accidental product of several different layers of textual history, of corrections, of additions, of transformations, all occurring during the preparation of one particularly costly manuscript but in none of which is Gower's own hand absolutely clear; which became an identifiable 'version' of the poem not from the circumstances of its origin but from the fact that it happened to be recopied. To conclude any differently is to confuse the history of this manuscript with the history of the text. Even its recopying was evidently an accident of its history. It is clear why a later scribe might have chosen it, as both a careful and a current text, but there is no support for Macaulay's suggestion (II, cxxx) that Gower himself prepared it for use as an exemplar. The later surviving copies that derive from Fairfax are all written by scribes well outside his circle, and it is clear that the recopying at least was well beyond his control. It is necessary to reconsider, therefore, exactly what we mean by 'recension'. If we mean a text that whatever its origin appears nearly uniformly in later copies then it is permissible to go on using the term. But that is not what Macaulay meant, and the exact meaning of 'recension' has important consequences both for the history of the poem and for the choice of manuscript for our edition.

'Recension two', as Macaulay defined it, is a great deal more complicated than 'recension three'. It is made up of a group of manuscripts that share a number of important similarities and additions to the text. But while some of these similarities – for instance, the accidental loss of exactly one column of text near the end of Book V – suggest that there was a common original exemplar from which they all derive, we do not have that exemplar as we do in 'recension three'; its relation to Gower's own copy is all the more unclear; and the manuscripts in this group are otherwise very diverse,

---

[25] In the first year of Henry's reign Gower alludes to his loss of sight, and in the second year he describes himself as *cecus*, 'blind'. See the Latin verses printed by Macaulay, IV, 365–6.

dividing in fact into two subgroups according to the selection and arrangement of the additional passages that identify the group as a whole.[26] The
relations among these copies are the thorniest of all the remaining problems
in the text of the *Confessio*. It is not yet possible to resolve all of the
difficulties in the origin of this recension, but there are a few things one
may say about the form in which it now survives.

The earliest known copy of this recension is the Stafford manuscript, one
of the most formal and most ornate of all of the surviving manuscripts of
the poem. Stafford shares with Fairfax that suspicion of having been
supervised by the poet. The evidence lies in its high quality and in the
armorial devices that it bears on its opening page – perhaps its most famous
feature – which suggest that it was prepared for presentation to a member
of the royal family. Macaulay concluded that it was written, under Gower's
supervision, between 1397 and 1399 for Henry of Bolingbroke, who is also
of course named in the dedication.[27] His view of the text that it contains
must be partly reconstructed by inference: he believed that 'recension two'
took form in the early 1390s, alongside of 'recension one';[28] that it reached
its final form in 1393, the date named in the dedication, with the presentation to Henry;[29] and that Stafford is a new copy prepared at the end of the
decade, just before Henry became king. He again treated the variations
among the different manuscripts as the stages in the poet's own revision,
though he was required in this case to take Stafford, the earliest copy, as
the representative of the last step in the creation of 'recension two'. There
are enormous problems here, particularly with the later manuscripts which
he thought embodied the earlier stage of revision.[30] His assumptions,
moreover, both that this form of the poem evolved that early in the
decade, and that the evolution can be reconstructed from the copies that
we have, do not bear up under a close examination of Stafford.

The first problem is posed by Macaulay's dating. His conclusion is
unlikely, not because the devices on the page are necessarily inappropriate
to Henry at the time he named but because anyone wishing to designate
Henry before he became king would not have done so in this way. The only
time when these particular devices in combination might have been used is
after Henry's coronation, and then Henry himself is not the only possible
designee.[31] Macaulay's belief that 'recension two' as we have it came
before 'recension three' rests largely on the dating of Stafford before

---

[26] See Macaulay, II, cxxviii–cxxix, cxxxiii–cxxxv.
[27] Macaulay, II, clii–cliii; *CHEL*, II, 512. See also Fisher, pp. 124–5.
[28] Macaulay, II, cxxix, cxxxiii.
[29] *CHEL*, II, 176.
[30] See my essay on 'Gower's Revisions', pp. 137–9.
[31] The argument for a date after 1399 will be presented in a forthcoming article by myself and
D'A. J. D. Boulton.

Fairfax; and if Stafford is later, much of the neatness of his account of the
textual history is destroyed.

It is also quite difficult to believe that Gower himself supervised this
copy, for however ornate it is, it has not been corrected, and the quality of
its text, though good in a relative sense, does not provide the slightest
evidence that it has been reviewed by the poet. The scribe himself is very
careful: in two important passages, for instance, he preserves very carefully
some of the peculiarities of orthography of his exemplar. His care here,
and the overall quality of his work, suggest that many of the faults that we
find – the loss of lines, the omission of many glosses, some obvious
misreadings – were already present in his exemplar, removing us one step
further from Gower himself.

The most interesting aspect of Stafford, however, is the evidence that it
too, like Fairfax, is a composite created rather late in the history of the
poem. The evidence lies in the differences in orthography in the revised
prologue and epilogue. These differences are especially noticeable in the
prologue, which also contains a higher than usual incidence of error which
the Stafford scribe evidently copied fully faithfully,[32] a remarkable circum-
stance if we believe that Gower himself had this copy prepared specially for
the dedicatee. It appears instead that Stafford was derived from an
exemplar much like Fairfax, that was written by more than one hand and
that had been altered at the beginning and the end by someone whose
spelling was different from the poet's.

The spelling of this reviser, moreover, is in all important respects
identical to that of the first revising hand in Fairfax, which opens up the
possibility that the same scribe was involved. Stafford was not derived
directly from Fairfax, of course, for the peculiarities of spelling are most
evident in Stafford's prologue, which in Fairfax was written by the other
scribe; and in any case orthography would provide a remarkably slim basis
for a new theory of the development of the text. The resemblance is most
interesting, not as evidence of direct affiliation, but when taken with all of
the other suggestions that the two manuscripts are the products of the same
milieu. For they have a great many other similarities: in page layout; in the
hierarchy of initials; and in the identical size and positioning of the
illuminations, which as Jeremy Griffiths has pointed out can have an

---

[32] The obvious differences in the prologue are a very different distribution of *i* and *y*; use of *i*
or *y* for unstressed *e* (e.g. *mannys*, l. 14); use of *gh* or *ʒ* where Fairfax normally has *h* (e.g.
tauʒt, l. 3, *knyghthode*, l. 89; *rigthwisnesse* in l. 109 may indicate that the *gh* spelling was
unfamiliar to the scribe); use of *u* for *o* (e.g. *schulde*, l. 43); and double *p* in *uppon* (ll. 27, 83,
125, 143). There are also exceptions to these irregular spellings on the same page. Compare
Macaulay, II, 548, on the spelling of the second scribe of Fairfax. More substantial differences
in the prologue occur in lines 15 (*Tho* for *To*, not noted by Macaulay); 29–30 (two lines
omitted); 49 (*tirantie* for *tirannie*); 51 (*is* for *was*); 63 (*Tho* for *To*); 92 *ver*. 2 (*antunas* for
antiquas, *urbe* for *orbe*); and 113 (*world* for *word*). In Book VIII, 2938–3146, the only
consistent departure from Gower's normal spelling is the use of *i* or *y* in unstressed syllables.

independent value in establishing the relations between copies.[33] They are also very similar in some accommodations that were made for the late copying of the text. For like Fairfax, Stafford contains at least two new additions to the marginal glosses in the prologue that have the same apparent purpose, of setting the historical context for Gower's harshest criticisms of his society by linking them to events that took place in the past.[34]

The total picture here is consistent. Stafford, like Fairfax, appears to be a complex product of several layers of revision, and reveals just as clearly as Fairfax the number of circumstances that go into the creation of a good manuscript of a long and important poem. It appears, moreover, to be a late product, created by the need to revise the poem after Henry's accession to the throne. Stafford is not directly derived, therefore, from the 1393–4 presentation copy for Henry, and is no better an indication of the form in which Henry first saw the poem than Fairfax is. If in fact it was produced after Fairfax then it has an arguably better claim to represent Gower's final intention for the poem. But even more importantly it confirms that speculation about the 'final' form involves too many prejudgements about the relations between these copies and Gower's own exemplar, and that we need to see each manuscript instead as a unique product compiled from available material under circumstances that we will probably never be able to reconstruct precisely.

Fairfax and Stafford provide only two examples of how the surviving condition of the *Confessio Amantis*, particularly in the 'revised' versions, was shaped by the scribes and editors who were responsible for making copies in the period following Henry's accession. If we include the manuscripts of the *Vox Clamantis*, with their many alterations, and the later

[33] Jeremy Griffiths, ' "Confessio Amantis": The Poem and its Pictures', in A. J. Minnis, ed., *Gower's* Confessio Amantis: *Responses and Reassessments* (Cambridge, 1983), p. 168. The leaf containing the opening of Book I in Stafford has been lost, and Griffiths is non-committal about the appearance of a second miniature. However, the number of lines missing from Book I (including the Latin verses) indicates that the scribe left a space of sixteen lines at the head of the second column of the recto, precisely the same size as the space now occupied by the miniature in Fairfax. Another thirty-four lines are missing from the end of the prologue, which are not enough to fill up the first column of the page. With the addition of the normal two lines for Explicit and Incipit there was evidently a ten-line space at the bottom of this column, insufficient for the miniature but awkward if left entirely blank. The scribe's solution may be preserved in Sidney Sussex College Cambridge MS △.4.1, which contains an obviously spurious ten-line passage at the end of the prologue (printed by Macaulay, II, 466). This MS is closely related to Stafford; Macaulay's argument (II, cliv) that it was not 'derived' from Stafford proves only that it was not copied directly, and it may well be descended by way of an intermediary. If this passage was in fact first added in Stafford to fill in the space then it is similar in function to the insertions made in the prologue and Book I of Fairfax, and provides additional evidence not only of the closeness in milieu of these two manuscripts but also of the absence of authorial supervision of the copying.

[34] Prol. 91, 331. Fairfax also has an addition at Prol. 194, where Stafford is lacking a leaf. See the discussion of these additions in my essay on 'The Dedications of Gower's *Confessio Amantis*', note 19, above.

manuscripts of 'recension two', in which editorial influence is even more apparent and in which we consequently find some quite odd arrangements of the text, then we have four different types of collaboration between poet and scribe represented here, all complicating our attempts to derive a single best notion of Gower's poem. The most obvious conclusion is merely on the side of caution: where Macaulay saw each form in which the poem survives as another stage in Gower's shaping of the text, we must instead look at the history of each manuscript individually and consider the diversity of influences on each scribe and editor before using these manuscripts as evidence of the poet's intentions. The caution applies even if we still suspect that Gower himself might have commissioned one or more of these copies, for there is still a vast difference btween the role of author and the role of editor. The surviving copies suggest that there may have been a variety of newly written passages available for later use, and that Gower's own exemplar was rather unorganised. They also suggest a particular need to provide a text that was current with political reality. From this situation our different versions evolved. The principal consequence for our understanding of the textual history is that we have to set aside the notion of 'recensions' as the basis for understanding Gower's revision of the poem. The 'recensions' are versions that were assembled in response to some immediate need, and then happen to have been recopied. They have no necessary relation to the process of revision, and that revision did not necessarily take place in the stages that are embodied in the copies that we have. It is also clear that the *Confessio* poses a special challenge for Gower's next modern editor, who will have to take into account both the original state and the later revision of the poem, without being able to resort to the chimera of Gower's 'final' intention. Ideally a new edition ought to reflect the unfixed nature of the text, and no single manuscript can do that on its own. As a practical matter, we may be obliged to select one manuscript as a base, and Fairfax, despite the complexity of its history, is still a defensible choice. This is of course the manuscript that Macaulay chose, though perhaps for the wrong reasons and though he presented it as something that it is not. To end upon a note of humility, however, our new edition might not in the end be very different from his. The principal difference might only be that we know a bit more about what we are doing, and have a somewhat different notion of the relationship between our edited text and Gower's conception of his poem.

EDITING *THE WARS OF ALEXANDER*

Thorlac Turville-Petre

There have been many interesting discussions of editorial theory, but practising editors are generally obliged to restrict an account of what they have done to a few paragraphs in their introduction headed 'This Edition'. It may be that an editor's report of the experience of editing is of more practical value to other editors than some of the more general enunciations of principle. Every text faces the editor with different problems, to which, in the end, every editor has to find individual solutions, but in my own experience it has been instructive to examine the range of solutions applied by editors to a wide variety of texts, and to consider whether their solutions might be applicable elsewhere. I have often wished that editors had room to explain in more detail the steps that they took. It is for this reason that I welcome the opportunity to offer these reflections on the experience of working on the long alliterative poem *The Wars of Alexander*.[1]

The fundamental decision that the editor needs to take concerns the nature of the edition. It is, of course, quite legitimate to reproduce the documentary form of the work as it exists in one of the manuscripts, as long as that aim is clearly stated and the editor explains his reasons for adopting such a course. There may also be circumstances where it is justifiable to attempt to recreate the readings of the common archetype of the surviving manuscripts. For most editors of literary texts, however, neither of these will be a final objective, but only a step on the path towards a critical edition, that is to say the re-creation of the author's intended text in most respects and as far as possible. 'In most respects', because editors go further in some particulars, by transforming into print what was originally in manuscript, expanding abbreviations, perhaps removing the yoghs and thorns that catch at the soft-skinned modern reader, and usually supplying modern punctuation. 'As far as possible', because the ideal of reproducing

---

[1] *The Wars of Alexander*, ed. H. N. Duggan and T. Turville-Petre, EETS (forthcoming). Line references are to this edition. Skeat's numbering is thoroughly eccentric. Our ll. 1–845 vary from Skeat's by no more than 1, but to calculate Skeat's later line-numbers subtract between 123 and 126 from our 846–5803. The arguments of this paper are based on our joint work for the edition and on discussions I have had with Professor Duggan, in particular about his metrics project.

the authorial spellings and morphology is almost never attainable.[2] Too often, though, editors assume that because there is no possibility of achieving such an aim, they do not need to reflect on the consequences of their failure to do so, for failure it is.

In some cases the prospects of recovering the authorial text would seem to be so very dim as to be hardly worth considering. In the case of *The Wars of Alexander* there are just two manuscripts: Ashmole 44 (referred to hereafter as A) and Trinity College, Dublin, 213 (hereafter D). Manuscript A is the earlier, from the mid-fifteenth century; D is from the end of the century. Both are copied by northern scribes; in fact the D scribe can be located in or near Durham. Neither manuscript is complete; A lacks 123 lines within the text and has lost the last few hundred lines, while D has a total of 2814 lines, a little under half the text. The A scribe is apparently more careful and accurate, and this impression is confirmed by the evidence to be discussed. Ashmole is the obvious manuscript to select for copy-text in those sections where both manuscripts are present.

Thus for half the poem there is only one manuscript, and where there are two the readings differ frequently. It is evident that both texts contain numerous scribal alterations, both mechanical (with words omitted, added or substituted), and also deliberate (most pervasively in the matter of dialect). The evidence of alliteration and relict forms strongly suggests that the poet was from the North West Midlands, perhaps Lancashire.[3] However the A scribe presents a remarkably consistent dialect translation, and the D text is also predominantly in the scribal dialect. So the task facing an editor attempting to recover the authorial text is a daunting one. Skeat, the previous editor, printed the two texts on facing pages, maintaining a very high level of accuracy.[4] He introduced sporadic emendations into the A text, and suggested improvements in footnotes and in his glossary.[5] Many editors might reasonably think that this was the best that could be done in such unfavourable circumstances. Rightly or wrongly, however, Professor Duggan and I believed that there was enough evidence to permit the establishment of a critical text, one that is demonstrably better than that of either manuscript, and at some points closer to the poet than their common archetype.

The crucial factor in the establishment of the authorial text is the

---

[2] For discussion of an exceptional case, see D. C. Greetham, 'Normalisation of Accidentals in Middle English Texts: The Paradox of Thomas Hoccleve', *Studies in Bibliography*, 38 (1985), 121–50; see also his essay above.

[3] G. Ronberg, 'The Two Manuscripts of *The Wars of Alexander*: A Linguistic Comparison', *Neophilologus*, 69 (1985), 604–10, concludes that there is no evidence of a West Midland original, but he has not seen the full discussion in our edition.

[4] *The Wars of Alexander*, ed. W. W. Skeat, EETS, ES 47 (1886).

[5] Many other emendations were suggested by J. B. Henneman, *Untersuchungen über das mittelenglische Gedicht 'Wars of Alexander'* (Berlin, 1889); and H. Steffens, *Versbau und Sprache des mittelenglischen stabreimenden Gedichtes 'The Wars of Alexander'* (Bonn, 1901).

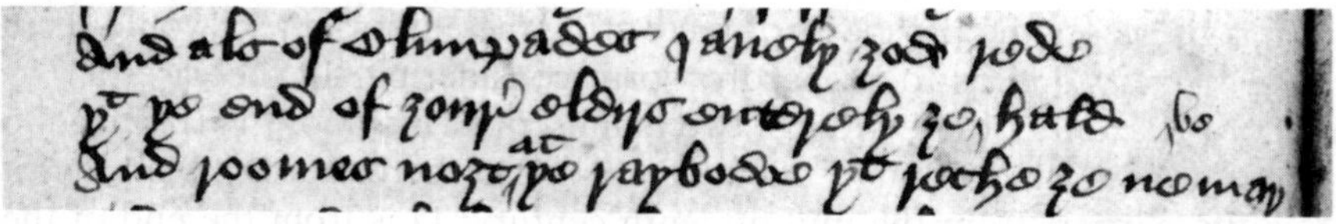

Fig. 1.

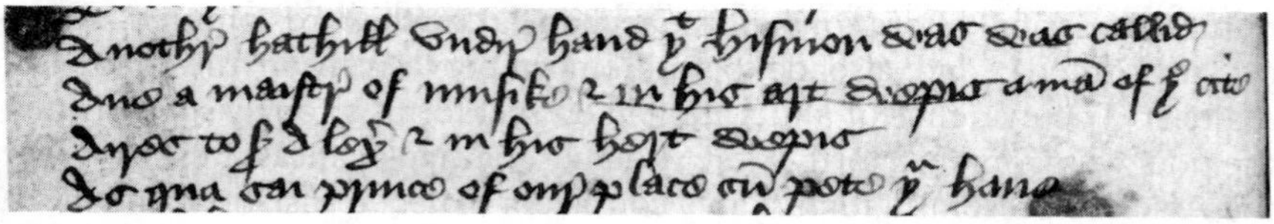

Fig. 2.

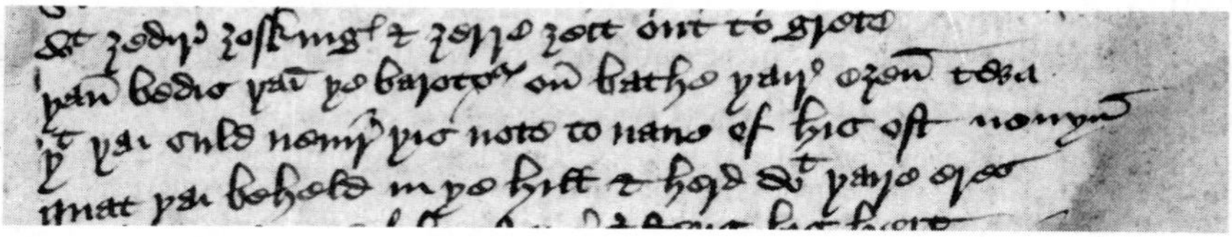

Fig. 3.

relationship between the two manuscripts, for though neither is particularly accurate, each differs from the other in ways that suggest that their archetype was extremely accurate. Only a handful of errors seem likely to be archetypal, and all of them could be examples of coincidental variation. There is no evidence of contamination, and it may well be that there were never many manuscripts for the scribes to contaminate from. Comparison of the two manuscripts made it possible to establish the text of half the poem with some confidence; once this had been done, we could then proceed to apply what we had learnt about the poet's practice and that of the scribes to that half of the poem for which only one manuscript survives.

A manuscript is properly chosen as copy-text because it most closely represents the dialect of the author, but neither of the manuscripts of the *Wars* qualified in this respect. Readings introduced into the text were given the forms and spelling-system of the copy-text, A, though we were uneasily aware that this involved distortions that were at times significant, which could not be handled satisfactorily or consistently. For example, the poet used two forms of the verb 'give' for alliteration, one with initial /j/ and one with /g/. Some of the /j/ forms were preserved by the scribes, but others were altered to the /g/ forms characteristic of northern dialects. It seemed reasonable to emend *geue* to *ȝeue* where necessary for the alliteration. However, we did not alter the frequent A spellings of 'catch' with initial *ch-*, even though the alliteration is always on /k/, nor did we alter the form *castite* alliterating on /tʃ/. These are illustrations of the kind of compromise involved in the unsatisfactory but inevitable situation of presenting a text in a dialect that is quite different from that of the author's. It is of even more significance that the grammatical forms of the poet are irrecoverable. These are generally referred to airily as 'accidentals', but they may at times be substantive. For example, the syllabic *-en* ending of the infinitive verb is very occasionally found in A, but rather more commonly in D. Probably such endings derive from the archetype, and perhaps, though not necessarily, from the poet. As I shall explain below, we came to the conclusion that the rhythm of the alliterative line was metrically significant, and yet in most cases we were unable to be sure whether the poet intended an *-en* or not.

Frequently the two manuscripts present variant readings neither of which is self-evidently corrupt. In such cases we drew on a wide variety of evidence to point to the better reading; we then used the cumulative evidence of postulated right readings to distinguish the poet's practice from that of the scribes, and with that information we were better equipped to suggest conjectural emendations in the situation where only one manuscript was present or where both were presumed corrupt. Of all evidence we had to draw on, the most valuable was the reading of the Latin source, the *Historia de Preliis*. Skeat had realised that the *Wars* was dependent upon the Latin work, but he used a text of the Latin that differed considerably from the poet's, and so failed to understand how very closely the poet was translating for much of the time.[6] This was a major handicap to him, for we were able to use the Latin as a running commentary on the English, always guiding the interpretation of the poem and the establishment of the text.[7] However, there were two reasons for exercising caution in this matter. Firstly, the *Wars* is a poetic translation, in which the poet feels free to expand on his source or occasionally to abbreviate it, though very rarely to say something quite different from it. Secondly, the Latin manuscript that the poet used is no longer extant, and therefore his source differed in certain respects from any text of the Latin now available. The relationship between the many manuscripts of the Latin is complex (see diagram), though there is a group of manuscripts copied in England that present a text that must be very close to the one the poet used.

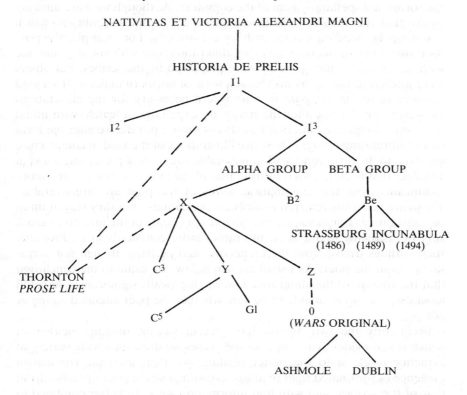

[6] See H. N. Duggan, 'The Source of the Middle English *The Wars of Alexander*', *Speculum*, 51 (1976), 624–36.

[7] For some discussion of the principles involved, see D. C. Greetham, 'Models for the Textual Transmission of Translation: The Case of John Trevisa', *Studies in Bibliography*, 37 (1984), 131–55. A number of the poet's techniques are briefly discussed by D. A. Lawton, 'The Middle English Alliterative *Alexander A* and *C*: Form and Style in Translation from Latin Prose', *Studia Neophilologica*, 53 (1981), 259–68.

All the versions of the Latin derive from the *Nativitas et Victoria Alexandri Magni,* a translation by Leo of Naples of the Greek *Pseudo-Callisthenes.*[8] The three interpolated versions of Leo are known collectively as the *Historia de Preliis:* I[1], and (independently derived from that) I[2] and I[3]. Forty-five manuscripts of I[3] have been identified, and its editor, K. Steffens – though basing his argument insecurely on only seven variants – has distinguished two families, Alpha and Beta.[9] Steffens' printed text is from Berlin MS lat. oct. 49 (B[2]) in the Alpha group. The text that Skeat used for comparison with the *Wars* was the Strassburg print of 1489, derived from, or at least closely related to, Bern Universitätsbibliothek MS 247 (Be) in the Beta group. The manuscript followed by the author of the *Wars* is closely related to a distinct set of manuscripts represented by St John's College, Cambridge, MS 184 (C[3]), Cambridge University Library MS Mm.5.14 (C[5]) and Glasgow University Library MS Hunterian 84 (Gl), though the poet's source was not quite as corrupt as they are. Therefore, in order to establish the readings of X, the common ancestor of C[3], C[5], Gl and the lost Latin manuscript (Z) used by the poet, it is necessary to refer to the readings of the Alpha family, and for purposes of comparison, to the readings of the Beta family and the I[1] recension from which the I[3] recension is derived. In practice, though, it was very rarely necessary to go beyond B[2], C[3], C[5] and Gl. An English text of some comparative value is *The Prose Life of Alexander* extant in the Thornton manuscript, Lincoln Cathedral MS 91.[10] This was translated from an I[3] text very similar to that used by the *Wars* poet, but the author also apparently drew on a text of the I[1] recension.

The relationship of the *Wars* to particular manuscripts of the *Historia de Preliis* is determined by numerous readings. Olympias' request to Anectanebus 'þat scho myȝt wetirly wete þe *will* of all þingis' (304) shows that the poet's source had not the B[2] reading 'omnem pandas *veritatem*', 'reveal the whole truth', but the corruption *voluntatem* in C[3] and related manuscripts. Similarly, Alexander, refusing to pay tribute to Darius, tells him that the 'lefe hen þat laide hire *first* egg' (1016) is now barren, which is prompted by the reading *antea* in C[3]; but the Latin author was referring to the story of the golden egg, 'ova *aurea*'. Olympias very oddly tells her lover that she will 'cherische þe with chere as þou my child were' (368). The poet's source presumably had the C[5] reading, 'quasi puerum te habebo', which in turn is an attempt to make grammatical sense of the reading of C[3] and Gl, which have 'pueri'; but the reading of B[2], 'quasi patrem pueri te habebo' shows that *patrem* has dropped out of the tradition. Olympias thus

---

[8] See G. Cary, *The Medieval Alexander* (Cambridge, 1956), pp. 9–11, 38, 43–4, 52.
[9] *Die Historia de preliis Alexandri Magni: Rezension J[3]*, ed. K. Steffens (Meisenheim am Glan, 1975), pp. xxv–xxviii.
[10] *The Prose Life of Alexander*, ed. J. S. Westlake, EETS, 143 (1913).

tells her lover, reasonably enough, that she will treat him as the *father* of her child – which, of course, he is.

The forms of place-names are particularly open to corruption in medieval manuscripts, and it is often necessary to trace them back through the stemma to discover what was intended. The place that is named *Capho Resey* in the *Wars* (1201) is *Tapho Resei* in C3, with the common misreading of *c* for *t*. B2 has *Thaphoseri,* which goes back to *Tafosiri* in the *Nativitas,* explained by Julius Valerius as 'the tomb of Osiris' (from Gk ταφος, 'tomb'). The English poet's *Detiraty* (5722) depends on the same *c/t* confusion, since C3 has *Deciracy.* This in turn is a corruption of *dicitur Titan* in B2 and the I1 recension (perhaps from a misreading of the abbreviation for *dicitur*). Here the Thornton *Prose Life* shows dependence on two manuscripts of the Latin, since it calls the place 'Cytan or Deciracy' (p. 107).

On very numerous occasions the source determines the choice between variant readings in the *Wars.* As a straightforward example, Darius on his deathbed warns Alexander that if a man forgets God, *wickidnes* (D: *wrychednes)* (3406) will be the result. The D reading must be right, since the Latin has *miserie.* So, too, Darius is not *at hame* (A), but *in hys trone* (D) (3116), translating 'in trono suo'. Variation between *thole* (A) and *dele* (D) in l. 1139 can only be resolved by reference to the source, since either makes excellent sense. Alexander's soldiers complain that they are too old 'strakis to *thole/dele*', that is, either 'to suffer misfortunes' (A) or, apparently more probably, 'to deal blows' (D). But A's *thole* is right, since C3 and B2 both have 'angustias substinere' (a phrase not included in many other manuscripts of the Latin).

At first sight the D reading at line 2590 makes poor sense, so that A's line seems evidently right. In D, Alexander warns his enemies 'þat þe ende of your elders enterly ȝe holden'. The A scribe copies out this line and then corrects what seems to be an obvious error by inserting *be* in front of *hald: enterely ȝe be-hald,* 'behold the end of your ancestors' (Fig. 1). However, the Latin shows that this is a misinterpretation, for there Alexander warns the Lacedaemonians to keep within the territory established by their forefathers: 'finem quem a vestris antecessoribus accepistis integrum conservetis' (C3, f. 11b). This is what the poet translates, providing an overliteral rendering of *finem,* 'boundary'; but the Latin manuscript in turn is wrong, for other I3 manuscripts have *fidem* in place of *finem.* Originally Alexander admonished his enemies to hold to the *faith* of their ancestors!

In these and many other cases the source is a valuable guide in the choice between the variants. To emend conjecturally on the basis of the source is a more hazardous undertaking, particularly since the exact text of the Latin used by the poet is not ascertainable and in any case the poet is at times rather free in his translation. Nevertheless, some conjectural emendations are convincingly supported by the evidence of the Latin. In a passage extant only in A, the text relates that the god who is to impregnate Olympias will have 'twa tufe hornes' (319). Since this translates 'arietina cornua duo', it seems clear that *tufe* should be corrected to *tupe,* used in the same sense of 'ram' in line 5692. So, too, the gold-plated bills and jaws (*chauyls,* l. 3824) of the artificial birds in Porus' temple must correctly be 'billis and þe clawis', since the Latin has 'rostra et ungule'. Even though the manuscript reading makes sense, it is harder to understand how *ungule* could be translated as 'jaws' than how an original *clawis* could be misread as *chawlis* and transcribed as *chauyls.* In the same way, although 'crestyns of clathe' (4814), 'cloth vessels', makes some sort of sense in the context, the reading of the source, 'vasa lutea', points to 'crestyns of *claye*' as the right reading, with the scribe misinterpreting *y* as *þ*.

On two occasions Alexander is attacked by beasts appearing out of a *marras,* 'marsh' (4021, 4060), yet the Latin at both points reads *arundinetum,* 'thicket of reeds'. A more exact translation would be *marram* (ON *marálmr).* This word is however not recorded in English before the seventeenth century, even though it was presumably in dialect use long before. Therefore, considering also that the poet might reasonably have translated *arundinetum* as 'marsh', we felt unable to make the emendation to *marram.*

Even more caution needs to be exercised over emending, on the basis of the Latin, readings shared by both manuscripts, and yet the argument for doing so is the same, for even manuscripts from a good archetype will share corrupt readings. A straightforward example will illustrate the procedure. A Persian prince writes a letter to his emperor Darius:

> Pan was a man, as me mynes, in þe morne qwile,
> Was of Sire Daris a duke, þe derfe emperoure.
>
> (2896–7)

Though *morne qwile* makes sense, there is no point to it, and since the Latin has 'Inter hec quidam ex principibus Darii imperatoris' (C3, f. 14a), the emendation to *meneqwile* seems secure. In this case an error in the archetype may be suspected, though coincident error is also possible, as is illustrated by the following rather extraordinary example. A Theban musician, hoping to persuade Alexander not to destroy his city, approaches the emperor and 'in his hert wepis' (the reading of both manuscripts in l. 2366). This is only superficially meaningful, for weeping in the heart is not a persuasive argument in a situation that calls for an open display of plangency. The Latin is quite different, for there the musician 'cepit per artem musicam lamentari' (C3, f. 10a), that is, he began to play sorrowful music. A daring conjecture would be 'in his *art* wepis', but few editors would confidently adopt such an elliptical reading. However, the A scribe shows that this must be correct, for he has mistakenly copied out 'in his art wepis' as the b-verse of the previous line, before deleting it and squeezing in the correction at the end of the line (Fig. 2). When he comes to the next line he has had time to consider and reject this odd phrase, and he substitutes the apparently more meaningful *hert* for the *art* in his exemplar. D, or his predecessor, 'corrects' the line in identical fashion. This is, then, a case not of a corrupt archetype but of coincident variation by the two scribes.

My final example of the value of the source is very curious. Darius compares Alexander's progress through Persia to a snowflake blown from a wall, a vivid though puzzlingly inappropriate image:

> Riʒt as a flaw of fell snawe ware fallyn of a ryft (D: þe drifte) ·
> Of a wysti wonn waghe with þe wynd blawen.
>
> (1880–81)

D's *drifte* seems to fit the snowy context better, and the source which is quite different at this point apparently offers no guidance. However, it is uncharacteristic of the poet to depart so oddly from the Latin, which likens Alexander not to a snowflake but to a mouse leaping from its hole: 'tanquam mus prosiliens de fissura' (C^3, f. 7a). How could a mouse turn to snow? The answer is, at a stroke of the pen. The word *mus* consists of five minims followed by *s*; one more minim and the word becomes (or can be read as) *niuis*. *Niuis* makes no sense, since it is genitive, but the poet was experienced at interpreting a corrupt Latin text; it just happens that his correction was the wrong one. So a mouse from its hole ('fissura') becomes the flake *of snawe* from the *ryft* ('fissura') of a wall, and thus D's *drifte* can be rejected, even though no Latin manuscript now extant has the error *niuis*.

The editor of a verse-text has additional information that can be used to confirm the correctness of the readings or to demonstrate error, and the rest of my discussion will be concerned with this. The first step the editor must take is to establish as securely as possible the techniques of the verse, though alliterative verse poses particular problems which have never been comprehensively studied or satisfactorily resolved. Our attempt to establish in detail the poetic techniques of the *Wars* breaks new ground; in effect we are proposing a number of theories about the techniques of alliterative verse in general and of this poet in particular. We believe that our hypotheses concerning alliterative patterns, formulaic usage, structural divisions and the rhythmic organisation of the line are based on firm evidence, but each is open to argument, and therefore the many readings based on these assumptions are questionable to the same degree.

The crucial supporting factor throughout is the survival of the poem in two manuscripts independently derived from an excellent archetype. Some years ago I attempted to establish that the alliteration of the poem is consistently according to one pattern, aa/ax (including the variant of this, aa(a)/ax, in which (a) may or may not have metrical stress).[11] The argument is essentially very simple. Both A and D quite frequently present patterns other than aa/ax, but they almost never *agree* on such patterns. Thus, where A reads 'And þe powere of þe Persens so truly ȝe traist' (2592), which is aa/bb, D has *purely* for *truly*, which is aa/ax. It is not possible to suppose that each manuscript preserved the rare patterns of the archetype at just those points where the other text corrupted it to the predominant pattern.

An examination of the readings presumed corrupt by this line of argument establishes the kinds of error to which each scribe is prone. Both tend to substitute an easier, non-alliterating synonym; for example one of the general words for 'man' for one of the 'chiefly alliterative' words: *man, kniȝt, lord, kyng* in place of *athell, renk, tulk, lede* and others. Commonly, too, a word or phrase will be picked up from a nearby line and accidentally substituted for the correctly alliterating phrase. In general, D tends to be simply careless and to produce obvious errors, while A rather more often deliberately replaces words or phrases that he takes exception to, so that he regularly drops *as* from the common half-line '*A*lexsandire *a*s belyue', meaning 'Alexander quickly . . .', perhaps because *as* has only a metrical function.

In that half of the poem where the two manuscripts run together, the regular alliterative pattern is presented in at least one of the manuscripts in all but a handful of lines. In a number of these lines that remain the readings of the manuscripts disagree, and it is possible to argue that both are independently corrupt. There are only fifteen lines which are substantially the same in both manuscripts to support the use of patterns other than aa/ax. Of these, three lines contain a non-alliterating *kyng*, as in 'Fra Alexsandire þe kyng as I am infourmed' (2041). Emendation to *athill* is straightforward, since it produces a very well-attested half-line, and since this precise error is frequent in both manuscripts. In another two cases, both manuscripts have /g/ forms of 'give' where /j/ forms would alliterate regularly. Ten lines remain of irregular patterns, which may, of course, be authorial. An editor is obliged to deal in probabilities rather than certainties, and to us it seemed unlikely that a poet who was careful to follow the aa/ax pattern would depart from the pattern on just ten occasions for no ascertainable reason.

In any case, the important conclusion to be drawn from this comparison of the readings of the two manuscripts was that an irregularly alliterating line in A is always, or at any rate nearly always, corrupt. This knowledge could then be applied to that half of the poem for which A is the only

[11] T. Turville-Petre, 'Emendation on Grounds of Alliteration in *The Wars of Alexander*', *English Studies*, 61 (1980), 302–17.

witness. Here we emended irregular lines conjecturally, building on our understanding of the kinds of error characteristic of the scribe, always checking for collocations in a computer-concordance and wherever possible selecting a word that the poet used elsewhere in the required sense in the same metrical circumstances. We realised too late that we should also have compiled a concordance of the variant readings to record words that A had substituted elsewhere. Instead we relied on memory, which is not the best guide.

There remain some knotty problems about the relationship between stress and alliteration which cannot be explored in any detail here. Editors sometimes suppose that any syllable in the line that has approximately the right initial sound will satisfy the alliteration. This is not so. Alliteration must coincide with stress; in essence it is as simple as that. Nearly always, the alliteration falls on the stressed syllables of words in 'open classes', that is on nouns, adjectives, verbs, and adverbs of more than one syllable. Alliteration only falls on words of other classes in special, well-defined circumstances, such as with inversion – 'On a *s*ege hire be*s*yde' (236), 'Ne had he *t*rispast him *t*o' (2510) – or where there is no word of higher rank within the phrase to carry the alliteration – 'As *h*e had bene a *h*iʒe gode' (596, 1246), '*A*lexsandire *a*s belyue' (2083, *et passim*). Furthermore, in all but a very few cases which may themselves be corruptions, alliteration falls on identical consonants or consonant-clusters, or on vowels. We adopted a rigorous approach to the question of alliteration, and did not find it necessary to 'manipulate' the evidence to fit our conclusions.

A notable feature of alliterative verse is the formula, of which, it is now recognised, there are several distinct types.[12] For present purposes it is helpful to distinguish between two kinds, the verbal and the syntactic. Some formulas consist of exact verbal and metrical repetition of half-lines or even complete lines; others involve the collocation of two or more words within a line, generally the alliterating words, though the other elements are not identical. In the syntactic frame, however, the syntax is identical but there is no significant verbal repetition of the alliterating elements. The computer provided an indispensable tool for identifying and sorting both kinds of formula. Verbal repetition showed up in the concordance and other kinds of word-list (which were also invaluable for compiling the glossary). The syntactic frame could only be identified by much more subtle and painstaking analysis undertaken by Professor Duggan, who coded every half-line of the poem in terms of its syntax and its metrical structure, and added to this a corpus of lines similarly coded from other alliterative poems. The total corpus consisted of 12,803 lines, which were

[12] See R. A. Waldron, 'Oral-Formulaic Technique and Middle English Alliterative Poetry', *Speculum*, 32 (1957), 792–804; H. N. Duggan, 'The Rôle of Formulas in the Dissemination of a Middle English Alliterative Romance', *Studies in Bibliography*, 29 (1976), 265–88.

sorted by computer so that the patterns could be compared not only within the *Wars* but also with other poems in the tradition.

Armed with this rather formidable array of information, we believed it to be possible to distinguish the variant that conformed to the poet's formulaic practice from the one that departed from it. The exact repetition of a phrase is the easiest type of formula to recognise. For example, on fifteen occasions the text offers a b-verse that ends with *out of nounbre*, meaning 'innumerable': 'a pake out of nounbre', 'a sowme out of nounbre', 'seggis out of nounbre', etc. In one line A reads '*withouten* nounbre' (1371), and although the poet certainly might have written this, the evidence points clearly to the preferability of D's reading which conforms to the poet's usual pattern. Every writer and speaker has, of course, habitual forms of expression of this kind. Similarly, two b-verses consist of the oath 'on bathe twa þine/his eȝen' (1908, 5329), meaning 'upon your/his life'. In another case Skeat's text reads 'on bathe þaire eȝen twa' (5169). Alerted by the departure from the word-order of the other half-lines, we examined the manuscript more closely here, and concluded that *twa* had been added to the end of the line in a different ink. (The same is true of *neuyn* in the following line; see Fig. 3.) The scribe had presumably intended the word *twa* to be included within the line but had forgotten to insert a caret to indicate its place after *bathe*.

The a-verse of line 1537 is 'quethirs out quarels', '(they) let arrows whizz out', in A, as against 'whirres owt quarels', 'let arrows whirr out', in D. At first sight *quethirs* is preferable as the harder reading (the word is restricted to Scottish and northern usage). However, on the only other occasion that *quarels* is used in the poem, it is collocated with *quirys/whirres* in both manuscripts (2353), so that the balance of probability favours the D reading in line 1537 also.

On a few occasions the evidence of formula was sufficiently strong to suggest that the readings of both manuscripts were corrupt. So in l. 2157 we discarded the variants *rais*, 'arrays', and *rachez*, 'hurries', in favour of conjectural *riches*, 'prepares', on the basis of the exact repetition of the whole line 'Riches him radly to ride & remows his ost' in l. 5182. In this view *rachez* is a misreading and *rais* the substitution of a synonym. However, we rarely made conjectural emendations in this kind of situation. There is undoubtedly a tendency for the poet to repeat certain collocations, and choices between variants need to take account of this. Yet it is equally clear that the poet was in no way bound by the collocation, so that in the absence of D there was no question of emending A's 'Quen he had lokid ouire þe *lefe*' (4170) to conform to the repeated half-line 'Quen he had lokid ouir þe *line(s)*' (2850, 3888, 4697).

In the same way we used the evidence of established syntactic frames principally to distinguish between variant readings and to test conjectural emendations that we were making for other reasons, and only rarely as the basis for a decision to emend conjecturally. In l. 1759 there seems little to choose between these variants:

þe   same gode at I in my slepe   saȝe in my days   (A)
Thame same god þat   in my slepe I sawe in þo days   (D)

Yet from an analysis of the structure of every half-line of the poem, it is now possible to say that the poet nowhere else has an a-verse with a subject pronoun between the relative and an alliterating prepositional phrase, whereas the a-verse as in D is readily paralleled both metrically and syntactically: 'A renke at in þa regions' (1326), 'þe domesmen þat fra Darius' (1937), 'Ane emperoure þat on erth' (1993), etc.

When faced with variants of this sort, a traditional editor would favour copy-text on the grounds that there was insufficient evidence for choice. If, however, further evidence becomes available, as in this case, it is the duty of the editor to make a choice, while always admitting the fallibility of his decision. Often enough an editor cannot say the choice is the right one, but only that he believes it to be the most likely of the options. In the cases discussed above, the complicating factor is that not only poets but also scribes tend to write in formulas. A scribe will impose his own habitual forms of expression on the text, and will, furthermore, become accustomed to the poet's formulas and will substitute them deliberately or mechanically in places where the poet does not actually use them. A clear example of this in the *Wars* is the b-verse 'authority tag' 'as þe buke tellis' which the poet uses frequently to refer to his source. To satisfy the alliteration the poet has a selection of variations on this expression, such as 'as the claus tellis', 'as þe writt shewys', 'as menys me þe writtes', etc. By accident or design, the A scribe often alters these, substituting 'as þe buke tellis/sais' (e.g. ll. 1004, 1738, 1815). Here it is possible to pick out the scribal formula because it fails to alliterate. Other formulaic substitutions are revealed by departure from the source, variation in the readings and so on. Yet the scribal formula is not always so obvious, and it is a complication that has to be taken into account.

Another point that needs to be emphasised is the importance of analysing the formula in detail. On the basis of a-verses such as 'Airis him to Sire Alexsandire' and 'Airis him on Sire Alexsandire', we at first believed there were sufficient grounds for supplying *him* or *Sire* in lines of this type where one of these words was missing. Only later did we realise the significance of the fact that two formulas of quite different grammatical construction are involved. In 'Airis him *to* Sire Alexsandire' (TYPE 1), 'Alexsandire' is dependent upon the preposition, whereas in 'Airis him *on* Sire Alexsandire' (TYPE 2), 'Alexsandire' is the subject: he 'travels/betakes himself onward'. If the patterns are examined in turn, the distribution of variants is much less clear-cut:

TYPE 1

		ASHMOLE			DUBLIN			
VB.	PRON.	+ PREP.	+ PREF.	PRON.	+ PREP.	+ PREF.	OBJ. N.	LINE
Airis		to	Sire		to	Sire	Alex	1741
		to	Sire	hym	to			2366
		to	Sire	hym	to			2805
		to	Sire	þaim	to			3237
	him	to	Sire	hym	to	Sire		2762
	þaim	to	Sire	þaim	to	Sire		2917

TYPE 2

		ASHMOLE			DUBLIN			
VB.	PRON.	+ ADV.	+ PREF.	PRON.	+ ADV.	+ PREF.	SUBJ. N.	LINE
Airis	him	on	Sire	hym	on	Sire	Alex	1196
	him	on	Sire	hym	on	Sire		2972
	him	in	Sire	hym	on	Sire		3044
	him	on	Sire	—				3956
		on	Sire	hym	on	Sire		2392
	him	on		hym	on	Sire		996

TYPE 2(a)

	him	furthe		hym	forth			872
		furth	Sire	—				5033
		furth	Sire	—				5609
	him	furth	Sire	—				5337

In type 1, no definite pattern emerges. A always has *Sire*, but sometimes has the reflexive pronoun and not at other times; D generally has the pronoun, but is as often without *Sire* as with it. If the poet had a fixed formula of this pattern, it is impossible to determine what it was. There seems at first sight to be more of a pattern in type 2. D always has both the pronoun and the prefix; A is generally the same but is once without the pronoun and once without the prefix. There would appear to be good reason to emend these two lines in A, until type 2(a) is considered. This formula is grammatically parallel, with *furth* as the adverb in place of *on*. Here all three possible variations occur, so that there is no rational choice between them, and the case for emending A in ll. 996 and 2392 is greatly weakened.

The two scribes of the *Wars*, like scribes of other poetic texts, are prone to omit or even to supply complete lines, and an editor of unrhymed alliterative verse may often find it impossible to know when this has occurred. A break in the syntax may be caused by some other corruption; a line that looks too hopeless to be authorial may have some dim and distant origin in the author's text. In 1892 Max Kaluza argued that the *Wars* was composed in 'strophes' of twenty-four lines, each divided into sentence-units of four lines.[13] This idea was generally dismissed, but careful examination of the text and the paragraph marks preserved in the manuscripts makes it certain that Kaluza's argument is essentially sound. To put it at its simplest, the number of lines in each *passus* is divisible by twenty-four. Where both manuscripts are present, a shortfall in one is always made up by the other, and the two lines in A and the two in D that are superfluous to the twenty-four-line scheme are in every case weak, unnecessary to the sense and unparalleled in the other manuscript. In those sections where the text is preserved in only one of the manuscripts, there is the same pattern of occasional shortfall or surplus. Where a line is entirely lost, there is little the editor can do except to point out the lacuna and compare the source, though Theodore Silverstein, supposing a line to have been dropped from *Gawain*, supplies an invented one, whose interest is that it shows how difficult it is to write even one good line of alliterative verse.[14] Where there are too many lines in the *Wars* it is generally quite easy to identify the interloper, but one passage (3456ff.) presents real difficulty in that, although it consists of a five-line unit making up a twenty-five-line 'strophe', there is no line that is markedly weak. The passage describes how Darius' crown is placed on Alexander's head:

> A coron ane þe costious þat euire kyng weryd,
> On þe propurest of proiecte þat euire prince bere.

The only cause for suspicion is that the lines say much the same thing and have b-verses of identical shape, which suggests that one line may be a revised version of the other which the poet had intended to delete.

One more formal feature of the verse remains to be discussed: the rhythmic structure of the line. Using rhythmic patterns as an editorial guide is no different in principle from using alliterative patterns in the way described above; the difference in practice is that the rhythms of alliterative verse have not been satisfactorily established,[15] so that it has been possible to believe that the distribution of stresses within the line is more or less random. In order to determine whether this is so, Professor Duggan applied the same procedures used to establish the alliterative patterns, concentrating on the rhythmic shape of b-verses which are much less varied than a-verses. On the assumption that the archetype is a good representation of what the poet wrote, readings shared by A and D are for the most part authentic. A rhythmic pattern presented by both texts is likely to be

---

[13] M. Kaluza, 'Strophische Gliederung in der mittelenglischen rein alliterirenden Dichtung', *Englische Studien*, 16 (1892), 169–80. See further, H. N. Duggan, 'Strophic Patterns in Middle English Alliterative Poetry', *Modern Philology*, 74 (1977), 223–47.
[14] *Sir Gawain and the Green Knight*, ed. T. Silverstein (Chicago, 1984), l. 1022a; first suggested by Sir Israel Gollancz, EETS, 210 (1940), p. 111.
[15] A start was made by R. F. Lawrence, 'Formula and Rhythm in *The Wars of Alexander*', *English Studies*, 51 (1970), 97–112.

authorial, even if it is quite a rare pattern. Other patterns may appear much more commonly in either manuscript, but have no good support from the two manuscripts together, and may therefore be judged corrupt. An examination of b-verses on these principles led to the discovery that the pattern with two 'dips' that are each of more than one syllable is not authentic.[16] If there is more than one syllable before the first stress of the verse, then that stress will be followed immediately by another stress or by a dip of no more than one unstressed syllable. In other words, the following b-verse patterns have good support (the bracketed elements represent optional unstressed syllables):

$$x \; x \; (x) \; / \; / \; (x)$$
$$x \; x \; (x) \; / \; x \; / \; (x)$$
$$x \; / \; x \; x \; (x) \; / \; (x)$$

But this pattern lacks support:

$$x \; x \; (x) \; / \; x \; x \; (x) \; / \; (x)$$

This rhythmic pattern, like the irregular alliterative patterns, is found in both manuscripts, but its distribution suggests that the poet did not use it. In almost 2700 lines where the text is extant in both manuscripts, the pattern occurs 27 times in A, of which 22 are regular in D. It occurs 41 times in D, corrected 36 times in A. There are only four lines where the manuscripts agree on a reading that has the pattern. Two are:

& all maner of bestis	(2979)
& al manire of nedis	(3547)

Here *of* is not necessary to the idiom in Middle English, and it can be assumed that it is a coincidental or archetypal error. The two other b-verses of this pattern in both manuscripts are:

quen þe son is to reste (D: at rist)	(686)
& before þe kyng bryngis	(2767)

In neither case is there one obvious emendation, though in the first, elision of *son is* is a possibility, and in the second, the poet might have used the aphetic form *fore*.

Remarkably few conjectural emendations are necessary to correct this pattern where only one manuscript is present, and all the corrections are minor – omission of &, postponement of a pronoun, adoption of an aphetic form of a word and changes of that kind.

More work needs to be done before the range of rhythmic patterns in the

---

[16] The subject is fully discussed by H. N. Duggan, 'The Shape of the B-Verse in Middle English Alliterative Poetry', *Speculum*, 61 (1986), 564–92.

alliterative line can be defined, but it does now seem to be possible to categorise the limited number of b-verse types that were acceptable to the poets, and thus to develop a procedure to assist the editor in distinguishing right readings from scribal corruptions. One difficulty is that the precise form and morphology of a word in the poet's dialect is sometimes uncertain, so that, for example, the past participle of 'call' may be monosyllabic *cald* or disyllabic *callid*, the form of 'follows' may be *foloȝes* (three syllables) or *foloȝs* (two syllables), and the infinitive of verbs may be with or without an *-en* ending.[17] Above all, there is the question of final *-e* which has so vexed the analysis of Chaucerian rhythms. Verses in which there are no such uncertainties permit the preliminary establishment of patterns that can then be tested on verses with words of ambiguous forms, to discover whether the ambiguities may be resolved to produce lines of regular rhythmic patterns.

The analysis of the rhythms of alliterative verse and its employment as an editorial guide have to proceed with great caution, since there are many questions that have yet to be answered. This analysis, so far at least, is applicable only to the shape of the b-verse, for there seems to be too much variety in a-verses to permit classification that is of real value to the editor. The other kinds of evidence we have used to determine the readings of the *Wars* are much more familiar to editors of Middle English poetic texts. A variety of information – from the source, the alliterative patterns, the 'strophic' organisation and the formulaic composition – provides the editor with a substantial amount of evidence, so that in that half of the poem where there are two manuscripts it becomes possible in most cases to distinguish the right reading from the corruption and even on occasions to correct common error in both manuscripts. This establishes a pattern of authorial and scribal practice which can in turn be applied to that half of the text preserved in only one manuscript. All in all I believe (perhaps a common misconception among editors) that we have been able to establish the text of the *Wars* with a considerable degree of confidence. What we have discovered about this poet's practices has, if it is accepted, obvious implications for editors of other alliterative poems; in particular, the alliterative line seems to us much more closely patterned than others have thought. Those works of this school of poets that are extant in more than one manuscript – *The Siege of Jerusalem* and *The Parlement of the Thre Ages* – appear to share the metrical features of the *Wars*,[18] and it may be inferred that the same is true of many other poems of the tradition, though their survival in only one manuscript means that direct evidence of this is

---

[17] See G. V. Smithers, 'The Scansion of *Havelok* and the Use of ME *-en* and *-e* in *Havelok* and by Chaucer', in *Middle English Studies*, ed. D. Gray and E. G. Stanley (Oxford, 1983), pp. 195–234.
[18] This is argued by H. N. Duggan, 'Alliterative Patterning as a Basis for Emendation in Middle English Alliterative Poetry', *Studies in the Age of Chaucer*, 8 (1986), 73–105.

generally lacking. If an editor of *Sir Gawain and the Green Knight* were to conclude that the poem was written within the same alliterative and rhythmic constraints as the *Wars*, and that the only surviving manuscript had thus been subject to a considerable degree of scribal interference, what should s/he do about it?

EDITING FOR *REED*[1]

Diana Wyatt

I originally began, when invited to give this paper,[2] by looking for a neat, arresting title which would define a precise area. But as I considered the possibilities, it occurred to me that 'editing for REED', while not perhaps particularly arresting, does indicate a very specific kind of editorial activity, defined at least partly by its differences from others which may be more generally familiar, and that it might therefore be worthwhile for me simply to offer some observations, from my own experience, about the peculiar features of editing for REED: the kind and range of materials used, and the editor's tasks as an individual and in relation to the whole REED project. I thought also that I might usefully draw on my own experience to illustrate briefly how one may meet different, or even conflicting, demands in attempting to edit the same materials simultaneously for two purposes – in my own case, for a doctoral thesis and for REED.[3]

A major characteristic of REED editing, which distinguishes it from the mainly literary editing discussed elsewhere in this volume, is that its materials are almost entirely historical, documentary manuscripts. They emanate usually from late medieval local authorities, that is, city corporations and town councils, from parishes and from local trade and religious guilds; a few are ecclesiastical records. Most, in any one case, will be original manuscripts (mainly of the fifteenth and sixteenth centuries); some will exist solely or additionally in antiquarian copies.[4] In most cases

---

[1] For convenience of frequent reference I adopt throughout this paper the now generally established acronym REED for Records of Early English Drama. The project, under its General Editor Alexandra F. Johnston, has so far brought out five sets of records, published by the University of Toronto Press: *York*, eds. A. F. Johnston and Margaret Dorrell (1978, 2 vols.); *Chester*, ed. Lawrence M. Clopper (1979); *Coventry*, ed. R. W. Ingram (1981); *Newcastle*, ed. J. J. Anderson (1982); *Norwich*, 1540–1642, ed. David Galloway (1983). Volumes on Devon (ed. John Wasson) and on Cumberland/Westmorland/Gloucestershire (eds. Audrey Douglas and Peter Greenfield) are .forthcoming; several others are in preparation.
[2] I am most grateful to Professor Derek Pearsall for inviting me to give this paper (for which he also suggested the title) at what proved to be a very enjoyable and stimulating conference.
[3] The thesis is *Performance and Ceremonial in Beverley Before 1642: an annotated edition of local archive materials* (2 vols., University of York, 1983); references in this paper are to *Performance and Ceremonial*. The REED volume *Beverley* is due for publication in the near future.
[4] The range of REED sources is much wider, varying according to particular volumes and their scope (city, smaller town, county). Those listed here are perhaps the commonest categories among civic or municipal records.

few, if any, 'literary' materials (texts of plays or of Royal Entries, ballads or song lyrics) will be found: these are predominantly functional records. The approaches and problems of editors tackling such materials are bound to differ from those of editors of literary – or indeed dramatic – texts.

The editor of a literary text, for instance, is likely to be faced with a number of manuscript versions, of which none may have obvious priority as the base text for the edition. Nevertheless the editor must establish one, must produce a single coherent version, and (in the case of a scholarly edition at any rate) must account for variations by a more or less laborious process of collation. Such a thing is by no means unknown to REED editors, but is likely to occur only here and there among the materials of a single REED edition. What is more likely for the REED editor is that he or she will have to deal with a miscellaneous collection of entirely *un*duplicated manuscripts set down by sometimes semi-skilled local scribes using inconsistent letter forms and idiosyncratic (and also probably inconsistent) abbreviations, determined – or forced – to write in Latin but somewhat hampered by ignorance of the language, which they often seem to have made up as they went along. Scribal ignorance, and efforts to compensate for it, must account for the weird unintelligibility of many of the abbreviations with which these records so often bristle, to their editors' despair. Rather than having to struggle to produce one version of a Canterbury Tale (to take an extreme example) from among the dozens of manuscripts available,[5] a REED editor is likely to be stuck with a single, faded, perhaps fragmentary manuscript of any relevant item, and no duplicate to help to reconstruct difficult, damaged or even vanished passages.

Another difference between the editing of literary texts and that of REED documents is one that adds a peculiar excitement, and by corollary a peculiar frustration, to the REED editor's life: whereas (to put it at its simplest) the editor of a literary text can begin at line 1 (or folio 1) and work methodically through to the end of the manuscript, the REED editor often begins by having to establish the *existence* of the relevant materials among a much larger body of manuscripts. That is, a prospective REED editor may embark on an archives search knowing – from work done by other REED researchers, or from published works on local history or drama – only that *some* potentially relevant material may be found among certain of the local records, which (in the interests of REED's aim of completeness) justifies a thorough search. Thereafter he or she will plough through all sorts of paper and parchment books, rolls and fragments – council minutes, annual accounts, guild ordinances and so on – attempting to find relevant items and then transcribe them, remembering always to

---

[5] On the particular problems of editing *The Canterbury Tales*, see the articles by Charlotte Morse and Ralph Hanna III in this volume.

make a description of each manuscript used and to keep precise references (a challenging task in the case of uncatalogued manuscripts or unfoliated books). Such a situation inevitably has depressing moments: a week spent peering into faded, semi-legible manuscripts may produce a mere handful of relevant but insignificant items. (My own 'favourite' such reminiscence is the twenty-three-foot Beverley Account Roll, written in great detail on both sides, which yielded, for my own and REED's purposes, one payment of 10s to a group of travelling players.) But editors survive to smile at past frustrations, while the excitement of future possibilities remains; it is the possibility of finding an unknown gem of information which will illuminate the history of performance – that, plus the fear of failing in the REED editor's duty of extracting every single relevant item – which keeps one going, and indeed awake, through that very laborious stage of the work.

Without trying to make further points of comparison between the editing of literary texts and REED editing (having experience only of the latter, I feel hardly competent to do so), I want to say something more about the aims and purposes of the REED editor. The title of this paper in fact focuses clearly on a major point about REED editing: that one is editing *for* REED, that is, within the established framework of aims, policies and editorial style of the whole project. The REED editor works as an individual in that he or she becomes the expert on a particular body of manuscripts and may – must – make the final editorial decisions on, for example, the relevance of individual items, the inclusion of specific notes or the treatment of particular scribal inconsistencies. But broadly speaking the aims and purposes of the editor are those of the project. They could be summed up by the phrase above: to illuminate the history of performance (of dramatic, musical and other related material) in Great Britain before 1642.[6]

In an obvious sense the manuscripts REED deals with are secondary rather than primary – primary, of course, in being original manuscripts, but secondary in that from the REED viewpoint, that of the student and performer of early drama, music and ceremonial, the records' usefulness consists in their ability to shed light on surviving playtexts in particular and, in general, on methods and conditions of the original performance of plays, music, entertainments and ceremonials of all sorts – which includes areas like staging, casting, financing and management, properties and costumes. Sometimes records and texts may have a close and direct relationship, as in the case of Chester, where a substantial collection of extant records supports a Corpus Christi/Whitsun cycle surviving in half-a-dozen (admit-

---

[6] The relatively late *terminus ad quem* was chosen to reflect the continuity of much performing (and wider cultural) tradition in Britain throughout the medieval and renaissance periods: the real break is marked not by the establishment of professional playhouses in London but by the closure of the theatres at the onset of civil war in 1642.

tedly very late and consciously literary) texts.[7] The same is true in cases
like York and, to some extent, Coventry. In a case like mine as editor of
the Beverley records, there is an obvious oddity in claiming that one's
edition will illuminate *local* performance to any precise extent, since not
the slightest vestige of text survives for any local play or pageant or Royal
Entry – or anything at all.

In such a case an editor must see herself or himself very much as part of
the entire REED project – the usefulness of the records must be general as
much as (or rather than) particular. The information furnished by the
extant records alone leaves our picture of the Beverley Corpus Christi
cycle, or of its rare Pater Noster play (one of only three recorded in
England), very faint and sketchy. The records do tell us that in the early
sixteenth century there were thirty-six plays in the Beverley cycle, for
example,[8] and that some of them were still performed then by the same
guilds as in the early fifteenth century;[9] that in the mid-fifteenth century the
Corpus Christi and the Pater Noster plays were both performed on the
same pageant route;[10] that the Pater Noster play was some kind of 'cycle'
dealing with the Seven Deadly Sins.[11] One document even gives a brief
(and probably incomplete) inventory of props for a single Corpus Christi
pageant.[12] But such a record remains tantalisingly limited in its application:
an extant play text would give it an immediate and and specific usefulness
which it otherwise lacks. Working with such a body of materials, the
REED editor, especially one who (like myself and many others) is first and
foremost a student and practitioner of drama, requires extra patience to
collect all those relevant pieces of information which have no immediate,
practical value.

That particular frustration, certainly, is balanced in positive ways: firstly,
the insights provided by the records into local history – social, political,
economic – are often fascinating in themselves, and frequently tempting (I
have found) to pursue, irrelevantly, for their own sakes. Of course the
irrelevance is so only in strict REED terms, and materials collected by
REED may well be starting points of real value to historians in other fields.
Secondly, even in an area where the records have no practical application
to a particular play text, work on those records may add to the drama-
historian's picture both of that area and of Britain generally – and that is
the ultimate aim of REED editing: each volume, whether or not its
contents can aid a producer in creating a workable and authentic revival of

[7] See David Mills, 'Theories and Practices in the Editing of the Chester Cycle Play
Manuscripts', above.
[8] *Performance and Ceremonial*, 1–2.
[9] Op. cit., *passim*: see Index, *Corpus Christi Play*.
[10] Op. cit., 256, 259, 284, 291 and Introduction.
[11] Op. cit., 241–42, 284–85, 290–91 and Introduction.
[12] Op. cit., 14.

a particular play, adds a piece to the jigsaw of performance history. Beverley does make its modest contribution there – for instance it provides fuller records of a Pater Noster play than either York or Lincoln, the homes of the other two; any student trying to piece together the Pater Noster jigsaw must use the information of all three towns together.

The individual editor, then, as I noted above, is in this case working very much within a larger scheme. Inevitably that has both advantages and disadvantages (and perhaps it depends entirely on the temperament of the individual editor which of them will seem the greater). On the one hand, to consider the disadvantages first, one is working within the constraints of an overall editorial policy on selection of material, transcription (details like the reproduction of decorations, flourishes, pointing, awkward letter forms *et al*), preparation of edited material for submission to REED, the nature and aims of all the editorial apparatus. Obviously one might, left to oneself, come up with a different set of approaches, and a different method of presentation of one's 'own' body of records. The REED policy, however, has been carefully formulated, with much revision over the decade since the inception of the project, aiming always to provide a framework able to accommodate the varieties of documents and information from many different sources: a volume from a northern city like York contains a great body of civic records of a Corpus Christi cycle, whereas a southern county volume such as that for Berkshire and Buckinghamshire[13] presents scattered parish records dealing largely with church ales and odd (often, indeed, 'strange') travelling entertainers. Two such volumes, if produced independently by different editors for their own purposes, might take very different forms; but it is in the nature of the REED project that separate volumes should have an obviously common purpose and a degree of uniformity in their presentation.

On the other hand, the advantages of *not* working in isolation are very great: as a 'trainee' editor, starting as a novice, I have found the immense expertise, and patience, of the REED editors and staff invaluable in helping me to transform the error-ridden products of my cross-eyed labours into a palaeographically respectable set of records, with Latin abbreviations correctly expanded and intelligibly translated.

My own awareness of the position of an editor working *for* REED, as I indicated at the beginning of this paper, was considerably enhanced almost from the start by the fact that I undertook to edit the Beverley records both for my DPhil thesis and for REED. It took me, in my innocence, some time to realise that this double task was *very* much more complicated than simply, as it were, making an extra photocopy of the thesis and posting it to Toronto. There is a basic, historical reason for that, certainly: I embarked on my research when REED was just beginning to establish itself and

[13] Ed. A. F. Johnston; in preparation.

develop firm editorial policies and the set of guidelines now enshrined in the invaluable *Handbook for Editors*.[14] (In fact 'enshrined' is misleading: the guidelines are by no means as inflexible as the word implies. discussions and alterations are continuous, and the *Handbook* incorporates blank pages to accommodate emendations.) The result of that historical fact was that I set out to develop a purpose, a framework and an editorial procedure for my thesis quite independently of REED, and found in due course that in all sorts of ways and on every level from the greatest to the least (in editing I have found the trivial problems to be the most infuriating), I was attempting to produce two quite separate editions. (Before detailing some of the differences I must make it clear that my guides and mentors at REED have always been most accommodating, accepting material in its thesis form and doing their own scissors-and-paste work, or something more technologically sophisticated, upon it.)

To take one broad and basic example of the divergence of the two editions, there was the question of organisation. At an early stage I decided to group the records in my thesis in sets according to the manuscripts; so all extracts from the Minute Books went together in folio order, then all those from the Account Rolls, in date and then in membrane order, and so on. I did so partly to allow the thesis to convey a sense of the overall variety, and the individual nature and purpose, of the original documents; I was also uneasy about attempting a purely chronological arrangement because in the early stages of my research I found a relatively high proportion of undated documents. REED however does arrange all materials in strictly chronological order, with undated extracts grouped in an Appendix to each volume. It is a straightforward, sensible plan, allowing a sense of historical development and change to emerge as one works through a volume. But the other arrangement seemed to me, originally at least, better suited to my thesis, especially since I intended to discuss historical developments in detail in the introduction to it: such a discursive and interpretative survey was, I felt, part of the task of a candidate presenting a thesis for examination. That, however, marks another difference between what I conceived to be the purpose of the thesis and REED's purposes: a REED editor should eschew, more or less rigorously, speculation and interpretation; because REED aims to present the manuscripts themselves in accessible form, with as much textual or background information as is necessary to make them useful to the reader.

---

[14] The REED *Handbook for Editors*, compiled by A. F. Johnston and S. B. MacLean (Toronto, 1980), is a comprehensive manual for actual and prospective editors, continuing information on the aims, policies, organisation and facilities of REED, on bibliographical aids and on approaches to manuscript repositories; advice on all stages of the records editor's work; and instructions on final preparation of material for submission. It is much more than a book of rules, and as an editorial guide comprehensive enough to be of general use to manuscript editors.

It is then for the *reader* to interpret or apply them, for academic or practical purposes.[15]

Many other examples could be chosen to show in how many different ways the same material may be tackled and presented editorially – every one raised questions or presented problems which altogether provided an exciting sort of editorial apprenticeship, one which constantly forced me to consider the reasons for my decisions and their implications. At times I came to feel strongly that, in the presentation of manuscript material, an editor's first priority is to be consistent at all costs – even that a particular decision might in itself be arbitrary, so long as it was adhered to once made. For example: a scribe may make no apparent distinction between small and capital 'a', using perhaps the same form but different sizes, or vice versa. The editor then must, as it were, make up his mind for him. Since the editor can never know the scribe's mind, the decision (however sensible) is bound to be arbitrary; but at all costs transcription and presentation should then avoid confusing the reader. That is a very minor example, but my many necessary discussions of similar items with REED made me acutely aware of the wider editorial issues.

Finally I want to present an illustration of some of the points I have discussed. It is, again, of minor significance in itself (the item is taken at random from the Beverley materials), but it does demonstrate some of the questions a REED editor must address, within the context of a single volume and of REED's wider purpose of presenting records of dramatic, musical and ceremonial activity.

Beverley: AR 1460–61
mb 1
Recep*cio* de l*a* dyng*es*
. . .
. . . Et (computantes respondent) de xx d *receptis* de Ioh*anne* panyff
p*ro* Aysiam*ento* Castelli Lignei Carp*entariorum* in la dyng*es* *per*
An*nu*m
. . .
Recep*cio* minut*orum* redd*itum*
Et (reddunt compotum) de xx d r*eceptis* de Ioh*anne* langton p*ro*
aisiam*ento* castelli Carp*entariorum* ad e*osdem* t*erminos* hoc Anno.
. . .

---

[15] Such avoidance of editorial intervention between records and their users is still REED's policy; more recent volumes, however, do point to a slight relaxation, accommodating a slightly greater expansiveness in editorial discussion of the records and their context than appeared in the earliest volumes. See, for instance, David Galloway's comments in his Preface to *Norwich 1540–1642* (vii, and note).

(Receipt from the Dings

. . .

. . . And (the accountants render account) of 20 d received from John panyff for easement of the wooden castle of the Carpenters in the Dings annually

. . .

Receipt of small rents

And (they render account) of 20 d received from John Langton for easement of the Carpenters' castle on the same terms this year

. . .)[16]

This extract from the Beverley Governors' (i.e. Town Council's) Accounts for 1460–61 concerns not in fact drama but local ceremonial tradition – the guilds' celebration of Rogation Monday, when the town annually mounted a St John of Beverley procession watched by the guild masters, in livery, from special viewing stands called 'castles', each guild having its own. The points of interest in this little manuscript extract are these:

1. Only two items, occupying one line each in MS, are relevant out of the several dozen items on the first membrane of this Roll; only three other items, also brief, were extracted from the Roll (5 mbb and 12 feet long).

[16] *Performance and Ceremonial*, 346

2. These items make fascinating but inevitably tantalising reference to their subject-matter, as do so many REED materials. Accounts are purely functional records; neither the scribe nor the Governors needed, for fiscal purposes, any of the extra detail that REED editors yearn for. The Carpenters' castle is mentioned as being accommodated in space rented from the governors; exactly what a castle was like – its size, shape, elaborateness of construction and decoration – and indeed the origin of the consistent local use of the term 'castle' for such a structure – is precisely the sort of thing *we* want to know and *they*, who knew it already, generally left out.[17]

3. The entries follow a common accounting formula and are heavily abbreviated. Once one has learnt to recognise such formulae, and how to expand the heavy abbreviations, a whole class of documents becomes accessible and for the most part intelligible. But it is a painstaking process, rather resembling code-cracking, and may be hampered by scribal errors and idiosyncrasies, or by oddities of local terminology.

4. The particular oddity here is that we have two almost identical entries, under two distinct sections of the account; one, under Receipts from the Dings (a property leased out piecemeal by the Governors for trading, storage and so on), notes payment of 20*d* by John Panyff for the accommodation (easement) of the Carpenters' castle 'per An*nu*m'; the other, under Receipt of Small Rents, notes payment of the same sum for exactly the same purpose but from a John Langton and 'hoc Anno'. Possibly the second entry contains a scribal error – 'Carpentariorum' being repeated in mistake for the name of another guild; if so, what should an editor do? Should he or she print both items, with or without a note drawing attention to the oddity? – or only one, mentioning the other in a note? And if both are included, how should the slight variation in recording the term of the lease ('per An*nu*m'/'hoc Anno') be tackled in translation? Is there any likelihood that a significant difference was intended, meaning that the first record concerns a repeated annual lease and the other an arrangement made for 1460–61 only?

A REED editor's duty is to intervene as little as possible between the original records and the reader, but even such a case as this suggests the extent to which not only transcription but translation may be bedevilled by possibly unconscious, but perhaps inevitable, editorial interpretation. The REED answer is generally to make translations as literal as possible, retaining rather than smoothing out any oddities, ambiguities or errors in the original. But here one *might* argue that the two items are so nearly

---

[17] On these grandiose-sounding 'castles' – apparently analogous in function, and perhaps also in structure and appearance, to viewing stands erected (in Beverley as elsewhere) for other sorts of public ceremonial, and for tournaments – see *Performance and Ceremonial*, Index: *Castles* and *Rogation*. The rather intriguing usage is, as far as I know, unique to Beverley.

identical that the scribe must have meant the same in each case, and so attempt to tidy up his Latin in the act of translating it. I found myself frequently so tempted – and in my thesis succumbing – in more important areas like that of performance terminology, a notoriously unstable category in both Middle English and medieval Latin. Again and again I had to try to answer the question: if these two records clearly, in context, refer to the same performers, viz. the Town Waits, but have been written by different scribes whose *in*different Latin finds dissimilar ways of rendering 'wait' in Latin, should not I as editor help the reader, in my translation, by making it clear that '*spiculator*' and '*mimus*' or '*ministrallus*' equally represent 'wait'? My answer, in the thesis, was yes; REED's was and is, very decisively, no.[18]

On the whole I am now glad that in most such cases REED's solution will be the one to be published. But my general point in this paper is simply that REED editing has its own peculiar interests and challenges, and that editing simultaneously for oneself and for REED more than doubles both, providing excellent exercise for the editorial brain.

---

[18] The REED Latin specialist Abigail Ann Young has recently written an interesting two-part article on medieval Latin performance terminology, 'Plays and Players: the Latin terms for performance' (REED *Newsletter*, vol. 9, No. 2 (1984), 56–62, and vol. 10, No. 1 (1985), 9–16).